T0374996

CZECH LAW IN HISTORICAL CONTEXTS

JAN KUKLÍK

CHARLES UNIVERSITY IN PRAGUE
KAROLINUM PRESS 2015

Rewiewed by: Doc. PhDr. et JUDr. Jakub Rákosník, Ph.D.
              PhDr. Jiří Noha, Ph.D.

CATALOGUING-IN-PUBLICATION – NATIONAL LIBRARY
OF THE CZECH REPUBLIC

Kuklík, Jan
   Czech law in historical contexts / Jan Kuklík. – 1st ed. – Prague : Karolinum, 2015. – 239 p.
Published by: Charles University in Prague
ISBN 978-80-246-2860-8

34(091) * (437.3)
– history of law – Czechia
– monographs

340 – Law [16]

Front cover: Allegory of the Faculty of law, Charles University in Prague.

ISBN 978-80-246-2860-8
ISBN 978-80-246-2916-2 (pdf)

CONTENTS

Introductory remarks

The legal system of the present-day Czech Republic would not be understood properly without sufficient awareness and knowledge of its historical roots and evolution. The trend of "harmonization" of European legal systems closely interconnected with the phenomenon of the European Union, of which the Czech Republic is a member, and with the profound changes after the so-called 1989 Velvet Revolution, form just a recent part of its complex interpretive framework. The 20th century in particular is very important for today's Czech state and law: this is connected with the establishment of an independent Czechoslovakia in 1918, which split in 1992 to give rise to the independent identities of the Czech Republic and the Slovak Republic. The 20th century encompassed periods of a democratic regime (in particular that between WWI and WWII) as well as of totalitarian regimes – both Nazi and Communist. The political, ideological, economic and social changes connected with such development were projected into, and reflected in, the system of Czechoslovak law; and it can therefore serve as a "case study" to those researchers interested in the transition of democratic legal systems into totalitarian regimes, and vice versa.

The historical development of Czech law is a good example of an application of the contradictory principles of continuity and discontinuity. It is interesting to observe how the original forms of Slavic law were influenced by the legal systems of neighbouring countries, primarily German and Austrian provinces, as well as by Canon and Roman law. It is equally interesting to see how a legal system originally based on customary law was changed into written and codified law. Czech law has been part of a broader Central European legal culture for centuries. It was so closely connected with developments within the Luxemburg, Jagiellonian and, primarily, Habsburg monarchies that many aspects of the development of Czech law can be observed in neighbouring states, although with some features remaining autonomous.

It is exciting to see the contradictions in the legal development of a changing society of the 18th and 19th centuries, when the Czech national revival and the creation of a modern Czech political nation collided with German ambitions both within the Czech lands and throughout the entire Austrian monarchy. Mutual relations between the Czechoslovak state and its nationalities and the concept of protection of national minorities under the auspices of the League of Nations are yet other aspects deserving the attention of foreign experts.

I believe that this outline of Czech and Czechoslovak legal history will stir the interest of its readers not only in law itself but also in the evolution of Czech and Czechoslovak statehood and culture.

/1/

Beginnings of the Czech state and law

The Czech Republic of today was historically made up of three main territorial elements: Bohemia, Moravia and part of Silesia, which together created the identity of the so-called Czech lands.[1] The first permanent settlement on this territory is connected with the Celtic tribes.[2] Some of their influence is still visible: for example, the original name of the country, Bohemia, was derived from the Celtic tribe of Boii and is still applied to the largest part of the Czech Republic.[3] In the first century of the first millennium, the Celts were replaced by the German tribe of Marcomanni. The territory of the Czech lands remained (with the exception of a Roman military camp in Southern Moravia near Mikulov) free of the influence of the Roman Empire.[4] This fact was important for

1   For the territorial development of the Czech state including maps see Semotanová, E.: Territorial Development and the Transformation of Landscape. In: Pánek, J. – Tůma, O. et al.: *A History of the Czech Lands*. Prague: Karolinum Press, 2009, pp. 25–54.
2   For Celtic period in Central Europe in broader context see especially classical works by J. Filip. In English Filip, J.: *Celtic Civilization and its Heritage*. Prague: Academia, 1977.
3   In more details Sláma, J.: Boiohaemum – Čechy. In: Teich, M. (ed.): *Bohemia in History*. Cambridge University Press, 1998, pp. 23–24.
4   Tejral J. – Bouzek, J. – Musil, J.: *The fortification of the Roman military station at Mušov near Mikulov*. Archeologica 45, 1994, pp. 57 and following.

the legal development in the Czech lands, as Roman law was not reflected at that stage.

From the 4th century AD, Slavic tribes, in the course of the worldwide Great Migration of Peoples, gradually settled down in Bohemia and Moravia.[5] After clashes between the Slavic population and invaders from the East, called Avars, the first attempt to create a loose state structure in the form of a tribal alliance was successfully accomplished by the Frankish merchant Samo. He was able to resist pressure from Dagobert, the King of the Franks. However, the empire disintegrated after Samo's death, around 658 AD. Some of the invaders from the East settled in Bohemia, later abandoned their nomadic lifestyles and became "Slavicized". [6] There are only a few written sources available for acquiring some knowledge about this period, the most important of them being a chronicle written by the monk Fredegar from Burgundy.

Another important Slavic state structure on the territory of the Czech lands was connected with the so-called Great Moravian Empire in the 8th century.[7] The establishment of the Empire gave a powerful impetus for the unification of Slavic tribes; it developed its own legal system and introduced Byzantine Christianity.

There are again very limited sources on legal development in that period. However, using archeological research,[8] comparative methods and even the methods of legal anthropology,[9] we can assume that the legal system was based on traditional Slavic customary law, comparable with that of other Slavic tribes. There is a notable exemption from customary law: one important written source of law was preserved from the Great Moravian Empire. It is called "Zákon sudnyj ljudem" – judge-made law for laymen, inspired by the Byzantine Ekloga. [10] It consists of 33 articles and deals primarily with criminal and property law and the law of marriage. The written law was intended as a subsidiary source, used in cases where original customs were to be changed or were completely missing.

During the reign of the Great Moravian Prince Rostislav, a Christian mission was sent by the Byzantine Emperor. The mission arrived at Moravia in 863 under the leadership of the brothers Cyril and Methodius. They instituted

5   In more details Třeštík, D.: Prehistory and Beginnings of Slavic Settlement (to the 8th Century). In: Pánek, J. – Tůma, O. et al.: *A History of the Czech Lands*, pp. 58–64.

6   Charvát, P.: *The Emergence of the Bohemian State*. East Central Europe in the Middle Ages 450–1450, Volume 13. Leiden and Boston: Brill, 2010, p. 113.

7   See for example Třeštík, D.: Great Moravia and the Beginnings of the State (9th and 10th Centuries). In: Pánek, J. – Tůma, O. et al.: *A History of the Czech Lands*, pp. 65–77. For archeological research see Klápště, J.: *Czech Lands in Medieval Transformation*, East Central Europe in the Middle Ages 450–1450, vol. 17. Leiden, Boston: Brill, 2012, pp. 14 and following.

8   *Ibidem*.

9   See especially the works by Leopold Pospíšil. For example Pospisil, L.: *Anthropology of law*, New Haven, 1971.

10 Dittrich, Z. R.: *Christianity in Great Moravia*. Instituut voor middeleeuwsche geschiedenis, 1962 p. 208.

a Slavonic liturgy comprehensible to ordinary people and developed a special script for the so-called Old Church Slavonic language. Cyril and Methodius translated the Bible from Greek into the Old Church Slavonic language. However, Rostislav's successor, the Moravian Prince Svatopluk (died 894), repudiated the supporters of Slavonic liturgy and switched to the Latin rite. As a result of church reforms new rules for the law of marriage were introduced and Christianity had an impact on changes to the original Old Slavonic family law.

The Great Moravian Empire gradually disintegrated during the reign of Svatopluk's son, Mojmír II (died 906), particularly due to the attacks of Hun (Magyar) nomadic raiders at the beginning of the 10th century.

The beginning of the Czech state (named after the Slavic expression for the Czech people – Bohemia) and its law is connected with clashes between the ruling Slavic families in the 8th and 9th centuries after Great Moravia was destroyed by Magyar tribes. In the end, the so-called Přemyslid dynasty (*Přemyslovci* in Czech) prevailed against its opponents in this struggle and, by the end of the 10th century, formed a nucleus of the Czech state, with its centre in Prague.[11] The first historically documented Přemyslid prince, Bořivoj, accepted (around 883) baptism from the hands of Methodius. In the beginning, the Přemyslid prince was loyal to the Great Moravian Empire, but Bořivoj's son, Spytihněv (died 915), took an oath of vassalage to Arnulf, the King of the Eastern Franks. The orientation of the society towards the West prevailed, including the Latin rite in the Church.

Among first Přemyslid princes the most important was Václav, or *Wenceslas* in English. He tried to pursue a policy of friendly relations, primarily with the mighty neighbour Saxony. Václav was murdered in a dispute with his brother Boleslav in the town of Stará Boleslav, most probably in 935. Václav was canonized and, as a patron of the Czech state, became a symbol of Czech statehood.[12]

In 973 the Prague Bishopric was instituted; a number of monasteries were built, with the first one founded in 993 for the Benedictine order in the quarter of Břevnov in Prague.[13] The second bishop of Prague, Vojtěch (*Adalbert* in English) promoted the basic principles of Christian life, affecting also the domain of law.[14] It should be noted in this context that the Přemyslid prince Boleslav II (died 999) enacted a set of privileges for the Church. In the doc-

---

11 For the development of Přemyslid domain in Central Bohemia and its transformation into early medieval state in English see Sláma, J.: *Boiohaemum – Čechy*, pp. 31–37.

12 In more details see Měřínský, Z. – Mezník, J.: Bohemia and Moravia from the tenth to fourteenth century. In: Teich, M.: *Bohemia in History*, pp. 40 and following.

13 Berend, N. – Urbańczyk, P. – Wiszewski, P.: *Central Europe in the High Middle Ages: Bohemia, Hungary and Poland*, c.900–c.1300. Cambridge University Press, 2013, pp. 115–117.

14 For Bishop Vojtěch see The Life of Saint Adalbert Bishop of Prague and Martyr. In: Klaniczay, G. (ed.): *Saints of the Christianization Age of Central Europe* (Tenth-Eleventh Centuries). Central European Medieval Texts, Vol. 6., CEU Press, 2013, pp. 77–182.

ument certified by Boleslav in 992 the Church was given jurisdiction over matters of marriage and was assigned the right to levy a bishop's tithe. This is the oldest known piece of legislation adopted by a ruler from the Přemyslid dynasty. The ill-fated policy pursued by Bishop Vojtěch led to open disputes with the prince and his followers; as a result, Vojtěch was forced to leave Bohemia and died during his attempt to Christianize Baltic Prussia. He was later canonized and became the second patron of the Czech state, after the first patron, sv. Václav (St. Wenceslas).[15]

The Czech Kingdom gradually became an autonomous part of the Holy Roman Empire (the "Roman Empire" revived by Emperor Otto II). Individual rulers of those territories comprising the Roman Empire as an artificial universal unit remained sovereigns within their own territory but formally received their titles from the emperor.[16] The first Přemyslid prince to be awarded the title of King was Vratislav II in 1085, although this title was entrusted to him just for life. Vratislav II (died 1092) was awarded the title in return for his support of Emperor Henry IV in his political struggle with the Pope. In 1158 Vladislav II (died 1174) was appointed the second Czech king; his nomination for life resulted from his support of the Roman Emperor Friedrich I Barbarossa in his military campaign in Italy. In 1198 Přemysl Otakar I (died 1230) was the first Czech king awarded the hereditary title. This fact was confirmed in 1212, when the so-called Golden Bull of Sicily was enacted by the Holy Roman Emperor Friedrich II, acting also as the King of Sicily.[17] Later Czech kings, as one of seven imperial electors, acquired the right to elect the Holy Roman Emperor.

The Czech lands became known as the "Czech Kingdom" and, later, as the so-called "Kingdom of the Crown of Bohemia". The Czech Kingdom under the Přemyslid dynasty was composed of several regions: Bohemia, Moravia (from 1182 called the Margraviate of Moravia), Upper and Lower Silesia. The Přemyslid dynasty ruled until 1306.

The emerging Czech state took over many cultural and legal aspects developed during the Great Moravia period. The legal system was based on customs, and much of its content was based on the Old Slavonic law of the pre-state period. For example, ownership was based on traditional forms of "common ownership" by extended families; family law was influenced by

---

15 The third Bohemian Saint was Procopius. In more details see Bláhová, M.: The function of the Saints in Early Bohemian Historical Writing. In: Mortensen, B. H. (ed.): *The Making of Christian Myths in the Periphery of Latin Christendom* (c. 1000–c. 1300). Copenhagen: Museum Tusculanum Press, 2006, pp. 83 and following.

16 For the royal titles and their significance see Třeštík, D. – Žemlička, J.: The Czech State in the Era of Přemyslid Princes and Kings. In: Pánek, J. – Tůma, O. et al.: *A History of the Czech Lands*, pp. 95–97.

17 The document is kept by the National Archives of the Czech Republic, Prague, the fund of the Archives of the Czech Crown. For the Latin text see Friedrich, G. (ed.): *Codex diplomaticus et epistolarius regni Bohemiae*, II. Prague, 1912, No. 96, pp. 93–94.

pagan traditions; criminal law was based mainly on private initiative, including the so called "blood revenge". Primitive court proceedings used ordeals (called after Christianization *iudicium dei* (the judgment of God)) – primarily ordeal by cold water, ordeal by hot iron and various forms of oaths.[18] Only later was the wager of battle (the duel) introduced into Czech law.

Ordeals as an integral part of court proceedings were known to other European legal systems, including the German law of neighbouring lands. However, some Czech "specials" existed, such as using only cold water, whereas the German, French and Anglo-Saxon legal systems knew ordeal by hot water. The accused person was forced to follow strict rules on ordeal corresponding to the nature of the case. 12th and 13th century sources suggest that an ordeal by hot iron was preferred, either in the form of walking on hot ploughshares barefoot or in the form of an oath with fingers on a red hot iron bar. Ordeal was considered a form of evidence, which is not rational from today's perspective. Courts observed detailed procedures prescribed for each type of ordeal and issued their judgment according to the result of the ordeal at issue. The outcome of an ordeal was certified by a priest who was present during the performance of the ordeal.

During the 10th and 11th centuries, the first attempts at kings legislation based on Christian principles emerged. The country was gradually Christianized in the Western "Latin" rite from the 9th century[19], and the last Czech monastery built near the Sázava river maintaining the above mentioned Slavonic liturgy ceased to practise it in 1096/97.[20]

The most important example of legislation based on Christian principles is the so-called Decrees of Prince Břetislav (died 1055) from 1039.[21] The Decrees introduced marriage based on the principles of Canon law, in addition to many other Christian principles, such as the necessity of burying in Christian graveyards or keeping Sundays and Church holidays.

The exact wording of the text of Břetislavs Decrees remains unknown. The Decrees were recorded later by the monk Kosmas in his famous Chronicle of Bohemians (*Chronica Boemorum*)[22] in the form retrieved from the original text of the Statutes of Hniezdno. Břetislav proclaimed his decrees on Polish territory (Hniezdno, or Gniezdno, is a city in central-western Poland), when he launched a military campaign to return the remains of St. Vojtěch back to

---

18 For legal aspects of ordeals see Bartlett, R.: *Trial by fire and water, The Medieval Judicial Ordeal.* Oxford: OUP, 1986.
19 In more details Sommer, P. – Třeštík, D. – Žemlička, J. – Doležalová, E.: *The Christianisation of Bohemia and Moravia.* Annual of Medieval Studies 13, CEU, 2007, pp. 153 and following.
20 Třeštík, D. – Žemlička, J.: The Czech State in the Era of Přemyslid Princes and Kings. In: Pánek, J. – Tůma, O. et al.: *A History of the Czech Lands*, p. 87.
21 An interesting account in Wolverton, L.: *Hastening toward Prague, Power and Society in the Medieval Czech Lands.* Philadelphia: University of Pennsylvania Press, 2001, pp. 28–29.
22 For English text see *The Chronicle of the Czechs, Cosmas of Prague*, translated with an introduction and notes by Lisa Wolverton. Washington D.C.: The Catholic University of America Press, 2009.

Prague. Břetislav assigned great importance to Christian principles, as his aim was to spiritually reconcile the memory of St. Vojtěch with "pagan" Czechs.

It is clear from the Chronicle of Kosmas that family law in particular was heavily influenced by principles conceived by Canon law. From the beginning of the 11th century Czechs living in the territory of Bohemia used an ecclesiastical form of marriage, followed the principles of monogamy (bigamy was prosecuted) and Canon law restrictions on marriage, such as the prohibition of adultery (sexual intercourse between a married person and someone other than his or her spouse), repudiation of one's spouse or desertion (leaving one's spouse with no intention of returning) and divorce. Basic principles of law of marriage were partly based on Roman law, including requirements and obstacles regarding the capacity to constitute a valid marriage. The Church acquired jurisdiction over all matters related to marriage law. The Břetislav Decrees included the application of ordeals in courts and a system of administration based on castles as regional centres. Restrictions on pubs were introduced as a possible source of revenue for the treasury and prohibition of trade on Sundays; however, it seems to be quite doubtful that these restrictions were followed in practice.

Břetislav is known for another piece of legislation, which is connected with his attempt to consolidate the Czech state. Before his death he proposed the so-called Act on "Seniority Rule", in 1054–1055.[23] The Rule provided that the ruler of Bohemia should always be the eldest member of the Přemyslid dynasty. This principle lead to a series of disputes among members of the Přemyslid dynasty; younger members of the dynasty were often given small portions of the territory as their dominions, especially in Moravia (úděly in Czech, or *deals* in English, with centres in Brno, Olomouc, Břeclav and Znojmo).[24]

The year 1189 is closely connected with yet another important legal achievement. The Přemyslid Prince Conrad II Otto (died 1191) called a congress of leading representatives of nobility (gentry) to the township of Sadská near Prague. During the meeting he proclaimed a set of rules known as the Statutes of Prince Conrad. The texts became known from the beginning of the 13th century, when the rules were certified for Moravian dominions of the younger Přemyslid princes.[25] According to those Statutes members of the emerging nobility were proclaimed to be free and hereditary landowners (close to the English term of *freehold*) of the gifts of land made to them earlier by Přemyslid princes. It was therefore possible to create a system of nobility

23 Třeštík, D. – Žemlička, J.: The Czech State in the Era of Přemyslid Princes and Kings. In: Pánek, J. – Tůma, O. et al.: *A History of the Czech Lands*, p. 83.
24 See for example Měřínský, Z. – Mezník, J.: *Bohemia and Moravia from the tenth to fourteenth century*, p. 44, and Marečková, M.: *Czech Legal and Constitutional History, Brief Summary*. Prague: Linde, 2006, p. 18.
25 Latin text published in Friedrich, G. (ed.): *Codex diplomaticus et epistolarius regni Bohemiae* II. Prague, 1912, No. 234.

domains, which became legal areas of their own, with their own jurisdiction and a special relationship between the lord and his subjects.

The Statutes confirmed the validity of several important customs; on the other hand, they introduced some changes to customary law and especially to its interpretation. For example, the law of succession was changed in favour of daughters should there be no male heirs. Changes were made in administrative matters, criminal law and court proceedings. However, the Statutes should not be regarded as a codification of law, because they covered only small parts of customary law; all other customs, not mentioned in the Statutes, remained fully in force.

During the 13th and 14th centuries, new settlers were invited by Czech kings, Church and nobility to Bohemia and Moravia to colonize areas with a low population density, in particular the border areas. The first German settlers had come to Bohemia much earlier; for example, in 1176–1178 Prince Soběslav II (died 1180) gave privileges (confirmed several times later) to German traders in Prague and exempted them from the law of the land.[26] However, the mode of colonization, both in its form and numbers, changed in the 13th century. This is why the Czech lands ceased to be inhabited solely by Slavs; German and Jewish populations settled on the territory of the Czech lands and lived there until the tragic events of WWII and immediately after the war in the middle of the 20th century.[27] In those early times, the population of Germans and Jews was regulated, as well as protected, by king's legislation, including the famous Jewish Privileges awarded by King Přemysl Otakar II. (died 1278) in 1254 (so called *Statuta Judaeorum*).[28] The Statutes granted Jews special permission to carry on financial business and exemption from local courts. They were subordinated directly to the king. In 1268 similar privileges were granted also to the Jews settled in Moravia.

German speaking settlers from Saxony, Bavaria, Swabia, Austria or even Rhineland brought with them not only advanced agricultural techniques and trade skills but also their own law. Initially, they could use it as a privilege certified by the king. Legal development in the Czech lands was therefore substantially influenced by legal patterns derived from neighbouring countries. This was visible mainly in the development of municipal law and in new ways of landlords' renting of land (real estate) during the internal colonization – this was known as *emphyteusis* or *purkrecht*. Its main effect was the impetus for

---

26 English translation in Wolverton, L.: *Hastening toward Prague. Power and Society in the Medieval Czech Lands*. Philadelphia: University of Pennsylvania Press, 2001, pp. 28–29.

27 In more details see Beneš, Z. – Kural, V. (eds.): *Facing history: the evolution of Czech-German relations in the Czech provinces 1848–1948*. Prague: Gallery for the Ministry of Culture of the Czech Republic, 2002, Chapter I. Historical Roots, pp. 10 and following.

28 For historical context see Agnew, H. L.: *The Czechs and the Lands of the Bohemian Crown*. Hoover Institution Press, 2004. For the text of Statuta see Bondy, B. – Dvorský, F.: *K historii židů v Čechách, na Moravě a ve Slezsku 906–1620*. Prague, 1906, pp. 15 and following.

the establishment of new villages and towns.[29] The newcomers from German lands were granted significant reliefs. The feudal lords contracted with their representatives (so-called locator) for the division of a designated area (for example a future village) into fields, and arranged for dwellings to be built for the use of the colonists. The rights and obligations of the new settlers were set down by the land lord in writing. It was customary to exempt the new settlers from taxes for a period of several years. After that period the relationship to the land was based on fixed monetary sums paid regularly, usually twice a year. The colonists were also given hereditary rights to their property, subject to their continued cultivation of the land. This "German law" (*ius teutonicum*) was different from and in most aspects more favourable to the original "Slavonic law" (*ius slavicum*). Under original Slavonic law the land of a peasant was subject to escheat and therefore reversed to the feudal lord upon the death of the original tenant.

At the same time yet another legal form typical for the feudal system developed within the Czech Kingdom. Besides the freehold there were forms of fiefs, in which a special bond between a feudal lord and his vassal developed. The vassal was obliged to be loyal to his lord, to assist him in arms (or, for example, to protect his castle), and to perform honorary services. The feudal lord, on the other hand, had to protect his vassals. Later, the law developed a special theory of division of ownership between the lord and his vassal. This field of law was also influenced by the law of neighbouring countries, especially Saxony. The object of the fief was not only land, but also dignity, office or certain rights.

In the beginning of the 13th century towns started developing their structures into special legal entities (corporations) – the number of town corporations amounted to 40 by the end of the century.[30] Towns were usually established directly by a Czech king (so called royal towns). Medieval towns were constituted as centres for trade and crafts, with most of them having developed from earlier settlements located close to important castles. Some of them were built from scratch as new settlements ("on a greenfield land"). The king usually awarded special privileges to a town, such as the right to conduct regular markets, to produce beer or have various other industries, to collect duties and to raise fortifications. For example, the town of Brno was granted by King Václav I (1205–1253) privileges called *iura originalia* (i.e. original laws). Inhabitants of towns were personally free; they were subject to their town's own jurisdiction and enjoyed a number of legal and economic

---

29 Třeštík, D. – Žemlička, J.: The Czech State in the Era of Přemyslid Princes and Kings. In: Pánek, J. – Tůma, O. et al.: *A History of the Czech Lands*, pp. 100–102. See also Žemlička, J.: *Přemysl Otakar II, Král na rozhraní věků* – Přemysl Otakar II. A King on the Turn of Ages. English resume, Prague: Lidové Noviny, 2011, pp. 701–702.
30 Berend, N. – Urbańczyk, P. – Wiszewski, P.: *Central Europe in the High Middle Ages: Bohemia, Hungary and Poland, c. 900–c. 1300*, pp. 448–449. See also Klápště, J.: *Czech Lands in Medieval Transformation*, especially pp. 350 and following.

rights and privileges. Their only lord (master) was the king, who exercised his powers over towns through his servants, so-called constables. Taxes paid by municipalities became important revenue for the royal treasury. Since royal towns were entitled to legislate on a number of issues in the form of statutory law, they established an autonomous administration – the town council and the court. The autonomous statutory law of royal towns dealt with a variety of issues, such as the regulation of individual crafts in guilds, the regulation of construction and development activities, the regulation of prostitution and the maintenance of public order.

Some municipalities, called dowry towns, such as Hradec Králové, were founded to serve economic purposes for the benefit of the queen. Other towns were built by the local nobility or by the Church; inhabitants of such towns were regarded as subjects of the founder of the town and their legal status was usually inferior to the status of the inhabitants of the royal towns.

There was no unified system of municipal law: practically every town of some importance had its own legal system. Nevertheless, a majority of towns in Northern Bohemia and Moravia were governed by Saxon law in accordance with the pattern of the Saxon town of Magdeburg. In other parts of Bohemia and Moravia an influence of Bavarian, Schwabian or Austrian municipal laws can be traced. The Old Town of Prague was developed from previous settlements which had originated during colonization with privileges granted by the king. The Old Town was also influenced by Nuremberg law (Schwabian law), as local merchants maintained close trade ties with this South German town.

The Prague Old Town and the Moravian capital of Brno gradually developed their own legal systems based on their original patterns supplemented by the statutes and findings of municipal bodies, customs and privileges often expanded and certified by kings. Municipal law became a vehicle for Roman law institutions to be introduced into the Czech legal system, particularly in the law of persons, the law of property and the law of obligations. Such development was closely connected with, and supported by, the University's teaching of Roman and Canon law and with the role of learned scribers and notaries working for town councils. The reason why Roman law was suitable for law applied in towns was particularly the trade and property matters to be resolved. Business or market negotiations, often concluded in town centres of trade (sometimes becoming even international), were an excellent environment for using traditional forms of contract developed by Roman law. Roman law was applied in developing the concepts of ownership, easements, the law of persons (including legal capacity), the law of succession, and the property aspects of family law. In towns, the application of modern forms of court proceedings based on Canon law and Roman law was possible. Municipal law was suitable for the development of new, written forms in which law was created and applied.

During the reign of King Přemysl Otakar II (died 1278) the Czech Kingdom acquired Austrian and Alpine lands and strengthened the position of the king.[31] Přemysl Otakar II is said to have started preparations for the codification of the law of the land (a name tailored to cover the "common law" of the Czech Kingdom and the law of nobility), but he failed to succeed in his initiative. The idea of codification was influenced by Canon law (including the teaching of just law and of the law of kings as law-makers), which could be found in private collections, including the legal textbook of Canon law by Gratian, called *Decretum Gratiani,* known in the Czech state from the middle of the 12th century, or in the rediscovered legislation of the Roman Emperor Justinian. Přemysl Otakar II is assumed to have planned to use some foreign models for his codification, including Saxon law. Přemysl's ambition to become the Roman Emperor was halted by Roman King Rudolf of the Habsburg dynasty during the Battle on the Morava Field in 1278, when Přemysl died.

During the reign of King Václav II (1271–1305) another attempt of the king to codify the law of the land failed, although the king invited Gozzius of Orvieto, a distinguished Italian lawyer, to prepare a code based upon his knowledge of both Canon and Roman law. The king only succeeded in codifying one of his sovereign rights, his *iura regalia* – specifically the law of mining. This law was closely connected with municipal law: the towns established by the king (e.g. Jihlava or Kutná Hora) were natural centres of mining. The law of mining was therefore regarded as a special part of municipal law. Between the years 1300–1305 the law of mining was codified.[32] The Code is known as *Ius Regale Montanorum,* or later as *Corpus Iuris Metalici*; the Code is a very good example of the influence of Roman law on Czech law (see Chapter 2). The proceedings were based on Roman Canon law proceedings.[33]

It represented the successful codification of existing legal, business, technical and even labour provisions promoting the expansion of mining activities. Some of its provisions were modern if seen from the perspective of medieval law. For example, corporations established for mining activities divided their capital into shares (*kuksy* in Czech), which served for the accumulation of capital, division of profit and for compensation to land owners who were forced to suffer mining operations on their land. The term "*kuks*" in the meaning of a share in mines, together with the right to start mining activities in given area, existed in Czech law until 1945, when mining companies were nationalized by the Czechoslovak state.

---

31 Třeštík, D. – Žemlička, J.: The Czech State in the Era of Přemyslid Princes and Kings. In: Pánek, J. – Tůma, O. et al.: *A History of the Czech Lands*, pp. 106–110.
32 For its new edition see Bílek, J. (ed.): Ius regale montanorum, právo královské horníkuov. In: České horní právo, volume II., 1978.
33 For more details see Ott, E.: *Beitrage zur Receptionsgeschichte der römisch-canonischen Processes in den Böhmischen Landern.* Leipzig, 1897.

The Code was also used in Silesian, Slovak and Hungarian mining centres and in the Saxonian town of Freiberg. The Code was enacted in Latin, but shortly after its issuance it was translated into German and Czech and later also supplemented by other sources of municipal or mining law and published.[34] The German text is known from the beginning of the 15th century, when the translation was done by Notary Jan of Gelnhausen and was used especially in the Jihlava mines. The Czech translation was the second and emerged in the middle of the 15th century in Kutná Hora. It should be noted that a century later (in the mid 16th century) the Code was translated into Spanish, to be applied to mining activities in new Spanish colonies (especially in Bolivian mines in Potosí).

The codification of mining law was connected with currency reform when Václav II introduced a new silver coin – the so called *Prague groschen*. The new coin symbolized the supreme position of the Czech king, and the right to issue the coin was regarded as another sovereign right of the ruler.

Václav II later became the Polish King, and he managed to secure the Hungarian crown for his son, Václav III (1289–1306). However, when Václav II died in 1305, his son lost his Hungarian crown and, trying to secure his Polish title, he was murdered in Olomouc in 1306 while making his journey to Poland. Thus the male line of the Přemyslid dynasty became extinct and short political crises followed during which the Church representatives and Czech nobility were searching for a new king.[35]

---

34 See for example two versions of *Ius regale montanorum* preserved in the collections of Czech National Museum and Czech National Library from 1515 and 1528 and the database of manuscripts available at www.v3.manuscriptorium.com

35 Měřínský, Z. – Mezník, J.: *Bohemia and Moravia from the Tenth to Fourteenth Century*, p. 53.

/2/

Development of law during the era of the Luxemburgs until 1419

After the short reign of Rudolf of Habsburg (1281–1307) and Henry of Carinthia (died 1335), one of the most important ruling dynasties in Medieval Europe, the Luxemburg dynasty, ruled the country between 1310 and 1419.[36] The first king of the dynasty, John (1296–1346), married Přemyslid Princess Eliška (Elisabeth). He reached significant success especially in foreign policy, such as acquiring Upper Lusatia and Silesia to enlarge the Czech Kingdom. He is also known as "Knight-errant King", which took part in the Hundred Years War on the side of French and died in the battle of Crécy.[37] The most important member of this dynasty was Charles IV (1316–1378) who became the "Holy Roman Emperor" in 1355.[38] Charles IV introduced a series of reforms: his Constitu-

---

36 Polívka, M.: The Expansion of the Czech State During the Era of the Luxemburgs 1306–1419. In: Pánek, J. – Tůma, O. et al.: *A History of the Czech Lands*, pp. 119–123.

37 The English King Edward highly regarded his bravery and this was regarded by historians like R. W. Seton Watson as the first direct link between Bohemia and England. Teich, M.: *Bohemia in history*, Introduction, p. 18.

38 Kavka, F.: Politics and Culture under Charles IV. In: Teich, M. (ed.): *Bohemia in history*, pp. 59 and following, and Polívka, M.: The Expansion of the Czech State During the Era of the Luxemburgs 1306–1419. In: Pánek, J. – Tůma, O. et al.: *A History of the Czech Lands*, pp. 128 and following. See also the foreword by F. Seibt in Balazs, N. – Schaer, F.: *Autobiography of Emperor*

tional Charter established the term "Czech Crown" designating expanding territories of the Czech Kingdom with Bohemia and Moravia as the "main lands", with the Principality of Silesia, Upper and Lower Lusatia as so-called "adjacent lands". Charles IV ordered a new crown of St. Wenceslas to be kept in Karlštejn Castle as a symbol of the state structure.

Charles IV established the relationship between the Czech Kingdom and the Holy Roman Empire in his so-called Golden Bull of 1355.[39] The Bull provided that the Czech king be considered the first elector of the Holy Roman King and Emperor. Charles IV established Prague as the capital of his Kingdom: he used his political influence to establish the Prague Archbishopric in 1344 and, three years later, to found the University of Prague.

The beginning of the University dates back to as early as 1347, when Pope Clement VI approved its foundation. Charles IV constituted a university (a so-called *studium generale*) in Prague on 7th April 1348.[40] The University was composed of four establishing faculties, the Law Faculty being one of these. The other three were the Faculties of Theology, Medicine, and Liberal Arts.

At its beginning, the University of Prague followed the pattern of universities in Paris and Bologna. It was the oldest university north of the Alps and east of Paris. Not only people living in Bohemia became members of the academic community of the newly established University, but also many foreign teachers as well as students came to Prague from Central Europe to join the University. The main subjects taught at the Law Faculty comprised the so-called learned laws, i.e. Canon and Roman Laws. Until the Decree of Kutná Hora was issued in 1409, persons of four nationalities – Saxon, Polish, Bavarian and Czech – had been students of law.[41] After 1409, the decision of King Václav IV (1361–1419) strengthened the position of domestic students and university masters.

From 1372 there was a separate University of Jurists in Prague – *universitas iuristarum*, sometimes called "the university of canonists". [42] The reasons why the University of Jurists was established were primarily disputes between leaders of the University of Prague and jurists over management of the institution. Many outstanding lawyers of that time taught at the University of Jurists,

Charles IV. And his Legend of St. Wenceslas. New York: Central European University Press, 2001, and the standard work in English by Jarret, B.: *The Emperor Charles IV*. London, 1935.

39   The text in English published by Phillips, J. T. (ed.): *The Fundamental Laws and Constitutions of Seven Potent States and Kingdoms in Europe*. London, 1752, p. 107 and following. See also www. avalon.law.yale.edu/medieval/golden.asp, Henderson, E. F. (ed.): *Select Historical Documents of the Middle Ages*, London: George Bell and Sons, 1896, pp. 39 and following.

40   In more details see Svatoš, M.: The Studium generale 1347/8–1419. In: *A History of Charles University*. Volume I. A History of Charles University 1348–1802. Edited by I. Čornejová, M. Svatoš with collaboration of P. Svobodný. Prague: Karolinum Press, 2000, pp. 22–93.

41   Šmahel, F.: The Kuttenberg decree and the withdrawal of the German students from Prague in 1409: a discussion. In: *History of Universities*, 4, 1984, pp. 153–166.

42   See part by J. Kejř in A History of Charles University. Volume I. *A History of Charles University 1348–1802*, pp. 149 and following.

such as Professor Bonsignore de Bonsignori from Bologna, its rectors Nicolas Geunher, Jan of Pernstein, and the distinguished masters Vilém Horborch, Bohuslav of Krnov and Kuneš of Třebovle. Students and graduates from the University of Jurists very often held prominent offices in the Church hierarchy or in the king's court. Only a smaller proportion of students obtained the formal degree – Bachelor or Doctor, due to very expensive and long studies, which often took more than seven years.

The establishment of the Law Faculty influenced the introduction of Roman law in the administrative offices and courts of Czech and Moravian towns. Instruction of Roman law helped lawyers in the Czech lands to understand the Roman law terminology and institutions in the sphere of private law.

In 1355 Charles IV proposed the first written codification of the law of the land for the whole Czech Crown called *Codex Carolinus* (the Code of King Charles); later, when it was rediscovered and published in 1617, the Code was known as *Maiestas Carolina*.[43] The codification was inspired by the Sicilian Constitutions of Melfi (*Constitutiones regni Siciliae* or *Liber Augustalis*) enacted in 1231 by the Roman Emperor Frederick II of the Hohenstaufen dynasty for the Kingdom of the Two Sicilies. It was based upon Canon law and, to a certain extent, upon Roman law, in particular when dealing with the position of the Czech king. The Code was drafted in Latin and Roman law institutions were often used to express the Czech legal terminology.

It was a combination of the traditional customary law of the land and of new provisions. The Code dealt with the position of a king, with religious matters, including provisions on the persecution of heretics, with administrative matters both at central and regional levels, with court proceedings, land registers, property, family and criminal law. The Code also provided that the Crown lands and most important castles could not be sold or otherwise disposed of without protecting adjacent forests. The Code stipulated that should a noble family become extinct the freehold property was to be returned to the king as royal escheat. Regarding court proceedings the Code proposed limits for the application of ordeals. At the time of drafting the Code, Charles IV, with the assistance of the Archbishop of Prague, had already put the limits into practice. Criminal law provisions in the Code preferred property punishments and fines collected by the royal treasury rather than corporal punishments; the criminal jurisdiction of nobility over their subjects was restricted.

However, Charles IV was forced to reject the Code because of pressure from the leading representatives of the Czech nobility; as a result, he solemnly proclaimed that the proposal for the Code had been destroyed by a fire. Nobility objected to the Code being drafted; noblemen were rather resistant

---

43 For its modern edition see Hergemöller, B. U. (ed.): Maiestas Carolina: Der Kodifikationsentwurf Karls IV. für das Königreich Böhmen von 1355. In: *Veröffentlichungen des Collegium Carolinum Bd. 74*. München, Oldenbourg 1995.

to changes in the traditional way of law-making – i.e. through findings of nobility courts. They were afraid that the codification would reduce their existing rights to only "freely searching for law and justice". Adoption of the Code would inevitably strengthen the powers of the king and, on the other hand, the privileges of nobility would be limited.

Despite their failure to codify the law of the land, the period of the Luxemburg dynasty rule marked profound changes in the Czech legal system. The changes are linked with the diversification of the legal system in accord with social class affiliation and other personal criteria, i.e. law based on privileges and personal and social status. The following main branches of Czech law may be listed: the law of the land (termed also as the "law of province"), which encompassed the law for nobility and public law for the whole territory of the Czech Crown; Canon law of the Catholic Church; municipal law for inhabitants of towns; peasant law for subjects; and some special branches of law, such as mining law or the law of vineyards.

During the 14th century new sources of written law were introduced into the Czech legal system for the first time; before then, changes had been based mainly on customs. So-called law books – private written aids for judges and other practising lawyers – represented the most important written source of Czech law of that period. They were written both in Czech and Latin and represented private recordings of customs and procedures applied in courts. The first law book in old Czech was written at the end of the 13th and beginning of the 14th centuries. Although there are several versions known, they preserved the title of the Law Book of Rožmberk. The modern edition was published in the 19th century and divided the text into 289 articles.[44] Unfortunately, the author of the Law Book remains unknown; it is presumed to have been ordered by the high official of the Crown and nobleman Peter of Rožmberk. The Law Book is a collection of customs from all branches of the law of province, including property law, criminal law and court procedure. Customs are followed by instructions to a judge on how to use and interpret them in a court and what kind of ordeal to apply. By the second half of the 14th century another law book originated as a direct consequence of the above-mentioned unsuccessful attempt by Charles IV to codify law. The title is "The Order of the Law of the Land", and the text was written both in Czech and Latin (as *Ordo iudicii terrae* in Latin). The book encompassed not only customs but also decisions (findings) of nobility courts. It dealt mainly with court procedure; a fictitious case of murder was introduced to show the sequence and purpose of individual stages of court proceedings. The book included various types of evidence, including a famous description of the wager of battle before court.

---

44 There are two editions from the second half of the 19th century: Brandl, V. (ed.): *Kniha Rožmberská*. Prague, 1872, and Gebauer, J. (ed.): Kniha Rožmberská. *In: Listy filologické a paedagogické 7*, 1880.

According to Czech law, a woman was allowed to take part in the wager of battle on condition that she was the only surviving member of the family and her male opponent was fighting at a disadvantage – he was to remain in a hole during the battle.

By the end of the 14th century, Ondřej z Dubé (Andrew of Dubá), a Czech lawyer and the chief justice of the Provincial court, wrote a manuscript (a law book) on the law of the land.[45] He used older legal writings, customs and findings of courts to prepare a useful aid for every person applying the Czech law of the land in practice. Ondřej z Dubé focused on court proceedings, the organisation of courts and offices and on land registers. Some impact of Roman law terminology and Canon law can be found in his book; however as a whole, the Czech law of the land resisted the influence of Roman law. Ondřej z Dubé tried to formulate some preliminary definitions regarding the law of the land, including his view on the priority of the law of the land over municipal law and other "special" laws.

Another important written source of law were the so-called *zemské desky* (the land records or registers), which emerged towards the end of the rule of Přemysl Otakar II.[46] These were not only public land registers of real property owned by nobility but also comprised precedential decisions of a nobility court called the Court of Province (*zemský soud*). The role of decisions of nobility courts in the Czech legal system of that time could be compared with the position of precedents in English common law. The law of nobility gave rise to some specific Czech institutions, in particular in the field of property law and the law of obligations, which represented a unique Czech legal culture different from Roman law. The Czech law of the land, for example, recognized collective ownership of property by the noble family as a whole, without any division of the property into individual parts (*nedíl* in Czech, "*undividedness*" in English).[47] Such collective ownership consisted of movable and immovable things and differed according to its "head", i.e. the person representing the ownership entity. There were units headed by the father of the family, grandfather or, even in some cases, the mother of the family. The "head" was acting on behalf of the whole entity.

Different provisions, if compared with Roman law, applied to the law of succession or to dowry. Special formal provisions were used in court proceedings, where ordeals ceased to apply just before the outbreak of the Hussite movement.

A number of legal writings and other forms of written sources connected with the application of law originated in Bohemian and Moravian towns. The

---

45 Čáda, F. (ed.): *Nejvyššího sudího království českého Ondřeje z Dubé Práva zemská česká*. Prague, 1930.
46 Žemlička, J.: *Přemysl Otakar II. A King on the Turn of Ages*, p. 702.
47 See for example Marečková, M.: *Czech Legal and Constitutional History. Brief Summary*, pp. 60–62.

oldest example of a document with legal content is the manuscript of the Prague Old Town developed between 1310 and 1518 and known according to its Latin title as *Liber vetustissimus statutorum et aliarum rerum memorabilium Veteris Urbis Pragensis*.[48] The manuscript was prepared by at least 16 different scribers, mostly in Latin but also in German and Czech. In Central Europe this is the oldest known manuscript on municipal law. It contains the privileges of the Old Town of Prague, lists of the members of municipal boards, statutes, individual legal deeds, decisions on admission to town "citizenship", and many other individual matters regarding the application of municipal law.

Between the years 1413 and 1419 another interesting manuscript was ordered and drafted by the Prague Old Town representatives. This was a handbook on the law of the land and municipal law, but also encompassed the law of fief (based on German patterns) and vineyards valid before the Hussite wars. The manuscript is a very good example of the overlapping of many various branches of law despite the existence of the principle of personality. It consists of 268 pages of laws written in Old Czech, and includes the above-mentioned Law Books of Rožmberk and by Ondřej z Dubé, as well as parts of laws of other Czech and Moravian towns. Today, the manuscript is stored and kept by the Archives of Prague. Handwritten notes on the margins of most pages prove that the manuscript was often used by the Municipal Court in the post-Hussite period.

Probably the best known legal book of the Czech provinces was compiled in the Moravian town of Brno in the middle of the 14th century (1353); it was based on previous collections of municipal law. The book is a large compilation, with 730 articles focusing mainly on the findings of municipal bodies. Attempts to use more general legal definitions based on excerpts from the Digest can be observed. The book dealt with all important aspects of municipal law as used in Brno, especially with the administration and position of the aldermen, proceedings before the town's court, the law of persons, the law of property and the modes of enforcement of court findings.

The law book served as an aid for the municipal council and court proceedings. It was written in Latin, and is therefore sometimes referred to as *Sententiae Brunensis*, and was influenced by Roman law. The book is usually known as the "Book of Scribe John", after its author, who was a notary in Brno, or as *Schoeffenbuch*, i.e. the book used by the representatives of the municipal council.[49] In the 1450s the book was translated into Czech in the town of Kutná Hora and published in 1498.

The Book of Scribe John inspired another known expert in municipal law John of Gelnhausen; at the beginning of the 15th century, he compiled a

---

48 The original is kept in the Prague City Archives; 22 facsimiles were published in 2010 by the Prague City Archives and Publishing House Tempus Libri.
49 For its edition see Flodr, M.: *Právní kniha města Brna z poloviny 14. století. volumes I.–III.* Introduction and text in volume I. Brno City Archives, Brno, 1990–1993.

general textbook on municipal law based mainly on the municipal law of Brno and Roman and Canon law sources, primarily definitions and principles from Justinian's Digest). This book is known as *Manipulus vel directorium iuris civilis* and was used mainly in the Moravian town of Jihlava, where John of Gelnhausen was working as a notary.[50] Jihlava and Brno therefore created their own legal circles, having an influence also on towns in Bohemia.

Roman law influence on Czech law before the Hussite period can be traced in the Code of Mining Law (*Ius regale montanorum*) by Václav II, as mentioned earlier. The Code, prepared by the Italian lawyer Gozzius of Orvieto, was inspired by Canon and Roman law, particularly by the division used by Gaius and Justinian in their Institutions. The Code is divided into four parts – the law of persons, the law of property, technical provisions for mining, and the law of court proceedings. Because of its Romanized contents, the *Ius regale montanorum* was included as part of municipal laws not only in mining centres like Jihlava and Kutná Hora, but also in other towns.

---

50 For its edition see Gelnhausen, J.: *Příručka práva městského (Manipulus vel directorium iuris civilis)*, edited by Flodr, M., Brno: Matice Moravská, 2008.

/3/

The Hussite period

At the beginning of the 15th century social and legal development in the Czech lands was interrupted by social and political crises, followed by the so-called Hussite religious movement. The movement got its name after Jan Hus – the Czech priest and follower of the English church reformer John Wycliffe.[51] The Hussites demanded a radical reform of the Church, society and law.[52] The Hussite revolt began when charges of heresy were brought against Jan Hus during the church Council of Constance.[53] Hus hoped that he would be able to convince the learned men of the Church of his ideas on how to reform

---

[51]   In more detail Kaminsky, H.: Wyclifism as Ideology of Revolution, *Church History 32*, 1963, and Hudson, A.: *Premature Reformation, Wycliffe texts and Lollard History*. Oxford: Clarendon Press, 1988.

[52]   In English Kaminsky, H.: *A History of the Hussite Revolution*. University of California Press, 1967, Fudge, T. A.: *The Magnificent Ride: The First Reformation in Hussite Bohemia*. Ashgate, 1998. From Czech literature see especially numerous works by F. Šmahel (in English The Hussite movement: an anomaly of European history? In: Teich, M. (ed.), *Bohemia in History*, p. 80 and following, or The Hussite Revolution 1419–1471. In: Pánek, J. – Tůma, O. et al.: *A History of the Czech Lands*, pp. 149 and following. For literature see also Zeman, J. K.: *The Hussite Movement and the Reformation in Bohemia, Moravia and Slovakia*. Ann Arbor: University of Michigan, 1977.

[53]   Kejř, J.: *The Hussite Revolution*. Prague: Orbis, 1988, pp. 48–50.

the Church; instead, he was sentenced to death by an Inquisition trial and burned at the stake in 1415.[54] A year later his follower Jeronymus of Prague was executed. Both men were seen as martyrs of the new religious reform movement. The events resulted in an open revolt, and tensions between the Hussite and Catholic sides rose. The Hussite movement had not only religious but also national and social dimensions.

In 1420 the Hussites adopted a programme known as the Four Articles of Prague.[55] The programme requested reforms of the church and society in accord with the principles of God's law. The First Article dealt with the freedom to preach the Word of God; the Second with the Sacrament of the Body and Blood of Jesus Christ being taken in the "two kinds" (*sub utraque speciae*, i.e. bread and wine for both priests and lay worshipers); the Third proclaimed the confiscation of the real property of the Church; and the Fourth outlined the punishment for mortal sins and all other trespasses to the law of God-these were to be punished according to the laws of the land.

The Hussites confiscated practically all real property of the Catholic Church and introduced their own church organization based on a "true understanding of the Bible". After the death of Václav IV of the Luxemburg dynasty the country had in fact no ruler, which led to open anarchy in some places and to permanent military clashes. There were differences even within the Hussite movement itself encompassing a whole range of factions, from quite moderate to rather radical.[56] The Hussites were united for some time, particularly because of crusades launched against them by the rest of Christian Europe. This period is known even in English history as the "Bohemian Wars": five crusades all ended with victory by the Hussite army.[57] Its military leader, Jan Žižka, enacted a special Military Order for the army in 1423. As a result, the Roman Emperor and hopeful (aspiring) Czech King Sigismud (1368–1437) of the Luxemburg dynasty was forced to negotiate a compromise with the Hussites during the Council of Basel in 1433.[58] In the end, the radical wing of the Hussites was defeated in 1434; the moderate wing, especially the new nobility and Hussite towns, came gradually to terms with the Catholics on the basis of so called "Compacta of Prague", formally promulgated in Jihlava in 1436.[59] Adult inhabitants of the Bohemian Kingdom were allowed to choose affiliation with either Hussite or Catholic worship. Sigismud was acknowledged as

---

54 Spinka, M.: Hus Trial at the Council of Constance. In: Rechcígl, M. (ed.): *Czechoslovakia. Past and Present, Vol II.* Washington D.C., 1968, pp. 1208–1220, and Fudge, T.A.: *The Trial of Jan Hus: Medieval Heresy and Criminal Procedure*, Oxford University Press USA, 2013.
55 English translation in Fudge, T. A.: *The Crusade against Heretics in Bohemia 1418–1437*. Sources and documents for the Hussite Crusades, Ashgate, 2002, doc. No. 39. See also Kaminsky, H.: *A History of the Hussite Revolution*, pp. 98–99.
56 Šmahel, F.: *The Hussite Movement: An Anomaly of European History?*, pp. 89–96.
57 Fudge, T. A.: *The Crusade against Heretics in Bohemia, 1418–1437*, pp. 45 and following.
58 Kaminsky, H.: *A History of the Hussite Revolution*, pp. 484–485, and Fudge, T. A.: *The Crusade against Heretics in Bohemia, 1418–1437*, doc. No. 183–190.
59 Kejř, J.: *The Hussite Revolution*, p. 143.

the Czech King; however, he was forced to confirm the confiscation of the real property of the Church, and prelates ceased to be represented at the Provincial Diet of the Czech Kingdom, which was the supreme representative body of the nobility. The Hussite movement could be regarded as a prelude to the European church reform movement, which later led to reforms which were demanded by Martin Luther, Jean Calvin, and other church reformers.

One event was of particular importance for the development of law, namely that, due to the Hussite movement, the separate University of Jurists was closed during 1418 and 1419. After the termination of the Hussite wars neither the University of Jurists nor the Faculty of Law of the University of Prague were reopened. Law studies were only available abroad at foreign universities, just as they had been before the establishment of the University of Prague in 1348. Lectures on Roman law and municipal law were delivered at the Faculty of Liberal Arts of the University of Prague. These lectures were read by Bachelor Prokop, the Highest Scrivener of the New Town of Prague, and, one century later, by Jan Kocín of Kocinét. The Hussite movement slowed down the introduction of the Roman law tradition in the Czech lands. On the other hand, it prepared the conditions and environment for a new legal period, characterized as the social and legal system of the Three Estates. The main direct legal outcome of the Hussite period could be seen in major changes in the free holding of land, as the Church and the King lost most of their land property. Professor František Šmahel later estimated that the changes had affected between 40 and 50 percent of the whole volume of real property of that time and especially the Catholic Church lost roughly four fifths of its farmsteads in Bohemia.[60]

There were two official churches in the Czech Kingdom (so-called Kingdom of Two Peoples) from the end of the Hussite wars to the Thirty Years' War in the 17th century. The Kingdom enjoyed a period of relative religious tolerance, or at least the co-existence of different religious beliefs. Interestingly, the first examples of legislation on religious tolerance can be found in the Czech law of the land of that period. The Czech Provincial Diet adopted an Ordinance on Religious Tolerance in Kutná Hora as early as 1485, the so-called Religious Peace of Kutná Hora, which had an explicit relation to the earlier mentioned Compacta.[61] The two main religions within the Czech Kingdom, accompanied later by Protestant religions in the 16th century, influenced the development of law primarily in family law and the law of marriages and some other parts of the law of persons.

---

60 Šmahel, F.: *The Hussite Revolution*, p. 162.
61 The Compacts were refused to be granted to the Czechs by new Pope Pisu II., but were confirmed by Czech Diets during the reign of George of Poděbrady. Heyman, F. G.: *George of Bohemia, King of Heretics*. Princeton University Press, 1965, p. 275 and following. See also Agnew, H. L.: *The Czechs and the Lands of the Bohemian Crown*, p. 53.

After the end of the radical Hussite movement, Jiří (George) of Poděbrady (1420–1471), a nobleman of Czech origin and moderate Hussite follower, was elected Czech King by the Czech Provincial Diet in 1458.[62] His reign was associated with a famous project (known also as *Tractatus pacis toti Christianitati fiendae* – Treaty on the Establishment of Peace throughout Christendom) to create a federation of leading Christian European states built upon their equality and sovereignty. In 1464, Jiří of Poděbrady asked Louis XI, the French King, to become the president of such a union.[63] The General Assembly of the federation was supposed to adopt common rules, and the Council of the leaders of States was planned as a representative of the executive power. The project proposed that a special Court would be established to solve conflicts between European states. The aim of the proposal was to guarantee permanent peace in Europe and to unite Christian states against the Ottoman Turks. Although the proposal was rejected, it could be regarded as a predecessor of integration projects in modern times, including the United Nations Organization or even the European Union.

62 For more details see Heyman, F. G.: *George of Bohemia, King of Heretics*, p. 147 and following. Odložilík, O.: *The Hussite King. Bohemia in European Affairs 1440–1471*. New Brunswick – New Jersey 1965, and Šmahel, F.: *The Hussite Revolution*, pp. 164–168.
63 For the document in English edited by J. Kejř see Vaněček V.: *The Universal Peace Organization of King George of Bohemia: A fifteenth Century Plan for World Peace 1462/1464*. Prague: Czechoslovak Academy of Sciences, 1964, pp. 81–90.

/4/
Law during the Estate Monarchy

During the second half of the 15th century and throughout the 16th century a new social and legal system gradually developed within the Czech Kingdom. It is called the Period of Estates, or the Estate Monarchy.[64] The same development could be observed in some other European states including the neighbouring lands or France. The powers of the king decreased profoundly, as well as the political power of the Catholic Church. The Estates were groups of free and privileged people with the same or similar political, legal, economic and social status within feudal society. However, the majority of inhabitants of the country did not belong to the Estates; they were regarded as subjects with limited legal capacity and inferior social status. The Period of the Estates strengthened the already existing principle of personality of law (i.e. the law is distinguished according to which estate it applies to) even more. There were three officially recognized estates – peers (higher nobility), knights (lower nobility) and free inhabitants of royal towns. The whole society

---

64 Macek, J.: The Monarchy of the Estates. In: Teich, M. (ed.): *Bohemia*, p. 98 and following. Boubín, J.: The Bohemian Crownlands under the Jagiellons 1471–1526. In: Pánek, J. – Tůma, O.: *A History of the Czech Lands*, pp. 176–179.

was organized in a hierarchical way, and the hierarchy applied also within the Estates themselves.

The peers were most powerful. In 1500 they formed a closed estate of higher nobility, with strict criteria for admission to the peerage, together with their internal hierarchy of forty-seven "traditional" aristocratic families, headed by the House (Dynasty) of Rožmberk. The most important bodies of the Estates were the Provincial Diet, Provincial Officials at the central and regional levels, and the Provincial Court. The peers dominated the government and the whole legal system, including decisions of the Provincial Court and adopted legislation. The peers acquired all the highest Provincial offices and the majority of judicial posts at the Provincial Court and its counterpart, the Chamber Court. The representatives of the peers decided a majority of the resolutions of the Provincial Diet, while the lower gentry, as a rule, only assented to them. Knights, as lower nobility, set rules for admission to their estate and closed its ranks in the middle of the 16th century. The main basis for the legal status of both the peers and the knights was the freehold of so-called patrimonial property. [65]

After the reign of King Jiří of Poděbrady, when the period of wars with the hopeful to the Hungarian crown, Mátyás Corvinus, for domination over the Czech lands was over, a new dynasty was installed on the Czech throne. This was the Jagiellonian House of Polish kings. It was through this dynasty (through the rule of Czech king Vladislav II 1456–1516) that the Czech Kingdom was personally united with other Central European states, primarily with Poland and Hungary. As a result of such political developments, Czech law began to be influenced even more by the legal systems of the neighbouring states, and a way was opened for the establishment of a Central European empire.

The systems of law and judiciary were divided according to the Estates. The law of the land (i.e. the law of the Czech provinces) not only became the law for nobility (for both peers and knights) but also the "common law" for the whole country. The Third Estate, the municipalities, had their own law and courts. The subjects, mostly peasants, were not regarded as free people, and special legal provisions applied to them. Generally, they were under the direct administration and jurisdiction of their landlords (masters). The whole state, which was composed of the Bohemian Kingdom, Moravia, Upper and Lower Silesia and Upper and Lower Lusatia, was decentralized. Each land (province) had its own Diet and Court, and their laws possessed certain distinctive features as well. There were differences in the composition of the Estates in the individual lands; for example in Moravia, spiritual lords, such as the Bishop of Olomouc, were regarded as the Fourth Estate.

---

65 Macek. J.: *The Monarchy of the Estates*, pp. 99–100.

The Czech law of the land was still based on customs and court findings (precedents), but new, written forms of law gradually prevailed. The Diet of the Bohemian Kingdom, in particular, issued its Proclamations (Acts), which were published from the beginning of the 16th century. The findings of nobility courts strengthened in their importance as a source of law, whereas the significance of customs gradually decreased. In 1500, the first codification of the law of the land was adopted by the Bohemian Provincial Diet and published. The king officially confirmed the Code as late as 1502. Unfortunately, the text was not systematic and the first publication did not even have numbers for its individual provisions. A modern edition of the Code published in 2008 consists of 576 articles.[66]

The codification committee, set up by the Provincial Diet in 1487 and controlled by the nobility, mainly used earlier customs, privileges awarded by the king, precedential court decisions and Proclamations of Provincial Diets. The result of the codification, known as Vladislav's Land Order, was not an exclusive code; other sources of law of the land were still valid and could be used in the courts. It was foreseen by the codification itself that the Land Order could be amended by new Proclamations of the Provincial Diet and that the Provincial Court could continue to produce new precedents.

Vladislav's Land Order is regarded as the first written constitution in Czech history, but it also dealt with other branches of the law of the land. It was not only a codification of constitutional and administrative law, but also of the private and criminal law of the nobility. Its constitutional character could be seen in the first part of the Order: it dealt with the competences of the administrative and judicial bodies of the Kingdom. Private law for the nobility covered part of family law, property law, including the law of succession, land registers and relevant court proceedings. The criminal law aspect could be seen in those parts dealing with the most typical crimes of that time and with criminal proceedings. There were provisions on the relationship between masters and their subjects, as well as on general rules on policing public order.

The Codification was approved by King Vladislav in 1502; however, the Land Order led to conflict with royal towns, which felt threatened by infringements of their rights and privileges. The Union of Bohemian towns, headed by the Old Town of Prague, rejected the Codification and refused to take part in the Provincial Diet. The tense situation led in some places to armed clashes between municipalities and local gentry. The unrest was ended by a compromise reached in 1517.

The Codification was amended and published three times in 1530, 1549 and 1564.[67] It was translated into Latin and German. The "revised and corrected"

---

66 For its modern edition together with introductory study see Kreuz, P. – Martinovský, I. (eds.): *Vladislavské zřízení zemské a navazující prameny (Smlouva svatováclavská a Zřízení o ručnicích)*. Edice. Příbram: Skriptorium, 2008.
67 Jireček, J., Jireček, H. (eds.): *Zřízení zemská království českého XVI. věku*. Prague: Všehrd, 1882.

edition from 1549 was the most important; it was ordered by King Ferdinand I (1503–1564) of the Habsburg dynasty after he had crushed the first rebellion of the Czech Estates against his rule. The text of the new edition strengthened the position of the king, and his powers were protected by criminal law when a new concept of so-called *crimen laesae majestatis*, crime against the majesty of the king, was introduced. The king used this powerful competence when he ordered confiscation of the property of the rebels and stripped the royal towns of some of their privileges.

There were some other important documents attached to the Land Order as annexes. Among these one should mention the Agreement of St. Václav of 1517, which ended the political disputes between the nobility and royal towns over the interpretation of the codification of the law of the land and over political and economic rights. The Agreement consisted of 51 articles and dealt with the jurisdiction of municipal courts, including a possibility for noble estates to be party before municipal courts, particularly in cases involving their property in towns.[68] Municipalities, on the other hand, reached a compromise over their economic rights.

The law of mining was amended by an Agreement between the King and the Estates on "mines and metals" in 1534, which was confirmed in 1575. The documents acknowledged the rights of the king regarding precious metals, but allowed the noble owners to take part in the mining business in all other instances. The last document annexed to the Codification was a legal instrument drafted by Jakub Menšík from Menštejn regarding disputes over land borders and published in 1600. Despite several proposals to revise the text of the Land Order, the last version from 1564 remained in force until 1618.

At the end of the 15th century, specifically between the years 1493–1499, the last influential law book on the law of the land was drafted. It was written in Czech in nine books by Viktorin Kornelius from Všehrdy (Všehrd).[69] The high quality of the Czech language in Všehrds work influenced not only lawyers but also Czech literature of the Age of Literary Humanism.[70] The law book dealt mainly with proceedings before the courts of the nobility, land registers, findings of Provincial Courts and with all other important aspects of the law of the land. Although the manuscript was of outstanding quality and Všehrd intended it to be used in practice (it was prepared as a counter proposal to Vladislav's Land Order), it was not regarded as an official source of law due to the existence of the above-mentioned Codification. In 1508 Všehrd prepared a revised version of his book and tried to harmonize it with the Land Order. This manuscript was published as late as in the 19th century, in 1841.

---

68 Kreuz, P., Martinovský, I. (eds.): *Vladislavské zřízení zemské*, pp. 269–284.
69 For its edition see Jireček, H. (ed.): *M. Viktorina ze Všehrd O právích země české Knihy devatery*. Prague 1894.
70 Macek, J.: *The Monarchy of the Estates*, pp. 110–111.

A different situation existed in Moravia, where the codification of the Moravian law of the land emerged in 1535[71] and 1545.[72] Even later, specific legal documents were used as official sources of law in Moravia, even though they were compiled by private persons. The legal book written by the Moravian statesman and lawyer Ctibor Tovačovský of Cimburk in the second half of 15th century (1481) was the most important source. His law book consisted of almost 200 articles on court proceedings and on provincial offices in Moravia, the law of succession, etc. There were at least ten annexes to the book, which had the authority of being an official source of the law of the land. In the 16th century, between 1523 and 1527, his book was revised by Ctibor Drnovský of Drnovice and published as the so-called Legal Book of Drnovice.

In 1535 the Moravian Provincial Diet in Znojmo adopted the Land Order in accord with the Czech pattern. However, it was not the same type of codification since it consisted of only 138 articles and most of its content dealt with court proceedings, private law of the nobility and criminal law. In 1545 the Moravian Estates enacted a new codification; however, this was not acknowledged by the Habsburg King Ferdinand.

Municipal law was also gradually codified and unified in the Czech lands. The first important step in this direction was taken when the Bohemian Provincial Diet adopted a proclamation in 1523 on the necessity of unifying municipal law in the Kingdom of Bohemia. In 1534 the Czech lawyer Brikcius of Licsko finished his proposal for the codification of municipal law, published two years later, in 1536.[73] However, his proposal was not officially adopted and was used in the practice of town councils and courts as a private aid. The Brikcius's proposal was merely a Czech translation of the Latin text of the Law Book from Brno (the Book of Scribe Jan) mentioned earlier, mixed together with the Prague Old Town's law. Brikcius used the vulgarized parts of Roman law, and on several occasions he referred to the Code of Justinian; he did this also in another book of his from 1534 on official titles.

Another step was taken when a special royal Court of Appeals for municipal law was instituted in 1548.[74] This was a court of a new type, functioning permanently and composed of professional lawyers, who used to decide cases not only according to valid municipal law but also according to Canon and Roman law principles. Municipal law was becoming unified through judicial practice. The codification of municipal law (the Municipal Law Code, or the so-called Koldín's Code) was prepared by Pavel Kristian of Koldín, a Czech

---

71 Čáda, F. (ed.): *Zemská zřízení moravské z roku 1535 spolu s tiskem z roku 1562 nově vydaným.* Prague, 1937.
72 Janiš, D. (ed.): *Práva a zřízení markrabství moravského z roku 1545.* (Pokus moravských stavů o revizi zemského zřízení). Historický úvod a edice. Brno, 2005.
73 For its edition see Jireček, H. – Jireček, J. (eds.): *Mistra Brikcího z Licska Práva městská, Codex Iuris Bohemici, IV, part III.* Prague, 1880.
74 For its role in broader historical context see Evans, R. J. W.: *The Making of the Habsburg Monarchy, 1550–1700, An Interpretation.* Oxford: Clarendon Press, 1979, pp. 105 and 150–151.

lawyer and representative of the Town of Prague's councils. It was approved by the King and the Czech Provincial Diet in 1579. The Code was sanctioned by the Court of Appeals and published.[75] In 1581, its "Short Summary", as a kind of Digest more suitable for practical usage, was published. The Czech version was soon translated into German. There were several later versions of the Code published with the authorization of the king. One version of the Municipal Law Code was composed as rhymes to enable smoother usage of the legal text in practice.

The Code is deeply influenced by Roman law, being derived mainly from the Digest and the Institutions. This can be observed primarily in private law (the law of persons and the law of property) and in the use of Roman law terminology. But the Code also dealt with many other important legal aspects of life in towns; and as such it reflected valid Czech law, especially that of the Prague Old Town. The Code referred to the relevant provisions of the Codification of the law of the land. Its text is divided into sections labelled alphabetically by the letters from A to T and subdivided into articles.

Koldín attempted to provide the main definitions that had regard to municipal law and the whole legal system. It is interesting to read, for example, his ideas on the importance of just (fair) law. The first part of the Code focused on the administration of towns, followed by the section on civil proceedings and its individual stages. It includes conditions for appeals and for enforcement of court decisions. The law of persons concentrated mainly on tutelage and curatorship and on the property aspects of marriage, including dowry. The law of things dealt first with the different concept of ownership in municipal law, with possession and forms of servitude. The law of succession followed, as this was very important for municipal law; the provisions for testamentary succession were very detailed. The part on contracts was influenced by the Institutions of Justinian, including the division of contracts and their types, such as consensual contracts of sale, hire of work or services, mandate or partnership and real contracts – for example, loans for use and consumption or deposit. Both the law of persons and the law of property were based on Roman law tradition. The Municipal Code covered some special fields, such as construction projects in towns. The last part of the Code was devoted to both substantive criminal law and criminal procedure; substantive criminal law encompassed crimes typical for municipalities, e.g. crimes against the person – murder, manslaughter, against property – arson, robbery or theft, and sexual offences. A list of fines for minor offences was published as a special annex to the Code.

The main importance and significance of the Code is that it gradually secured the unification of municipal law – initially in Bohemia, then later

---

75 Its new edition with commentaries was published in 2013, see Malý, K. et al. (ed.): *Práva městská česká*. Prague: Nakladatelství Karolinum, 2013.

in Moravia and Silesia. The introduction of the Code in 1610 finally ended the usage of Saxon municipal law in its Czech centre, Litoměřice. Because of Koldín's Code the end of the 16th century could be regarded as an important milestone in the introduction of the Roman law tradition into the Czech legal system. During the 17th century Koldín's Code, along with Roman law, began to be used as a subsidiary source for the law of the land and for manor courts. With certain amendments, the private law part of the Code remained valid until 1811, when the modern codification of the Austrian Civil Code was adopted.

One of the most distinguished lawyers of his era and the drafter of the Municipal Law Code, Pavel Kristian of Koldin was also a patron of, and counsel to, the University of Prague. Other legal experts, Šimon Skála and Jan Matyáš of Sudet, were assigned to restore systemic studies of law at the University at the beginning of the 17th century; however they were not successful in their attempt. Canon law was taught at the Catholic Jesuit College from 1556; this College was situated at the Clementinum in the centre of Prague.[76]

In 1526 the Czech Estates elevated the Austrian Archduke Ferdinand I of the Habsburg dynasty to the Czech throne, and the Czech lands became part of the emerging Habsburg Empire in Central Europe.[77] This important fact governed Czech developments until World War I. The Czech Kingdom gradually ceased to exist as an independent entity and became part of the Central European multinational empire consisting of the Austrian lands, the Czech lands and Hungary. The process of rapprochement between their different state and legal institutions began.[78] Until 1618 the new Habsburg rulers tried to curtail the original powers and privileges of the Estates, focussing these efforts on non-Catholics and royal towns. Ferdinand I. benefited mainly from the situation after the first rebellion of Czech Estates against its king was defeated in 1547. Not only were its leaders punished, but the Estates lost a lot from its previous dominance.[79]

The Habsburgs especially tried to strengthen the position of the Catholic Church, for example, by inviting the Jesuit order to come to Central Europe, and they advocated the advantages of centralization. At that time, the former moderate Hussites (called Utraquists, after the Sacrament of the Body and Blood of Jesus Christ being taken in "two kinds" – *sub utraque speciae*) very

76 *A History of Charles University.* Volume I (1348–1802), pp. 217–236.
77 In more details Pánek, J.: The Czech Estates and the Habsburg Monarchy. In: Pánek, J. – Tůma, O.: *A History of the Czech Lands*, p. 191 and following. Dillon, K.: *King and Estates in the Bohemian Lands 1526–1564.* Brussels, 1976. Kann, R. A.: *A History of the Habsburg Empire 1526–1918.* Berkeley: University of California Press, 1974, pp. 18–25.
78 In more details see van den Berg, P. A. J.: *The Politics of European Codification. A History of the Unification of Law in France, Prussia, the Austrian Monarchy and the Netherlands.* Groningen: Europa Law Publishing, 2007, pp. 85–88.
79 Fichtner, P. S.: *Ferdinand I of Austria: The Politics of Dynasticism in the Age of Reformation.* New York: Columbia University Press, 1982, esp. pp. 140 and following.

often changed their belief for a more radical Protestant (Evangelic) one. Specific non-Catholic religions, such as the Czech Brethren, came to be.[80] The issue of religion once again became part of the ideological and political struggle in the whole of Central Europe and an object for specific legislation. The religious tolerance promised by the Habsburg King Maxmilian (1527–1576) in 1575 was known as the "Bohemian Confession" (*Confessio Bohemica*); it was finally confirmed by the Letter Patent of His Majesty, King Rudolf II (1552–1612) of Habsburg dynasty in 1609.[81] The issue was discussed by the Provincial Diet, and the final document approved by King Rudolf represents far reaching concessions to the freedom of religious beliefs not only for the nobility but also for the wider strata of Czech society.

The Protestant estates tried to form parallel power structures to the Catholic "kings" Government and Provincial Diet. They established the so called "Body of defendants" (of the Protestant Faith) and the Diet of Protestant Estates. It was only a matter of time before the two religious and political camps would enter the final show down.[82]

The issues of religion became extremely important during the Thirty Years' War: The Czech Protestant Estates took part in an open revolt against their Catholic Habsburg king.[83] The war started in 1618, when Protestant rebels threw two pro-Habsburg high officials out of a window of the Prague Castle. This "defenestration" led to the proposal to establish a Confederation of Protestant Estates of the five independent lands of the Czech Crown – Bohemia, Moravia, Silesia, Upper and Lower Lusatia. The Habsburg dynasty was stripped of the crown, and protestant estates elected a new king, Prince Frederic of the Palatinate. A Constitution for the Confederation was enacted by the General Diet of Czech provinces in July 1619. [84] It consisted of a Preamble and 100 articles. The Confederation, or Union, was based on the equality of all lands, with priority given to the Bohemian Kingdom in certain affairs. The head of the Confederation was the Czech king, answerable to the Estates.[85]

---

80 In more details see Brock, P.: *The Political and Social Doctrines of the Unity of Czech Brethen.* Leiden, 1957; recently Atwood, C. A.: *The Theology of the Czech Brethren from Hus to Comenius.* Pennsylvania state University, 2009, especially pp. 189 and following.

81 Reich, E.(ed.): *Select Documents Illustrating Mediaeval and Modern History*, London, 1905, pp. 630–631. For the historical context see Válka, J.: Rudolfine culture. In: Teich, M. (ed.): *Bohemia in History*, pp. 120–124, and Pánek, J.: *The Czech Estates and the Habsburg Monarchy*, p. 221.

82 Pánek, J.: *The Czech Estates and the Habsburg Monarchy*, pp. 219 and following.

83 Classical account in Polišenský, J. V.: *The Thirty Years War.* University of California Press, 1971, especially Chapter IV – Bohemian war: the local conflict and its Wider consequence, p. 98 and following. See also Evans, R. J. W.: *The Making of the Habsburg Monarchy, 1550–1700*, pp. 102 and following.

84 Pursell, B. C.: *The Winter King. Frederick V of the Palatinate and the Coming of the Thirty Years War.* Aldershot: Ashgate, 2003, p. 80 and following. For legal aspects see English summary in Adamová, K.: *První česká federativní ústava z roku 1619.* Plzeň: Aleš Čeněk, 2009, pp. 163 and following.

85 See *A declaration of the causes, for the which, we Frederick, by the grace of God King Bohemia, Count Palatine of the Rhine, Elector of the Sacred Empire, & c. have accepted of the crown of*

The Estates were given the right to oppose the king with arms in the event that he would misuse his powers. The executive power was in the hands of the *Directorium*, with representatives of all three Estates. The General Assembly was established as the supreme legislative body of the whole Confederation. The Confederation favoured non-Catholic religions, and Catholics were restricted in their access to certain offices, including those of municipalities.

The Protestant coalition, however, lost a decisive Battle of White Mountain in Prague in 1620, and the Habsburg dynasty took full advantage of the victory. King Frederic (1596–1632), known also as the "Winter King"[86], fled the country, and the leaders of the rebellion were put before a martial court – twenty-one of them were publicly executed on the main square of the Prague Old Town. Large scale confiscations and redistribution of property followed. [87]

Bohemia, and of the countries there unto annexed signed in Prague Castle on November 7, 1619 (edited by T. Carter) at www. aquinas.edu/history/pdf/carter_paper.pdf

86 See for example the monograph by Pursell, B.C.: *The Winter King. Frederick V of the Palatinate and the Coming of the Thirty Years War.*, especially pp. 93 and following.

87 Mikulec, J.: Baroque Absolutism 1620–1740. In: Pánek, J. – Tůma, O. et al.: *A History of the Czech Lands*, pp. 233–234. Petráň, J. – Petráňová L.: The White Mountain as a symbol in modern Czech history. In: Teich, M.(ed.): *Bohemia in History*, pp. 144–145.

/5/

Law during the Age of Absolutism

In 1627 and 1628 a new provincial constitution, the so-called Renewed Constitution of the Province, was adopted for Bohemia and Moravia.[88] The document commenced a new period of a centralized absolute monarchy governed primarily from the Austrian capital, Vienna. This period is often designated as a period of absolutism, although in many respects the King governed together with the nobility.[89] The Habsburg dynasty treated the title of the Czech kings as hereditary. The privileges of the Estates were significantly reduced; towns were subject to, and suffered from, restrictions and discrimination. As a result of the Counter-Reformation, only the Catholic religion was allowed to exist in the Czech lands. Those members of nobility practising religious beliefs other than Catholic were either forced to switch (convert) or go into exile (so

88 For 1627 version of the Czech Kingdom see Jireček, H. (eds.): *Obnovené právo a zřízení zemské dědičného království českého.* Codex iuris Bohemicii, díl 5/2, Prague, 1888; for Moravia 1628 version see Jireček, H. (ed.): *Obnovené zřízení zemské markrabství moravského 1628.* Brno, 1890 (or Codex Iuris Bohemicii, díl 5/3, Prague, 1890). See Mikulec, J.: *Baroque Absolutism 1620–1740*, pp. 234–235. Mikulec speaks about "Renewed Land Ordinances".

89 See especially Evans, R. J. W.: *The Making of the Habsburg Monarchy, 1550–1700. An Interpretation.* Oxford: Clarendon Press, 1979, pp. 198–206 and Mikulec, J.: *Baroque Absolutism 1620–1740*, pp. 245 and following.

called *ius emigrandi*). As a result Bohemia and Moravia lost several hundred aristocrats and among the emigrants were also burghers from royal towns or leading scholars and intellectuals including famous Czech philosopher and reformer Jan Amos Komenský (Comenius).[90]

The Canon law of the Catholic Church resumed its position as the only source of the law of marriage; as such, it influenced the whole branch of family law. Affiliation with the Catholic Church and Catholic belief became compulsory prerequisites for holding land and high office. Catholic prelates, as Lords Spiritual, resumed their membership in the Czech Provisional Diet and were proclaimed as the "first" among the Estates.

The practice of absolutism resulted in profound changes being introduced into the legal system. The Habsburg rulers became the supreme and sole legislators. In order to support and justify their exclusive position, the Habsburgs applied and enjoyed one part of Roman law tradition, namely the legislation of the Roman emperors. The importance of customs and precedents further declined, and new sources of law were introduced, based upon letter patents, decrees or mandates issued by the King. Czech law was influenced by Austrian legislation; as a result, the official language of new law gradually changed from Czech to German. As can be read in the Constitution, the Czech and German languages were proclaimed to be equal. However, it should be emphasized that the text of the "Renewed Constitution of the Province" was published only in German, and the corresponding Czech version was not even completed – the translation stopped at Article F I.

The content of the Constitution was divided into parts, A to Z. It dealt mainly with the "constitutional" matters of the land, especially those relating to the powers of the King, the Provincial Diet and the Provincial Court. There were changes made in court procedure, property law and criminal law. For example, the Constitution put to an end the earlier mentioned existence of family ownership, but, on the other hand, introduced a new law of succession, including an institution of *fideicomissum*, parallel to the English institutions of fee tail (freehold interest in land restricted to a particular line of heirs, who are not free to sell it or give it away), as well as trust. The St. Václav Agreement of 1517, as well as the Agreement on the Law of Mining of 1575, were annexed to the Constitution and published again.

In 1640 the original text of the Constitution was amended and explained by Ferdinand II in the *Novellae et Declaratoriae*.[91] To a certain extent the amendments curtailed the original sharp absolutistic wording of the Renewed Constitution of the Province. In Moravia a similar explanation was published

---

90 Mikulec, J.: *Baroque Absolutism 1620–1740*, p. 237. For Comenius see Pánek, J. (ed.): *Comenius in World Science and Culture*. Prague, 1991, and Pánek, J.: Comenius: *Teacher of nations*. Prague, 1991.

91 Its recent edition in Malý, K. et al. (edd.): *Vývoj české ústavnosti v letech 1618–1918*, pp. 793–873. Prague: Nakladatelství Karolinum, 2006.

in 1650, and the amended version of the Constitution was published in 1573. The amended text stipulated that the Municipal Law Code (Koldíns Code) was a subsidiary source to the law of the land. This actually meant that Roman law became a subsidiary source for the whole legal system.

Political developments connected with the Battle of White Mountain in 1618 and the Thirty Years' War resulted in large scale transfers of real property. The defeated Estates were proclaimed as rebels and prosecuted and convicted for committing a crime against the King (*crimen laese maiestatis*). According to the law of the land the punishment for such a crime encompassed the death penalty, attainder and confiscation. The institution of confiscation has its roots in Roman law (from Latin verb *confiscare*); it means the seizure of private property as punishment, and the transfer of the seized property to the royal treasury without compensation.

Half of the Bohemian nobility, at least 178 individual cases, were affected by confiscation of their property in the 17th century. As a result, the social and economic status of the Bohemian nobility declined markedly. Where rebels were condemned to death, the punishment implied the denial to their legal heirs of the inheritance of their noble titles and other possessions. In some cases the Emperor allowed a fine to substitute for confiscation, mainly when an accused person did not possess immovable property. Despite the efforts of the Emperor and his officials to obtain sufficient financial resources for maintaining his army, the confiscated property was insufficient to fill the royal treasury because the property was, in most cases, sold below cost. The confiscated property was frequently given to the supporters of the Habsburgs. Almost half of the new noble land possessors in the Czech Kingdom came from foreign aristocratic houses. A second wave of property redistribution followed the assassination of Count Albrecht of Wallenstein in 1634.

In consequence to the Thirty Years' War, the number of inhabitants of the Czech lands rapidly declined. As a result, peasants were forcibly tied to their landlords and to the land. They could not, for example, move freely without the consent of their master (landlord) and had to carry out compulsory labour or pay financial duties. Marriages among peasants were concluded only after the landlord of the prospective spouses and his subjects had given his consent to their marriage (as well as to other important activities). The period of the so-called "second serfdom" began.[92] The second half of the 17th century saw the introduction of official land surveys and the registration of land and subjects for the assessment of tax revenues.

The harsh conditions of peasants gave rise to several rebellions, the most important of these in 1680. On the other hand, there was also a response from legislation, where provisions for the regulation of compulsory labour were enacted. The best example would be a decree issued in the same year, 1680,

92 Mikulec, J.: *Baroque Absolutism 1620–1740*, pp. 233 and following.

by Emperor Leopold (1640–1705) setting limits on compulsory labour. This decree was later followed by two decrees issued by Charles VI (1685–1740), in 1717 and 1738.

The legal development in the 17th century was influenced by the resumed teaching of law at the University.[93] The Faculty of Law was restored at Prague University as late as 1622 by a decision of Emperor Ferdinand II Habsburg (1578–1637). Teaching commenced two years later. The Law Faculty suffered from instability due to the Thirty Years' War and disputes with the Jesuit Academy. However, such instability disappeared with the merger, initiated by the so-called Union Decree issued by Ferdinand III in 1654, of the previously mentioned Jesuit Academy (*Clementinum*) and Prague University (*Carolinum*). The newly established university was called Karl-Ferdinand University.

Teaching in the second half of the 17th century was based primarily upon Roman law and Canon law. Professors were assembled into four departments – Institutions, Digest, Codex, and Canon Law. In addition to regular professors, appointed directly by the King, extraordinary professors were gradually involved in teaching. The number of law students increased until the end of the 17th century. Teaching was conducted as public lectures held in one room of the Carolinum university building. At the same time, professors provided private tutoring for money. The course of study usually took three years, without examinations. After that, anyone who wished to be awarded a degree had to pass an oral and a written examination, called *tentamen* and *examen* respectively, followed by a ceremonial disputation. The applicant had to pay the required amount of money and further arrange for a dinner for the professors. The graduation ceremony was also very expensive. From the 17th century, two types of degree were awarded: a lower licenciate, and a higher degree of doctor.

The interest of students in positive law of the land began to increase at the Law Faculty of Prague University within the school of Roman law, called *usus modernus pandectarum*. Kryštof Kyblín of Waffenburg was among the most outstanding representatives of the Law Faculty of that time. He acted as Dean of the Faculty several times and became Rector of the whole University. In addition, he was the author of a prominent comparative treatise dealing with domestic and general (Roman) law. After his death, a second generation of professors emerged, among whom Jan Krystof Schambogen was the most eminent.

At the beginning of the 18th century the existing codifications of land law and municipal law became a major obstacle for modernization of the whole legal system. It was necessary to unify laws valid in Bohemia and Moravia. A new codification of constitutional, administrative, private and criminal

---

93 Kuklík, J. et al.: *Faculty of Law of Charles University in Prague*. Prague: Havlíček Brain Team, 2008, pp. 13–16.

law to be valid in the Czech lands was envisioned. In 1709 Emperor Joseph I (1678–1711) entrusted a Codification Committee with the preparation of a draft.[94] The full name of this body was the Committee for the Codification of the Law of the Czech Province and Unification of the Law of the Bohemian and Moravian Provinces.[95] The Committee was headed by the Chief Justice of the Court of Appeals, J. Löw of Erlsfeld. There were in fact two separate committees, one in Prague for Bohemian law, and the other in Brno for Moravian law. The proposal was associated with the introduction of teaching based on the theory of natural law at the Law Faculty in Prague. It was also connected with the academic performance of Václav Xaver Neumann of Pucholtz, who, in addition to serving as Rector of the University and Dean of the Faculty of Law, became famous due to his involvement in the above-mentioned Codification Committee.

The proposal drafted by the Prague Committee divided the envisioned Provincial Code into nine parts: 5 parts were to be connected with the new concept of unified private law, including the law of persons, the law of property, the law of succession and the law of contracts. This proposal remained incomplete due to the political situation after the death of Charles VI and is known as *elaboratum bohemicum*. However, the proposal represented an important step towards the codification of private law instituted by the Habsburg Empress Maria Theresa, this time with a clear aim to unify private law for the Austrian and Czech lands.

---

94 Agnew, H. L.: *The Czechs and the Lands of the Bohemian Crown*, pp. 79–80.
95 See also Loschelder, M.: *Die österreichische Allgemeine Gerichtsordnungvon 1781 Grunlagen- und Kodifikationsgeschichte.* Berlin: Duncke a Humblot, 1978, p. 26.

/6/
Enlightened Absolutism

At the beginning of the 18th century the Austrian branch of the Habsburg dynasty was forced to resolve problems regarding the law on succession, and this led to serious consequences. Emperor Leopold died in 1705 and was succeeded by his son Joseph. After a short period of reign, Joseph I died on 17th April 1711, leaving two unmarried daughters – Maria Josepha, who later, in 1719, married Augustus II, the future Elector of Saxony and King of Poland, and Maria Amalia, who married Karl Albrecht (1697–1745), Elector of Bavaria, in 1722. His brother Charles became Emperor of the Holy Roman Empire, as Charles VI, and inherited the Habsburg lands in accord with the so-called Succession Pact. In 1711 Charles VI wrote a will in which he gave his daughters precedence over those of Joseph or Leopold in the event that his male line should become extinct; this violated the Family Pact of 1703. The leading officials of the Privy Council and the Ministers of the Emperor approved this modification on 19th April 1713. The notarized publication later received the name "Pragmatic Sanction of 1713".[96] The Pragmatic Sanction became the law

96 Bernatzik, E.: *Die österreichischen Verfassungsgesetze mit Erläuterungen.* Second edition. Wien: Manzsche k.uk Hof-Verlags, 1911, dok. No. 2, p. 15.

of the Habsburg House of Austria. It was confirmed by Provincial Diets in Bohemia, Moravia and Silesia in October 1720 and it became an integral part of the Austrian constitution until 1918.[97]

Charles VI's only son died as an infant in 1716, and it soon became clear that Charles VI himself was likely to be the last male Habsburg. He therefore took part in a long diplomatic struggle to preserve his own inheritance for his daughter Maria Theresa (1717–1780) and to have the Pragmatic Sanction accepted not only by the Crown lands of the Habsburg empire but also by other European powers. Charles VI concluded several international treaties to guarantee the Pragmatic Sanction, such as the Treaty of Vienna of 30th April 1725, with Spain, or 6 years later with Great Britain and the Netherlands, and then with France in 1738.

However, when Charles VI died in 1740, France, Bavaria, Spain and Saxony contested the claims of his eldest daughter, Maria Theresa.[98] Prussia also took part in the so-called War of Austrian Succession by seizing Silesia. Joseph Is son-in-law, Karl Albrecht of Bavaria (1697–1745), was crowned King of Bohemia in December 1741 and elected Emperor, as Charles VII, in January 1742. But he lost his own Bavarian lands when these were taken by Austrian troops. Charles VII died in 1745. His son preferred to support the claims of Maria Theresa in return for recovering Bavaria. Maria Theresa's husband, Archduke of Tuscany, was elected Emperor of the Holy Roman Empire, as Francis I, in 1745. The Habsburg dynasty was transformed into the House of Habsburg-Lorraine. By the Treaty of Aachen in 1748 Maria Theresa's inheritance of the Austrian lands, including the Czech Kingdom and Moravia, was recognized on condition that a larger part of Silesia was ceded to Prussia and Austria lost some territories in Italy.

After this difficult period of time, Marie Theresa decided to create a modern monarchy capable of competing with the leading European powers. Initially, reforms in state administration were introduced. The aim of the reforms was to create a united nucleus of the centralized monarchy from the Austrian and Czech provinces, whereas in Hungary legal and administrative differences persisted. The Czech lands became more and more closely connected with the Austrian lands, as German hereditary lands.[99] Traditional Czech offices were dissolved in Vienna, and new central administrative and judicial bodies common to the Austrian and Czech lands were established. The reforms initiated the "bureaucratisation" of state administration. They laid the foundations for a centralized system of state administration consisting of paid

---

97 *Ibidem*, pp. 15–47.
98 In more details Ondo Grečenková, M.: Enlightened Absolutism and the Birth of a Modern State, 1740–1792. In: Pánek, J. – Tůma, O. et al.: *A History of the Czech Lands*, pp. 263–268 and Kann, R. A.: *A History of the Habsburg Empire 1526–1918*, pp. 170–179.
99 See for example Olechowski, T.: *Rechtsgeschichte, Einführung in die historischen Grundlagen des Rechts*, Wien, 2006, pp. 33–35.

state servants at regional, provincial and central levels, with the exception of the first instance administrative procedure, which remained in the hands of landlords. The reform of administration was supplemented by a reform of the judicial system. Reforms of regional and municipal administration followed.[100] For example, the number of towns with their own criminal justice system decreased. In 1784, as a result of bureaucratisation of the "magistrates", four originally independent towns of Prague (the Old Town, the New Town, the Lesser Quarter, and the Castle) were united, and a board of municipal authorities was appointed to sit at the Old Town Hall and to replace their respective self-governing bodies.

The law reform was seen as an important part of the whole reform movement, with new legislation becoming an important tool for central administration to implement its reform projects. As a result, a modern legal system originated in the Czech lands as well as in the whole Habsburg monarchy in the second half of the 18th century. This period of legal developments was influenced by so-called "enlightened absolutism" and its social and economic reforms. Enlightenment was closely linked with the philosophy of natural law and brought in a new era of large scale and significant codifications.[101] The results of enlightened reforms were very impressive, particularly in Prussia. Prussian achievements caused the Habsburg monarchs, Marie Theresa and her son Joseph II (1741–1790), to use law reform as one of the main tools for the modernization of Central European societies.[102]

The significance of the age of Enlightened Absolutism is substantial due to its installing profound changes in the legal system. Legal reforms were connected with the unification of law, which was intended both for the Austrian and the Czech lands.[103] As a starting point, a new Criminal Code (*Constitution Criminalis Theresiana*), including Criminal Procedure, was adopted in 1768 during the reign of Maria Teresa.[104] Its Czech translation was published in Vienna in 1771. This Code was not the first attempt to codify criminal law. Joseph I enacted the Criminal Code as early as 1707; its Czech translation was published in 1708 by the Justice of the Court of Appeals, Kašpar J. Kupec of Bilenberg. The Code was intended for Bohemia, Moravia and Silesia and was inspired by Emperor Ferdinand III's codification of Austrian criminal law in Lower Austria in 1656. The Code was relatively brief: there were only

---

100 Ondo Grečenková, M.: *Enlightened Absolutism and the Birth of a Modern State, 1740–1792*, pp. 270–276.
101 Recently see Beales, D.: *Enlightenment and Reform in Eighteenth-century Europe.* International Library of Historical Studies, I. B. Tauris NY, 2005, especially pp. 28–59; instead of enlightened absolutism Beales uses the term "enlightened despotism".
102 See Agnew, H. L.: *The Czechs and the Lands of the Bohemian Crown*, pp. 86–90, Okey, R.: *The Habsburg Monarchy c. 1765–1918. From Enlightenment to the Eclipse.* European Studies Series, Basingstoke, 2001, pp. 3–67.
103 See for example Bernard, P. P.: *The Limits of Enlightenment: Joseph II and the Law.* University of Illinois Press, 1979 p. 5 and following.
104 Kann, R. A.: *A History of the Habsburg Empire 1526–1918*, pp. 179–180.

twenty-three articles plus some separate paragraphs, and it dealt mainly with criminal proceedings. The Code was used by the Court of Appeals as a source subsidiary to both the Renewed Constitution of the Province and Koldín's Municipal Code. It helped to unify criminal proceedings primarily in the practice of municipal courts.

The Criminal Code of Marie Theresa was divided into two parts and consisted of a total of one hundred four articles. The first part dealt with criminal proceedings and the second part covered substantive criminal law. The Code unified Austrian and Czech criminal law and repealed earlier legislation, including parts of the Renewed Constitution of the Province and Koldín's Municipal Code. Although the codification and unification effects could be regarded as modern features of legal development, the Criminal Code was still materially based on early modern and even medieval criminal law relics, such as torture (as a "crown" of evidence), a limited possibility of defending oneself before court with the assistance of a lawyer, punishment of witchcraft, etc. The application of analogy was permitted, and the whole concept of crime and punishment was still based on the assumption that punishment is, to a certain extent, a revenge for the crime committed. Punishment embodied deterrent and symbolic effects. Substantive law considered the most serious crimes to be those against religion, Church, Emperor and State, while crimes against person and property were of a lesser importance. The Code, and especially the use of torture, was criticized by legal experts, including Josef Sonnenfels and his pamphlet on abolition of torture from 1775. The torture was repealed a year later, in 1776.

Changes in the whole concept of criminal law were brought about as a result of discussions initially held at universities in Vienna and later also in Prague. Austrian academia was influenced by the Italian lawyer and philosopher Cesare Beccaria, in particular by his famous book "On Crimes and Punishments", from 1764.[105] Beccaria criticized the death penalty and torture and demanded that punishment should be adequate to the crime committed; and he determined educational, social and economic roles for punishment to perform. He advocated that rationality and effectiveness be applied in criminal proceedings. [106]

Leopold (1747–1792), Joseph IIs brother, brought some of Beccaria's ideas into practice in Tuscany by enactment of the so-called *Leopoldina*, the Leopold Criminal Code, in 1786. The ideas of enlightenment and natural law attracted Josef Sonnenfels, an Austrian lawyer, professor and high official, who was

---

105 Beccaria, C.: *Dei delitti e delle pene*, Milano, 1764. Original English translation was entitled *An Essay on Crimes and Punishments* and published in London in 1767 with preface by Voltaire. Beccarias work was translated into German and published in Prague by Josef Ignác Butschek in 1774.
106 In more details see Shaffern, R. W.: *Law and Justices from Antiquity to Enlightenment.* New York: Rowman and Littlefield, 2000, pp. 205–208.

entrusted by the Emperor with carrying out the reform not only of criminal law but also of the whole so-called "police sciences".[107]

As a result, modern principles of criminal law were introduced by Joseph II's Criminal Code in 1787, the General Code on Crimes and their Punishment.[108] A year later, a new and unified Criminal Procedure followed. The Criminal Code applied to the whole Habsburg Monarchy, and it was a significant step towards a modern and unified criminal law.

The Code, consisting of two parts, was enacted in German and translated into Czech. In addition to unifying criminal law for the Austrian and Czech lands, it was an exclusive code, repealing all earlier criminal legislation. It was a very good example of the application of new and modern legislative techniques including the enactment of general, brief and clear provisions. The principles of *nullum crimen sine lege* (no crime without a law) and *nulla poena sine lege* (no punishment without a law) were introduced for the first time. The Code was based on a new approach to punishment, which was supposed to reflect the extent and nature of injury caused to society or an individual by the crime committed. The Code attempted to apply the above-mentioned new functions of punishment, including social, educational and economic.

The first part dealt with crimes and relevant punishments. It was divided into seven chapters. There was the legal definition of a crime as a single act, or a series of acts, punishable by law, forbidden by statute, and connected with a guilty state of mind and free will. A crime must have been committed intentionally, knowingly and wilfully. The limit of the age of responsibility for a crime was set at twelve years. Not only offenders but also accomplices or accessories were liable for a crime committed. An attempt to commit a crime was itself a crime as soon as substantial steps to perpetrate the crime were taken. The second chapter set conditions for the application of punishment by a judge. The judge had to take into account the low age of an offender, or that he had committed a crime for the first time, etc., in favour of the offender. On the other hand, the extent of the damage caused by a crime, or previously committed crimes, was to be taken into account against the offender.

The Criminal Code restricted the imposition and execution of the death penalty. Death penalty was reserved only for high treason during a state of emergency. The sentence of imprisonment was served in a strict prison, called a penitentiary. There were three categories of prison and imprisonment was usually accompanied by forced labour or stocks. Gaol-keepers held a wide array of other tools for disciplining their inmates. There were cruel

---

107 Wandruszka, A. – Urbanitsch, P. (eds.): *Die Habsburgermonarchie 1848–1918. Volume II.* Verwaltung und Rechtswesen, Verlag der Österreichischen Akademie der Wissenschaften, 2nd edition, Wien, 2003, Chapter I, pp. 33–39. For its English translation see *The Emperors new code of criminal laws,* published at Vienna, the 15th of January, 1787. Printed by John Rea for Messr. Moncrieffe [and 3 others], 1787 (google e-book).

108 Padower, S. K.: *The Revolutionary Emperor. Joseph the Second 1741–1790.* New York: Ballou, 1934, pp. 193–195.

and publicly executed corporal punishments, including beating, defamatory display on the pillory (racks) or burning of signs of guilt.

The ensuing chapters of the first part of the Code dealt with individual categories of crime. Crimes against the State, prerogative rights and public order came first; the second category of crimes against person (murder, manslaughter, assault, battery and rape) was followed by the third and last part encompassing crimes against property, such as arson, larceny (theft), robbery or forgery.

The second part of the Code was divided into five chapters and focused on so-called "political misdemeanours". They were of a lesser danger to society, subject to different punishment. An example of such a misdemeanour could be damage caused by careless performance of craft or trade, misdemeanours against property, and misdemeanours against public order.

In June 1788 the codification of criminal procedure was adopted as the General Criminal Procedure (*Allgemeine Kriminal-Gerischtsordnung* – KGO in German).[109] If compared to the Code of Maria Theresa, a certain modernisation in the field can be seen; however, there Inquisition proceedings remained the basic type of criminal proceedings, including a written process with exclusion of the public in most cases.

The reform of private law also began during the reign of Maria Theresa. These brought changes in various aspects of private law, the most important of them being an attempt to prepare a new general Civil Code.[110]

The Code was intended to combine valid private law in various Austrian and Czech lands (both customary and written) with new principles based on Roman law and the theory of rational natural law. At the beginning of the codification process, the leading role was played by Jozef Azzoni, an outstanding lawyer from the University of Prague. He proposed including the law valid in the Czech lands, mainly Koldín's Municipal Code. The Austrian legal tradition was represented by Joseph Ferdinand von Holger. By 1758 the first part of the Code was finished; the whole draft was completed after Azzoni's death in 1766.[111] The proposal for the new Code is known as *Codex Theresianus universalis* and was divided into three parts: the law of persons, the law of property and the law of obligations. There was a proposition to add a fourth part dealing with civil proceedings; however, the fourth part was not included, which led to the preparation of a separate procedural code. The draft of the Code was

---

109 For its text in German see Johann Thomas Edlen von Trattnern *Allgemeine Kriminal- Gerichtsordnung*, Wienna, 1788 (e-book Google).

110 In more details Strakosch, H. E.: *State Absolutism and the Rule of Law: The Struggle for the Codification of Civil Law in Austria, 1753–1811.* University of Sydney Press, 1967, p. 12 and following.

111 Ph. Harras von Harrasowsky: *Der Codex Theresianus und seine Umarbeitungen*, Volume I, Wien, 1883, pp. 5 and following. Harrasowsky published not only the original draft but in the years 1883–1886 next four volumes including the drafts by Horten and Martini. See his book *Geschichte der Codification des Österreichischen Civilrechtes.* Wien, 1868; van den Berg, P. A. J.: *The Politics of European Codification*, pp. 91–97.

quite a large compilation of private law in force; it was a compromise between the traditions of the individual lands. Roman law combined with natural law principles was used mostly for defining the institutions of private law and for strengthening the position of the Emperor as legislator.

The draft was not suitable for practical application, and there were many complaints from various quarters of politics, administration and the individual lands. The whole draft was highly casuistic, and some experts regarded it as a legal textbook rather than a code. There were other political and legal arguments against the Code, especially among the State Councillors.[112] The Empress herself was not prepared to enact the draft; as a result, it was put under review by a special committee headed by Johann Berhard Horten.[113] Together with Karl A. Martini, another leading Austrian lawyer and professor of Roman and natural law at Vienna University, they revised and shortened the whole draft. The changes in the proposal were influenced by the German natural law philosopher and legal theoretician Christian Wolff.[114] It should be noted that his impact led to decreasing of the role of Roman law.[115] Despite the successful completion of the new draft, it became clear during the revision process that there was a growing opposition to a uniform codification. This halted the process until the death of Maria Theresa.

The process of codification was influenced by the arrival of theories of natural law, which were connected mainly with new developments at various Law Faculties. Legal education, not only in Vienna but also in Prague, underwent substantial changes, in particular in its structure. Regular lectures on Czech case-law and proceedings were held from 1740. In 1746 a new Department of History and Rhetoric was established and a Department of Natural, Public and Feudal Law was constituted two years later. In 1755 the original system of final examinations was replaced with strict, so-called *rigorous* examinations.[116] After 1761 the degree *juris utriusque doctor* was the only degree awarded. In 1774 three rigorous examinations were prescribed, and their content reflected the changes that had occurred in legal education. The first examination was composed of natural law, state law and Canon law. The second rigorous examination included Roman law and criminal law. And the third examination consisted of German state and feudal law and the legal history of the Empire. In 1784 new political subjects were incorporat-

---

112 They included the lack of exclusivity and that the draft was too wordy, too doctrinal and overly influenced by Roman law. Van den Berg, P. A. J.: *The Politics of European Codification*, p. 101–102. See also Hausmaninger, H.: *The Austrian legal system*. Hague: Kluwer Law International, 1998, p. 217.
113 Strakosch, H. E.: State *Absolutism and the Rule of Law: The Struggle for the Codification of Civil Law in Austria, 1753–1811*, pp. 95–96.
114 For his personality and work see H. M. Bachmann: *Die naturrechtliche Staatslehre Christian Wolffs*. Berlin: Duncker und Humblot, 1977, especially pp. 117 and following.
115 *Ibidem*, p. 205.
116 For reforms of this period see Odložilík, O.: *The Caroline University, 1348–1948*. Prague: Orbis, 1948, pp. 59–61.

ed into the rigorous examinations, namely state administration, the police, business and finance. New subjects, such as statistics, were introduced to the system of legal education, which expanded the professional qualification of future lawyers. German became the language of instruction, and the whole course of study took four years. The increasing significance of legal education corresponded with the importance of the above-mentioned changes in the legal system as an instrument for the centralisation, bureaucratisation and improved efficiency of state officials as well as for deep social changes, which were highly appreciated and enforced by the enlightened emperors.

After the death of Empress Marie Theresa in 1780 the preparations for codification were almost successfully completed during the reign of her son, Joseph II.[117] Joseph II launched a new and more radical campaign on modernization and unification of law.[118] At first he finalized the enactment of the General Code on Civil Procedure (*Allgemeine Gerichtsordnung* – AGO in German) on the 1st May 1781.[119] As was already mentioned, the Civil Procedure was originally meant as a fourth part of the General Code of the whole of private law, and the draft of the Civil Procedure Code was completed in 1776.[120] The proposal of the Code was prepared by Swiss born lawyer Joseph Hyacinth von Froidevo (Froidevaux).[121] The Code was divided into thirty-four chapters and was published in German, Latin and Italian and there was also a Czech translation arranged. It was based on new principles of civil proceedings, including the enforcement of judgments, and separated from criminal proceedings.[122] Its Article 1 stipulated that civil proceedings should start on the initiative of a party to the dispute (action), and ex officio proceedings were permitted to start only when there was an explicit statutory authorization. Parties to proceedings were essentially equal; the main intention of the legislature was to diminish formalities and to enforce efficient and expeditious proceedings. The intention failed, especially because there were three instances of proceedings with two stages of appeals. Another important change was an introduction of more opportunities for the representation of parties by lawyers (attorneys-at-law). The Code brought changes to the judiciary. To become a judge it was

---

117 For his reforms in civil law see Beales, D.: *Joseph II. Volume II: Against the World, 1780–1790.* Cambridge University Press, 2009, p. 526 and following. Padower, S. K.: *The Revolutionary Emperor, Joseph the Second 1741–1790*, pp.193–195. Paul P. Bernard: *The Limits of Enlightenment: Joseph II and the Law*, pp. 24 and following.

118 Van den Berg, P. A. J.: *The Politics of European Codification*, pp. 106–107.

119 In more details see Loschelder, M.: *Die österreichische Allgemeine Gerichtsordnung von 1781 Grunlagen–und Kodifikationsgeschichte*, especially, pp. 80 and following.

120 Caenegem, R. C.: *International Encyclopedia of Comparative Law*. Volume XVI, Chapter 2, History of European Civil Procedure, p. 96.

121 For his personality, Loschelder, M.: *Die österreichische Allgemeine Gerichtsordnung von 1781 Grunlagen- und Kodifikationsgeschichte*, p. 55.

122 Wandruszka, A. – Urbanitsch, P. (eds.): *Die Habsburgermonarchie 1848–1918. Volume II. Verwaltung und Rechtswesen*, Chapter IX., W. Ogris, Die Rechtsentwicklung in Cisleithanien, 1848–1918, p. 572.

necessary to prove one's professional expertise, which needed to be acknowledged by passing state exams at a Law Faculty within the Empire.

In the years 1783 and 1784 the reforms of proceedings before municipal courts followed; in 1786 Joseph II ordered that specialized professional justices for individual manors should be introduced. The West Galician Civil Proceedings Code (*Westgalizische Gerichtsordnung* – WGO) was enacted in 1796, which inspired changes in civil procedure in other Austrian lands.[123]

In 1781 Joseph II issued the Decree on Religious Tolerance.[124] According to this Decree not only Catholic but also Protestant (Lutheran and Calvinist) and Orthodox religious creeds were allowed to be practised. The document had an impact primarily upon changes in family law: marriages among Protestants concluded before their priests, or even cross-religious marriages, were permitted. The people of Jewish religion were still not enjoying full rights. In 1726 so called "family system" was introduced to limit the number of Jews in the Habsburg monarchy. Only oldest sons were allowed to enter into marriage and establish their own family. Joseph II. improved also their legal status, but discrimination in the Jewish law of marriage was not removed. In 1797 the so called Jewish systematic patent, *Judensystemal-patent*, was enacted.[125]

In 1781 the Decree on the Abolition of Serfdom followed. According to this Decree, subjects, especially peasants, were allowed to freely enter into marriage, to move, to study or to gain knowledge of crafts in towns. However, certain feudal obligations of peasants towards their masters, in particular their obligation to work on the land or to pay a certain amount of money, remained in force until 1848.

Both decrees modified the proposals of the Codes of private law. In January 1783 a special Decree regarding marriages was issued. State law, for the first time in centuries, set rules for the conclusion of a contract of marriage; disputes arising from the law of marriage and all marriage-related matters were transferred from the Church to state civil courts. In May of 1786, the law of succession (or the law of inheritance, as it was also called) was officially proclaimed as a unified reform for all inhabitants of the Austrian and Czech lands. It unified lines of succession for all classes of inhabitants, with the only exception being the privileges of aristocratic families.

Joseph II used the existing partial reforms to revise the proposals for the codification of civil law. Horten was again entrusted with the task; his proposal, known as "Horten's Draft", promoted and strengthened the role of natural law. The Emperor decided that individual parts of the Code should be enacted

---

123 *Ibidem*, p.573.
124 In more details see O'Brien, Ch. H.: *Ideas of religious toleration at the time of Joseph II: a study of the enlightenment among Catholics in Austria*. American Philosophical Society. New series. Vol. 59, part 7, 1969, pp. 22–24.
125 Mischler, E., Ulbrich, J.: Österreichisches Staatswörterbuch II. Wien, 1906, pp. 964–969, Bihl, W.: Die Juden. In: *Die Habsburgermonarchie 1848–1918* III./2, Wien, 2003, pp. 890–892.

step by step. On the 1st November 1786 the first segment of the Civil Code was promulgated. It was officially published under No. 591 in a newly created Collection of Judicial Laws. This part of the Civil Code dealt with the law of persons, family law and guardianship and curatorship.[126]

After the death of Joseph II, the new Emperors Leopold II and Franz I (1768–1835) suspended the codification of the remaining parts of the Code. The Habsburgs returned back to more absolutistic and conservative forms of government. The period between 1790 and 1848, sometimes designated as a period of Police Absolutism, was a reaction of the conservative nobility and high administrative officials connected with the House of Habsburgs to the French Revolution and conquests of Napoleon.

Subsequently, the project of the codification of private law was transformed into a more fragmentized approach. Individual provinces tried to preserve as much of their own law as possible, which resulted in slowing down the progress of codification. Individual provinces, including the Czech lands, established their own coordination committees attached to Courts of Appeal, referring their outcomes to the Central Committee, established by the Imperial Court and headed by the outstanding Austrian lawyer Karl Anton von Martini. This approach resulted in the decision to prepare a draft of the Code, which would be put into practice in one Province only. It was decided that a unified code for the Austrian and Czech lands would be prepared only after the evaluation of enforcement of such a single code in the respective Province. The proposal was drafted by 1797, when the Civil Code was approved by Emperor Franz I for the territory of Western Galicia. The Western Galician Civil Code thus became a direct predecessor of the General Civil Code.[127]

Some changes were made in the codification of criminal law. On the one hand, Leopold II continued humanizing criminal law in accordance with Beccaria's views. As a result, exhibit on the pillory, publicly executed beating or burning of signs were abolished. On the other hand, criminal law was more strictly applied to political crimes.

In 1795 new Emperor Franz I reinstalled the death penalty for high treason and other political crimes and ordered a revision of the Criminal Code to be done. The revising committee was composed of leading judges, state officials and university professors, including Josef Sonnenfels and Matthias W. Haan, who also took part in the codification of private law.[128] The revision of the Criminal Code was pursued in full with respect to the historical traditions of individual provinces. The revised Criminal Code (known as Haans Draft),

126 Van den Berg, P. A. J.: *The Politics of European Codification*, p. 108.
127 Van den Berg, P. A. J.: *The Politics of European Codification*, p. 113.
128 Wandruszka, A. – Urbanitsch, P. (eds.): *Die Habsburgermonarchie 1848–1918*. Volume II. *Verwaltung und Rechtswesen*, Chapter IX., Ogris, W.: *Die Rechtsentwicklung in Cisleithanien 1848–1918*, p. 562.

intended for the whole of the Austrian and Czech lands, was enacted in 1797 only for the territory of Western Galicia.

Having considered the experience in enforcement of the Western Galician Criminal Code, a new codification of Criminal law was enacted in September 1803.[129] This Code was divided into two parts, the first dealing with crimes, and the second with misdemeanours; both parts contained a special subdivision for criminal procedure. The Code was applied in the Austrian and Czech lands, but not in Hungary. The final stages of codification were influenced by the teaching of the leading German expert in criminology, Paul Johann Anselm von Feuerbach.

The Code contained in its first part a legal definition of crime using again the principle *nullum crimen sine lege* and a so-called formal concept of crime. A crime must have been committed intentionally, knowingly and wilfully. Children under fourteen years of age were not liable for their criminal acts. Not only offenders but also accomplices and accessories were liable for the commission of a crime. An attempt to commit a crime was itself a crime should substantial steps towards committing the crime have been taken. It was possible to claim lack of criminal responsibility using the defence of infancy, insanity, duress or necessity.

The principle *nulla poena sine lege* applied for sentencing. However, the Code returned to the possibility of imposing the death penalty as a capital punishment executed by hanging the convict. The death penalty was reserved for the most serious crimes against the State, high treason, and for certain degrees of murder or arson. The second most severe punishment was imprisonment served in provincial penitentiaries. The sentence of imprisonment was divided into three degrees, according to the conditions and daily regime of inmates. It was possible to impose other types of punishment, e.g. forfeiture of property, forced labour, deprivation of titles of honour, awards and military rank, or banishment. Corporal punishments were not explicitly prohibited.

The second category of criminal conduct, misdemeanours, were punished with different types of penalty, including imprisonment in jail for up to six months, house arrest, monetary fines or prohibition from performing professional activities, banishment, or prohibition from staying at particular towns or even provinces. Misdemeanours were treated before courts in a different way, and the mode of criminal proceedings with regard to crimes and misdemeanours differed. The Code dealt with some modern principles of sentencing: the judge was obliged to take into account the personal and social conditions of the perpetrator, and the danger or consequences of the crime in favour of the offender or against him.

The Code, however, brought about stricter punishment for particular types of crime, especially crimes against the Emperor, State or public order. The

---

129 *Ibidem*, pp. 555–556.

Code used, for example, the Latin term *vis publica* (public might) to cover several different crimes. These categories were seen as the most dangerous to the society, and they were enacted first, followed by crimes against the person. The Code enacted a more detailed division between murder and manslaughter, and crimes against property mainly encompassed the definitions of robbery, theft and fraud. Crimes against religion, bigamy, adultery and libel were also defined.

/7/

Codification
of Austrian civil law

On August 11th 1804, Emperor Franz II, the "Head of the House and the Monarchy of Austria", assumed the title of "Hereditary Emperor of Austria". When the Holy Roman Empire finally broke up in 1806, a new Austrian Empire was announced. All its parts, including the Czech lands, but with certain exceptions with respect to Hungary, were seen merely as administrative provinces of the Empire. Such an approach strengthened centralist tendencies, which also naturally found their expression in the law.

Despite the absolutist form of government, the most important codification of civil law within the history of Central European law was adopted in 1811 as the so-called General Austrian Civil Code – *Allgemeines Burgerliches Gesetzbuch* (ABGB).[130] The Code was influenced by the French Civil Code of 1804 (*Code civil* or *Code Napoléon*) and by the Prussian codification of provincial law of 1794. The final draft of the Austrian Civil Code was prepared by Franz

---

130 For its text in English see *General Civil Code for All the German Hereditary Provinces of the Austrian Monarchy*. Translated by Joseph M. Chevalier de Winiwarter, Wien, 1866, and modern version Baeck, P. L. (transl.): *The General Civil Code of Austria*. Oceana, 1972.

Anton von Zeiller, Professor of Roman and natural law at Vienna University.[131] He not only conducted the work on the wording of a final draft, but also compiled an analysis comparing the draft with the principles of Roman law and with the leading codifications of civil law in other countries.

The Austrian Civil Code stems from the Roman law tradition and Roman law institutions, as well as from the concept of natural law.[132] The principles of natural law were allowed to be used by judges during civil proceedings where no provision of the Civil Code could be directly applicable or where it was impossible to apply the provisions of the Code by analogy. Such an approach was connected with the introduction of common law principles – such as justice, common sense, or equity into valid law and practice. Natural law was behind the principle of the equality of persons before the law: the Code provided that people, as human beings, are born free and are equal before the law; slavery was prohibited on the territory of the Austrian Monarchy.

The basic principles set in the introductory part of the Code applied universally to the whole legal system; they tried, albeit insufficiently, to define the term private law itself. Article 1 read as follows: "The entirety of laws that regulate private rights and obligations of inhabitants of the state amongst themselves shall form civil law". [133]

The Introductory Patent of the Emperor stated the reasons for codification and proclaimed it as an exclusive code: the General Civil Code introduced unified private law for all inhabitants of the Austrian and Czech lands, along with the reservation that the Code was not applicable in Hungary.[134] The patent repealed all "old law" including the first part of the Civil Code of Joseph II and the Western Galician Civil Code. The Introductory Patent provided for a possible division of private law into civil law and business law. However, the envisaged Commercial Code was enacted much later, in 1862. The General Civil Code was enacted in the German language as the authentic language version for its interpretation. The Czech translation of the Code was published immediately in 1811 and was widely used in practice.

The Code was divided into three books and one thousand five-hundred two sections. The first book dealt with the law of persons. It provided definitions of natural and juristic persons and of their different types of capacity in private law. The concept was based on three statuses of persons – the status of

---

131 Strakosch, H. E.: *State Absolutism and the Rule of Law: The Struggle for the Codification of Civil Law in Austria, 1753–1811*, pp. 209 and following.

132 See analyses by Robinson, O. F. – Fergus, T. D. – Gordon, W. D.: *European Legal History, Sources and Institutions.* Butterwords, London, 1994, pp. 254–255. Hausmaninger, H.: *The Austrian legal system*, pp. 218–219.

133 Translation from 1866 reads as follows: "The complex of laws, by which the private rights and obligations of inhabitants of the State towards one another are determined, constitutes the Civil Right (law)". General Civil Code for All the German Hereditary Provinces of the Austrian Monarchy, p. 5.

134 *Ibidem*, pp. 1–4.

liberty, the status of citizenship, and the status of "family". The first status was connected with the natural law concept of people being born free and equal before the law. The second status gave rise to the enactment of provisions regarding state citizenship. The third status dealt with the law of marriage and family law. Marriage was still concluded before the Church, but it was in a form of contract, and the Code regulated the property issues of marriage. Civil marriages were allowed only after the enactment of Imperial Act No. 51/1870, which provided for a civil marriage between persons not belonging to any religion recognized by the law.

The parties to a marriage contract were not equal, because a wife had to obey her husband and the husband had a stronger position regarding the alimentation of his family and power over his children. Interreligious marriages were allowed, with special provisions regarding Jewish marriages. The possibility of divorce was opened only for the non-Catholic population and for strictly stipulated reasons. The Code set the concept of "legal separation" with respect to the Catholics. However, in the case of a so-called defective marriage, the marriage might be legally nullified by the innocent party through a court action, and, as a result, both parties would have their status as unmarried persons restored. There were many restrictions imposed on marriage, such as the principle of monogamy, blood relations, insufficient age, insanity, etc. These restrictions were construed as the lack of capacity to conclude the contract of marriage.

The whole concept of family law was based upon the institution of the so-called power of the father of the family (*patria potestas*). It governed the relationship between the father and children born to legally married parents, including alimentation, education, the mandate to act on the behalf of the children and consent to their marriage. Should the father of the family die, there were strict rules on tutelage (from Latin *tutela*): the tutor had general control over his ward's affairs, particularly in property and educational matters. The first book of the Code regulated the legal capacity to act with respect to age and mental health. Should the capacity to act be limited, an institution of so-called curatorship (from Latin *cura*) was introduced, with the curator taking care of the interests of the (partially) incapacitated person.

The second book of the General Civil Code dealt with the law of things (property). Its introductory part provided basic definitions and categories concerning things: (a) things in public ownership (ownership of the state, natural resources, seas, rivers, etc.); (b) things in private ownership, subdivided into (i) corporeal things (could be "touched", were tangible) and incorporeal things (intangible, such as rights, copyright); and (ii) things movable and immovable.

The introductory chapter was followed by two parts, one focusing on property law, connected with so-called rights *in rem*, and the other on the law of obligations. The property part dealt with the institutions of possession, ownership, co-ownership, servitudes (easements), mortgage and the law of succession; the second part regulated obligations arising from contracts and from civil wrongs (damages).

The concept of ownership was essentially based on Roman law; however, there were certain feudal relics reflecting the feudal division of ownership over fiefs or special conditions laid down for the usage of land by peasants and for Church property. Natural law played an important role in defining public interest with respect to entitlement to expropriate. Ownership could not be curtailed or limited except for the sake of public interest, and then for adequate compensation as determined by law, should any restrictions have occurred.

The Roman law institution of servitude has left its mark on the modern Central European law. Usufruct as personal servitude was a classical method of creating a life interest; "real" servitude was used for easement relating to the use of land in villages as well as neighbouring houses in towns. Provisions for the forms of legal mortgage of land were very important for the establishment of hypothecation of immovable property subject to registration. On the other hand, the establishment of gage was applicable to movable property. Very detailed provisions were laid down for the law of succession. This part of the Code was based on the previous reform introduced by Joseph II. It covered both testamentary and intestate succession.

The law of contracts regulated not only general conditions for making valid contracts but also the most important types of contracts, including contract of sale, donation, hiring work or services, mandate, partnership, loans for use and consumption, and deposit. It opened a way for using innominate contracts, which helped the legal practice to be more flexible. The part of the Code which dealt with contracts was also used for emerging branches of commercial and labour law.

The third book of the General Civil Code commenced with common provisions for parts I and II, such as legal consequences relating to setting time limits, the Roman law concept of *usucapio* as an original mode of constituting ownership after possession exercised in good faith and for a legally determined period of time, termination of contracts, security for claims, etc.

In conclusion, the General Civil Code may be described, in spite of some feudal relics, as a modern code which remained in force until the very end of the Austro-Hungarian Empire in 1918. Substantial amendments regarding the removal of feudal ownership of real estate were adopted in the 1860s; an amendment concerning the declaration of the death of a person was passed in 1883 after a terrible fire in the Vienna theatre; and, eventually, three important partial amendments (so called *Teilnovellen* in German) were enacted between 1914 and 1916 changing or adding 180 provisions in accordance with the German Civil Code of 1900.[135] However, it should be noted that the part

---

135 Hausmaninger, H.: *The Austrian legal system*, p. 222.

of the Code regulating the law of marriage did not apply to Catholics between 1855 and 1870, due to an international treaty concluded between the Holy See and the Austro-Hungarian Empire.

The Austrian General Civil Code represented a natural basis for the development of university instruction and legal science in private law. At first the adoption of the Code led to the stagnation and decline of Austrian legal science, "whose perspective quickly narrowed to the practical tasks of explaining the Code and making it work".[136] During the second half of the 19th century Joseph Unger (and therefore the German oriented historical and pandectist school) became the leading personality of the Austrian school of civil law.[137] Among other representatives an important role was played by Czech university professor Antonín Randa (especially in the field of property law).

The interpretation of the General Civil Code (it contains interpretation rules especially in its Articles 6 and 7)[138] was also influenced through court decisions. In 1863 a private edition (register) of the civil law decisions of the so called Austrian High and Appelate Courts (*Oberster Gerichts- und Cassationhof* in German) was introduced by Josef Unger, Julius Glaser and Joseph von Walther and published in Vienna by C. Gerolds Sohn.[139]

The Austrian General Civil Code was in force in the Czech lands until 1950 as a result of their reception of Austrian law. This is the main reason why Czechoslovak law could be regarded as law based on the legal culture of Central Europe and on the Continental Roman law tradition.

Austrian law in the 1850s also dealt with some areas of private law left originally outside the Civil Code. The Order for Manufacturers and Individual Proprietorship in 1859 prohibited abusive practices in labour contracts. It was connected also with the development of social legislation. In 1855 the eleven-hour working day was introduced and in 1867 trade unions were allowed to exist. In 1888/1889 the Imperial Council enacted Acts on social insurance to cover sickness and disabilities.[140]

---

136 *Ibidem*, p. 220.
137 *Ibidem*, p. 221. See also Unger, J.: *System des österreichischen Allgemeinen Privatrechts.* Leipzig: Breitkopf u. Härtel, first edition, six volumes 1856–1864.
138 For their meaning and English translation see Hausmaninger, H.: *The Austrian legal system,* p. 28.
139 See *Sammlung von civilrechtlichen Entscheidungen des k. k. Obersten Gerichtshofes.* Wienna, 1863. (2nd volume from 1864 is accessible as google e-book). For its importance for central European legal culture see Kühn, Z.: *The judiciary in Central and Eastern Europe: mechanical jurisprudence in transformation?* Martinus Nijhoff Publishers, 2011.
140 Hausmaninger, H.: *The Austrian Legal system,* p. 222.

/8/

Austrian constitutional development 1848–1914 and Czech national movement

In 1848 and 1849 Austria saw the beginning of a certain kind of constitutional progress within the Habsburg Monarchy. In 1848, a majority of the society, with the exception of the conservative nobility, ceased to be satisfied with the ongoing absolutistic trends within the Habsburg Monarchy.[141] This social distress was primarily connected with the arrival of new liberal concepts of society. As a result, the establishment of a constitutional monarchy was demanded as a minimum concession to be made by the ruler, and basic civil rights and freedoms were requested to be incorporated. The year 1848 is widely known for revolutionary upheavals that occurred not only in Austria but in the whole of Europe.

Civil rights within the territory of the multinational Habsburg Monarchy were closely linked with the issue of national rights, especially those relating to national language and culture. Pressure was also visible in the Czech

---

141 The so called period of Die Vormärz (Pre-March i.e. the period before March 1848), started in 1815 at the Wienna Congress. See Taylor, A. J. P.: *The Habsburg Monarchy 1809–1918. A History of Austrian Empire and Austria-Hungary*. London: Hamish Hamilton, 1948, pp. 47–57.

politics of 1848.[142] Czech politicians formed the so-called St. Wenceslas Committee; on the 14th March 1848, the Committee drafted a Petition, consisting of eleven requirements, including claims of linguistic and civil rights, communal self-government, the right to vote, the freedom of press and publication of court proceedings.[143] The petition was sent to Vienna. The Emperor promised that he would "give consideration" to the issue of the equality of the Czech and German languages and other demands submitted. A second Petition, of the 29th March 1848, requested the right to vote representatives to the Provincial Diet for all inhabitants regardless of their social and property status.[144]

These petitions created the basis for a visible outcome: in 1848 Czech politicians formed their own modern political program. They demanded that traditional rights of the Czech Kingdom should be recognized, particularly national rights, including the equality of the Czech and German languages, the existence of Czech schools, Czech organizations and associations, etc. They combined these with liberal claims for civil rights and liberties. The important issue was the equilibrium between the two types of claims, i.e. between the requirement to resume the Czech constitutional tradition and the requirement to install civil rights and liberties. The Czech politicians, represented mainly by František Palacký, refused to participate in the activities of the German National Constituent Assembly in Frankfurt.[145]

Meanwhile, the revolt in Vienna gave rise to changes in the government. The First Austrian Constitution was promulgated by the Emperor Ferdinand V on the 25th April 1848;[146] the Emperor was exposed to, and acted under, extensive pressure caused by various revolutionary events throughout the whole Empire. The Constitution of April 1848 was called the *Pillersdorf Constitution*, after its author, Franz von Pillersdorf, Minister of the Interior. The Constitution was provisional and proclaimed only limited civil rights, and it set certain constitutional limits upon the rule of the Emperor. Its text was relatively brief, consisting only of seven parts and fifty-nine simple articles.[147] The Constitution promised the equality of the nations of the Empire, religious freedom, freedom of speech, freedom to move, protection of home, protection of postal secrecy and a reform of court proceedings. The Constitution envisaged

---

142 In more details see Urban, O.: Czech society 1848–1918. In: Teich, M. (ed.): *Bohemia in History*, p. 203 and following. Hlavačka, M.: Czechs during the Revolution and Neo-Absolutism 1848–1860. In: Pánek, J. – Tůma, O. et al.: *A History of the Czech Lands*, p. 319 and following. Pech, S. Z.: *The Czech Revolution of 1848*. The University of North Carolina Press, Chapel Hill, 1969, especially pp. 343 and following.
143 Hlavačka, M.: *Czechs during the Revolution and Neo-Absolutism 1848–1860*, p. 314.
144 *Ibidem.*
145 Letter by Palacký was translated into English and published in 1947 in Slavonic and East European Review 26, pp. 303–308.
146 Bernatzik, E.: *Die österreichischen Verfassungsgesetze mit Erläuterungen*, doc. No. 36, s. 102–109. See also Brauneder, W.: *Quellenbuch zur österreichischen Verfassungsgeschichte.* Wien: Manz, 2012, doc. No. 2, pp. 1–5.
147 *Ibidem.*

a bicameral system of Parliament (the Imperial Diet), composed of a House of Deputies and a Senate. The Emperor was limited in his executive power, because, while he nominated and recalled ministers, ministers were answerable to the Parliament. Justice was administered in the name of the Emperor. The Pillersdorf Constitution is sometimes referred to as an "imposed" constitution, as it was issued by the Emperor and not passed by a Parliamentary assembly. It was proclaimed for all provinces of the Austrian Empire except Hungary, Croatia and the Italian territories. It was an attempt to strengthen centralization in the rest of the Empire, namely the Austrian and Czech lands, which were regarded as Crown provinces only. The Constitution did not meet with general approval and was never applied in practice as a whole.

The first Austrian Parliament – the Imperial Diet, or *Reichstag* – was elected in May 1848[148] and its sittings were inaugurated by Archduke Johann in Winter Riding School on July 22. The Imperial Diet declared itself as a Constitutional Assembly.[149] It consisted of only a Lower House. Due to the revolutionary atmosphere in Vienna in 1848, the Assembly moved to the Moravian episcopal town of Kroměříž (Kremsier in German) in October, became known as the Imperial Diet of Kroměříž, and the work on a new liberal constitution began.[150] It was proposed that the Austrian Monarchy change into a constitutional monarchy and a federation of nations and peoples based upon equality.[151] However, before the draft constitution could have been completed[152] the Assembly was pre-emptively dissolved by the new Austrian Emperor Franz Joseph I (1830–1916), who, instead, promulgated his own Constitution on the 7th March 1849.[153] The only outcome from the activities of the Kroměříž Constitutional Assembly was a decree ensuring equality of all citizens before the law and abolishing all kinds of feudal subjugation.

The Constitution of March 1849,[154] by its form of introduction, was again an imposed constitution; it was named after its main author, Franz Stadion, Minister of the Interior. The Emperor attempted through the Constitution to calm the population that had been disappointed by the dissolution of the

---

148 Bernatzik, E.: *Die österreichischen Verfassungsgesetze mit Erläuterungen*, doc. No. 37, p. 110. For elections see Krejčí, O.: *History of Elections in Bohemia and Moravia.* Columbia University Press, 1995, p. 51. There were indirect elections, every 500 urban voters elected 2 electors and every 500 rural voters elected just one.
149 Brauneder, W.: *Quellenbuch zur österreichischen Verfassungsgeschichte*, doc. No. 3, p. 5.
150 Kann, R. A.: *The Multinational Empire, Nationalism and National reform in the Habsburg Monarchy 1848–1918. Volume II. Empire Reform.* Columbia University Press, New York, 1950, pp. 21–39.
151 Brauneder, W.: *Quellenbuch zur österreichischen Verfassungsgeschichte*, doc. No. 4, pp. 5–14.
152 For the drafts of the Constitution and Fundamental Law see Bernatzik, E.: *Die österreichischen Verfassungsgesetze mit Erläuterungen*, doc. No. 39, pp. 115–145.
153 Brauneder, W.: *Quellenbuch zur österreichischen Verfassungsgeschichte*, doc. No. 6, pp. 19–28.
154 It was enacted in the form of the Imperial manifesto, Imperial patent and Fundamental Law (No. 149–151/1849 RGBL). Bernatzik, E.: *Die österreichischen Verfassungsgesetze mit Erläuterungen*, doc. No. 40, 40 a) and 40 b), pp. 147–169.

Kroměříž Assembly. However, the Constitution initiated a gradual return to centralization and absolutism.

Part I of the March Constitution dealt with the Austrian Empire. The Empire of Austria consisted of the so-called Crown Provinces, including Bohemia, Moravia and Upper and Lower Silesia; the Constitution also applied to Hungary and the Italian territories (the Lombardo-Venetian Kingdom). Equal justice was promised to all nations of the Empire, as well as the right of preserving and maintaining their own national affiliation and language. Provincial Diets within the Empire were abolished as another step towards centralization.

Part II of the March Constitution dealt with the person of the Emperor. The Crown of the Empire was hereditary within the House of Habsburg-Lorraine in accord with the Pragmatic Sanction and domestic laws of the House. The Emperor was obliged to abide by the Constitution; the imperial oath was to be taken by his successors at their coronation. The person of the Emperor was sacrosanct, inviolable and not answerable to anyone. The Emperor headed the Executive, Legislative and Judicial branches and, either in person or through his generals, had command over the whole armed forces, having the exclusive right of declaring war or making peace. He received and sent ambassadors and concluded treaties with foreign powers, promulgated laws and issued necessary regulations. Regulations were subject to a countersignature by a minister in charge of the respective issue. Ministers were named and dismissed by the Emperor. Justice was administered in the name of the Emperor, and judges were appointed according to the Emperor's will. The Emperor had the right of granting full pardon, of mitigating punishments and of giving amnesties.

Part III dealt with Austrian state citizenship and basic civil rights. All Austrian citizens were equal before the law and were liable to the same legal treatment. The citizens were promised freedom of person, their right to leave the country was restricted by the State only in so far as the duty of military service was concerned. Every kind of serfdom and every kind of feudal subjection was abolished forever. For example, it was stipulated that "on touching Austrian soil, or the deck of an Austrian ship, every slave becomes free". Public offices and positions in service for the State were open to all who were capable of performing them. Property was under the protection of the State; it could not be curtailed or limited except for the sake of public interest and for some compensation determined by the law. Every Austrian citizen had the right to settle in any part of the Empire and to exercise trade.

Part IV dealt with communal affairs, including self-government. The fundamental right of self-government for communal and municipal corporations subsisted in the election of their representatives, the reception of new members into communal corporations and in the independent administration of their affairs. Details of these rules, including the establishment of districts as administrative units for implementing self-government, were to be enacted through a Model Communal Act. Such an Act was adopted in 1849; however, it was never implemented in practice.

Part V and Part VI of the Constitution divided competences between the Empire and Provinces. Provinces were promised to be able to have their own legislation in agriculture, to have the administration of public buildings covered from public funds, to run charitable institutions, to acquire revenues from land, and to levy taxes for public purposes. In addition, they could legislate in the affairs of self-government, or affairs of the Church and education; however, their laws must be enacted within those limits set by the legislation of the whole Empire.

Under the March Constitution, the Legislative power was exercised by the Emperor in conjunction with the Parliament, where the affairs of the Empire were dealt with; where the affairs of Provinces were subject to legislation, the Emperor in conjunction with the Provincial Diets acted as legislature.

The Constitution foresaw a two-chamber Parliament – an Upper and a Lower House. The Upper House was composed of members who were chosen from the Provincial Diets of their respective Crown domains. The Lower House was elected. The right to vote was possessed by every Austrian citizen of thirty years of age and fully enjoying his political rights. The right to vote was to be further determined by an Electoral Act; it was envisaged that the voting right would be based on one's yearly amount of direct taxes. The Constitution provided that each Province should be represented by its Provincial Diet and that Provincial Constitutions should be enacted. The rest of the Constitution dealt with the Executive power vested in the Emperor and his ministers, with the Privy Council, with the judicial branch, revenues and armed forces.

The March Constitution of 1849 was never fully implemented in practice; in particular, Slavic and Hungarian politicians did not accept the new centralizing tendencies.[155] The Constitution was repealed on the 31st December 1851 by the Sylvester Patents.[156] What followed was called a period of neo-absolutism, or the period of Bach's absolutism, as its leading figure was Alexander Bach, Minister of the Interior.[157] The Habsburg Empire was ruled without a proper constitutional basis; practically all civil rights and freedoms promised in constitutions drafted in 1848-1849 were suspended, with the exception of

---

155 See Paar, M.: *Die Gesetzgebung der österreichischen Monarchie im Spiegelbild der Normen und der staatsrechtlichen Literatur.* Series II. Law, Frankfurt–Wien: Peter Lang, 2008, pp. 38–43.
156 Published in Reichsgesetzblatt as No. 2, 3 and 4 in 1852. Bernatzik, E.: *Die österreichischen Verfassungsgesetze mit Erläuterungen*, doc. No. 48–50), pp. 208–210. Brauneder, W.: *Quellenbuch zur österreichischen Verfassungsgeschichte*, doc. No. 12, pp. 37–38.
157 Taylor speaks about neo-absolutism and system of Bach–Schwarzenberg, because Count Felix Schwarzenberg presided over the Council of Ministers in 1851, when the system was introduced. Taylor, A. J. P.: *The Habsburg Monarchy 1809–1918*, p.83 and following. See also Kann, R. A.: *The Multinational Empire, Nationalism and National reform in the Habsburg Monarchy 1848–1918, Volume II*, pp. 66–87.

the equality of citizens before the law, the limited religious freedom and the replacement of manorial administration by the civil administration.[158]

As a kind of paradox Bach's regime supported business and trade activities and laid down the foundation of liberal capitalism for the subsequent decades. As Milan Hlavačka pointed out economic prosperity was to contribute to further the integration of various lands of the Austrian empire.[159] It is possible to add that this policy served as compensation for the restraint of political activities.[160] From 1852 it was possible to establish economic and financial legal entities on the basis of Imperial Act on associations. For example the Lower –Austria Discount Bank was established in 1853, followed by the special Austrian Credit Institute organized as a joint stock company. The regime also initiated the establishment of business and trade Chambers as self-governing bodies of entrepreneurs and traders to consult economic legislation. At the very end of Bach's regime a new "Order for Manufacturers and Individual Proprietorship" was enacted in 1859 to foster small and medium sized enterprises under special state licences and trade tax rules.

In place of a constitution only basic organizational rules for state administration, court proceedings and legislation were enacted.[161] The rules dealt with new administrative units and introduced three instances of the judicial system. Court proceedings ceased to be public, and juries, typically engaged in cases regarding the press and the freedom of speech, were abolished. On the other hand, some reforms were introduced; for example, in criminal proceedings the State was, for the first time, represented by a new type of state servant – the public prosecutor. The most important change regarding legislation was that, for the first time, Austrian codifications and laws were valid on, and applied to, the territory of Hungary.

The period of neo-absolutism ended in 1859 when Minister of the Interior Bach was removed from office. The Austrian army suffered a devastating defeat in the war with forces unifying Italy, supported by France. The military debacle was accompanied with a collapse of State finances. The Emperor was forced to enact the so-called October Diploma of 1860, in which he promised to retreat to a constitutional form of government with a parliament and a more decentralized version of the Austrian State.[162] The Imperial Council was summoned, in which representatives of financial and business circles of

---

158 Okey, R.: *The Habsburg Monarchy c. 1765–1918*, pp. 160–161. Agnew, H. L.: *The Czechs and the Lands of the Bohemian Crown*, p. 126.
159 Hlavačka, M.: *Czechs during the Revolution and Neo-absolutism 1848–1860*, p. 325.
160 Agnew, H. L.: *The Czechs and the Lands of the Bohemian Crown*, p. 127.
161 Brauneder, W.: *Quellenbuch zur österreichischen Verfassungsgeschichte*, doc. No. 13, pp. 38–41.
162 There was an Imperial Manifest ordering to publish the October Diplom (No 225 and 226 /1860 RGBL). Bernatzik, E.: *Die österreichischen Verfassungsgesetze mit Erläuterungen*, doc. No. 55–56, pp. 222–227.

bourgeoisie took part.[163] It was a beginning for the renewal of parliamentary representation, which was important for the legitimization of taxation.

The Czech political elite took the opportunity and established a predominantly upper middle class Czech National Party led by František Palacký and his son-in-law František Ladislav Rieger, which aimed at cultural and political autonomy of the Czech lands within a devolved or perhaps federated Austria.[164] Also new patriotic and cultural societies emerged.

On February 26, 1861, a new – again imposed – constitution was adopted, called the February Constitution (February Patent), or Schmerling Constitution, after Prime Minister Anton von Schmerling.[165] The Constitution failed to incorporate the promises of decentralization embodied in the October Diploma of 1860.[166] The February Constitution was not a single constitutional bill; it consisted of three patents (No. 20–22/1861) and forty-eight annexes, including the Land Orders for Bohemia, Moravia and Silesia.[167] In many aspects, it was based on the principles embodied in the March Constitution of 1849.

One of the Constitutional components, namely the Patent on Imperial Representation, constituted a two chamber Imperial Parliament (called the Imperial Council, or *Reichsrat* in German) for Austria as the whole,[168] with a possibility to renew Diets in individual provinces, including the Czech lands.

The Parliament was composed of a House of Deputies and a House of Peers (so called *Herrenhaus* in German). Representatives to the House of Deputies were appointed by Provincial Diets to which elections were held. Adult princes of the House of Habsburgs, the high nobility and Church dignitaries were entitled to sit in the House of Peers. The Emperor had the right to appoint certain outstanding persons to become life peers of the Upper House, having considered their achievements in public life, the Church, or the arts and sciences. The Presidents and Vice-Presidents of the House of Peers, as well as the Presidents and Vice-Presidents of the House of Deputies, were appointed by

163 They were selected by the Emperor either directly or from nominations of Land Diets. Krejčí, O.: *History of Elections in Bohemia and Moravia*, p. 54.
164 Urban, O.: *Czech society 1848–1918*, pp. 203–205. Carver, B.M.: *The Young Czech Party 1874–1901 and the emergence of a multi-party system.* New Haven: Yale University Press, 1978, pp. 30–31.
165 Bernatzik, E.: *Die österreichischen Verfassungsgesetze mit Erläuterungen*, doc. No. 71–101, pp. 255–303. A. J. P. Taylor speaks about the so called "constitutional absolutism" and "the system of Schmerling". Taylor, A. J. P.: *The Habsburg Monarchy 1809–1918*, pp. 109–123. Kann, R. A.: *The Multinational Empire, Nationalism and National reform in the Habsburg Monarchy 1848–1918. Volume II.* pp. 115–124; Kann speaks more precisely about German oriented centralism.
166 Brauneder, W.: *Quellenbuch zur österreichischen Verfassungsgeschichte*, doc. No. 16, pp. 42–44.
167 Bernatzik, E.: *Die österreichischen Verfassungsgesetze mit Erläuterungen*, doc. No. 92–97, pp. 301–303. Kann, R. A.: *The Multinational Empire. Nationalism and National reform in the Habsburg Monarchy 1848–1918. Volume II,* appendix IV, pp. 311–31.
168 For the history of Austrian parliamentarian system see especially Schambeck, H. (ed.) *Österreichs Parlamentarismus. Werden und System.* Berlin: Duncker und Humblot, 1986 (especially chapter I – Der Parlamentarismus in der Monarchie, parts Die Entstehung des Parlamentarismus 1861/67 und seine Weiterentwicklung und Die Funktion des Reichsrats elaborated by W. Brauneder); in English *The Austrian Parliament*, published by Parliamentary Administration, Wien, 1998, especially pp. 7–28.

the Emperor. The February Constitution did not provide for any parliamentary immunities.

It was proposed that the House of Deputies meet in two forms: a "wider" House, where representatives of Hungary and Lombardy were present, and a "narrower" House, which did not include the Deputies from Hungary and Lombardy. Due to the resistance from the representatives of the eastern part of the Empire, the Imperial Parliament never met in the wider form. Hungary, with its own Diet and differences in legal and administrative systems, enjoyed a special position within the Austrian Empire.

The Emperor, as Head of State, was in charge of the military forces, declared war and concluded peace. Should there be no sittings of the Parliament, the Emperor, together with his Government, issued decrees having the force of the law.

As a result of the February Constitution the Czech and Moravian Diets were re-established. Elections to the Provincial Diets were held in March 1861. Those elections were based on a system of so-called electoral *curiae*.[169] The *curiae* represented various groups of voters – land owners registered in the land records, municipalities, business and trade chambers and peasants, with the system being combined with property qualification (*census*). Certain Church dignitaries and University rectors were honorary members of the Diets. After elections, the Provincial Diets appointed their representatives to the House of Deputies of the Imperial Council. Deputies served a six-year term. The division of competences between the Imperial Council and Provincial Diets was very similar to the provisions of the March Constitution of 1849, mentioned earlier.

The majority of representatives from the Czech and Moravian Provincial Diets refused from June 1863 to participate in meetings of the Imperial Council because, as they claimed, the historical rights of the Czech lands were not taken into account.[170] Czech politicians (mainly the new coalition of the Czech National party and conservative noble landowners in the Czech Provincial Diet) focused primarily on the so called Czech "historical state rights", i.e. the programme of greater political autonomy within Austria based on the continual existence of the state of the Czech Crown. In practical politics they succeeded in the promotion of Czech industry, language, schools and culture; they took an active part not in the Vienna Parliament but in the local, municipal and district self-governments re-introduced after 1860. Nevertheless, this policy of so-called passive resistance did not bring sufficient rewards, and Czech political representatives did not participate in important discussions on key issues of the Empire. Therefore a new generation of more pragmatic

169 In more details Krejčí, O.: *History of Elections in Bohemia and Moravia*, pp. 56–57.
170 *Ibidem*, p. 58.

Czech politicians criticized such an approach and advocated an active defence of national claims within the framework of Austrian politics.

There were no specific provisions for civil rights and freedoms in the February Constitution; however, the Constitution stipulated that legislation in that field was within the competence of the Imperial Council. In 1862, the Imperial Council decided to guarantee personal freedom and the inviolability of one's home. The Council adopted two Acts of the 27th October 1862, regulating the protection of personal freedom and the protection of one's home.[171] In December 1862 the Council also voted for the new Press Act to guarantee limited freedom of speech, even though the printing was subject to many restrictions and regulations including official licensing, police supervision and responsibility of the editor.

The year 1867 was a turning point in the development of law in the 19th century. However, the process had started two years earlier, in 1865, with the suspension of the February Constitution due to the pressure of Hungarian politicians demanding "dualization" of the Monarchy.[172] After a disastrous defeat of Austrian Armies by Prussia at the Battle of Hradec Králové in 1866, the internal instability and reshuffling of the Government (headed instead of Count Richard Belcredi by Count Friedrich Beust) led to changes in the whole structure of the Austrian Empire. It was divided into two relatively independent parts and formed a union called Austria-Hungary.

This development is referred to as the "Austrian-Hungarian settlement". The union was close to a confederation; in addition to a common Head of State where the Habsburg monarch ruled as the Austrian Emperor and the Hungarian King, the union had common foreign policy, common national defence and common finances. Count Andrassy was appointed as Hungarian Prime Minister on February 17, 1867. Austrian Emperor Franz Joseph accepted the coronation as king of Hungary on June 8, 1867 and formally approved Hungarian Law No. XII/1867 on the Austrian-Hungarian settlement.[173] A common representation, called Delegations, was established from amongst representatives of the Austrian Parliament (20 from the House of Peers and 40 from the House of Deputies) and the Hungarian National Assembly to deal with common matters. Agreement on tariffs, taxes, coinage and military conscription had to be made every ten years with the approval of both parliaments.

---

171 Andreas, G., Guttenfeld, E. (eds.): Österreichisches Recht: *Textausg. österreichischer Gesetze, Verordnungen und Erlässe in einem Band; mit Hinweisen, Literaturangaben und einem ausführlichen Sachregister*. 4th edition. Wien 1950, doc. No. 5 and 6, p. 32. See also Hausmaninger, H.: *The Austrian legal system*, p. 148.

172 For the so called "Sistierungspatent" or "September manifesto" of September 20, 1865 see Brauneder, W.: *Quellenbuch zur österreichischen Verfassungsgeschichte*, doc. No. 20, p. 55, and Bernatzik, E.: *Die österreichischen Verfassungsgesetze mit Erläuterungen*, doc. No. 107, zákon č. 89, pp. 317–318. See also Kwan, J.: *Liberalism and the Habsburg Monarchy 1861–1895*, Palgrave Macmillan, 2013, pp. 46–48.

173 Okey, R.: *The Habsburg Monarchy c. 1765–1918*, p. 193.

The Czech lands belonged to the Austrian part of Austria-Hungary, called also "Cisleithania" (i.e. lands of this side of the river Leitha). Hungary was analogically called Transleithania.

Changes connected with the Austrian-Hungarian Compromise were reflected in a call for amendments of the February Constitution of 1861 and especially for constitutional guarantees of civil rights and liberties.

There was an interesting debate on the constitutional affairs within the Government as well as within both houses of the parliament.[174]

In November 1867, two important Imperial Acts (No. 134 and 135) were adopted regarding the freedom to associate and the freedom to assemble.[175] In December 1867, a whole new constitution followed. The so-called December Constitution of 1867 applied only to the Austrian part of Austria-Hungary and remained in force until 1918.

It consisted of five so-called "Fundamental Laws of the State" (Acts No. 141–144/1867 Austrian RGBl), supplemented by a special Act on the Austrian-Hungarian Compromise.[176] The December Constitution of 1867 established Austria as a genuine constitutional monarchy.[177] The Constitution was based on the division of powers between a two-chamber Parliament, the Emperor and his Government and the judicial branch. The Constitution introduced a Constitutional Court (called the Supreme Court of the Realm) and an independent judiciary. However, the position of the Emperor was in practice so powerful, that he was able to curtail many democratic and liberal features of the Constitution, including the suspension of Parliament and civil rights.

The first Fundamental Law of the Constitution dealt with the legislative branch. The December Constitution in fact amended the Patent of the 26th February 1861, concerning Imperial Representation. As already stipulated by the February Patent, the Imperial Council (*Reichsrat*) in Vienna consisted of the House of Peers and the House of Deputies. The competences of the Imperial Council included all matters which were of common concern of the Provinces represented in the Parliament, including the common budget. For the first time, the Austrian Parliament was entitled to vote annually on taxes. The division of competences between the Imperial Council and the Provincial

---

174 For the documents see Haider, B. (ed.): *Die Protokolle des Verfassungsausschusses des Reichsrates vom Jahre 1867, Fontes rerum Austriacarum. Österreichische Geschichtsquellen*. Abt. 2. Diplomataria et Acta. Bd. 88, Wien Verlag der Österreichischen Akademie der Wissenschaften, 1997. Paar, M.: *Die Gesetzgebung der österreichischen Monarchie im Spiegelbild der Normen und der staatsrechtlichen Literatur*, pp. 57 and following.

175 Bernatzik, E.: *Die österreichischen Verfassungsgesetze mit Erläuterungen*, doc. No. 131–132, pp. 381–389.

176 For documents see *Ibidem*, doc. No. 133–137, pp. 390–439. Brauneder, W.: *Quellenbuch zur österreichischen Verfassungsgeschichte*, doc. No. 21, pp. 56–70. Okey, R.: *The Habsburg Monarchy c. 1765 –1918*, pp. 187–190.

177 For extracts translated into English and comments see Macartney, C. A.: *The Habsburg Empire, 1790–1918*. London, 1968, p.562 and following. Hobelt, L.: "1867: The Empire Loyalists Last (But One) Stand". In: *Parliaments. Estates & Representation 23*, 2003, pp. 131–141.

Diets was stipulated in more detail; however, the most important matters concerning foreign policy, national defence, state administration, economy, finances and the judiciary remained reserved for the Imperial Council.

Presidents and Vice-presidents of the House of Peers were appointed by the Emperor, whereas the House of Deputies was entitled to elect its presiding officers on its own. The December Constitution of 1867 enacted, for the first time, provisions for the immunity of the members of Parliament.

The Fundamental Law of the State governing the Executive and Administrative Branches dealt with the executive power vested in the Emperor and his ministers. The Emperor was again proclaimed "sacrosanct, inviolable and not answerable". The Emperor appointed and dismissed his ministers. Ministerial accountability to Parliament was finally achieved. The first such government was appointed on December 31, 1867 and was headed by Karl Auersperg with Eduard Taafe as his Deputy Prime Minister. All ministers of this Government were also members of the Imperial Council. This was regarded as a major liberal achievement.[178] A two-thirds majority in one of the Houses was required to impeach a minister before the Supreme Court of the Realm (*Staatsgerichtshof* in German). A minister was obliged to answer regular Parliamentary questions.

The Fundamental Law of the State concerning General Rights of Citizens represents the most liberal part of the Constitution. The Fundamental Law guaranteed a wide range of civil rights and freedoms, such as the right of free association and assembly, the right of inviolability of domestic rights, the right to acquire real and movable property, the right to have private ownership protected, the right of petition, postal secrecy, the liberty of instruction and teaching, the freedom of speech and scientific research, the freedom of religion, etc. Since the exercise of individual rights was closely connected with individual laws needed to implement them and decisions taken by state administration, the Supreme Administrative Court was established in 1873. It was regarded as an important safeguard of civil rights: it could decide that the individual decision of an administrative body was issued contrary to the law and, as a result, it provided for an effective remedy. On the other hand in 1869 special Imperial law no 60 allowed the imperial Government in case of war or serious domestic unrest to declare a state of emergency (sanctioned by the Emperor and when sitting also by both houses of Parliament) and suspend in whole or in part political rights (including right of free association and assembly and freedom of speech) guaranteed by the Constitution. This law was quite frequently used by the Government in the 1880s and 1890s to cope with political unrests and opposition activities including those connected with Czech political life or with the policies of the Austrian Social Democratic Party.

178 Kwan, J.: *Liberalism and the Habsburg Monarchy 1861–1895*, pp. 63–64.

The December Constitution dealt with the rights of individual nations living within Austria-Hungary. It laid down the principle of the equality of nations and individual language communities, which was meant as the possibility to use their national languages and an introduction of schools for individual language communities. In fact, constitutional promises in this respect were not implemented in practice. The German nation was regarded as superior to other nations living in the Austrian part of Austria-Hungary; Magyars were considered superior in the Hungarian part of the Empire. Language rights were governed by special provisions adopted for individual provinces – such as the Governmental Ordinances in the case of Bohemia adopted by the Austrian Governments (especially Stremayr's Ordinance of 1880 and Badeni's Ordinance of 1897) , and the regulation was based on the results of regular censuses.[179] For example, the Czech language in the Czech lands was not equal to German and it was possible to use Czech in dealings with State administration only under strict conditions and only in regions where more than 20 percent of the Czech population resided. The situation in self-government bodies was more convenient in predominantly Czech regions; conditions were set for the establishment and financing of Czech schools. The so called two-tracked system of government, which divided administration between centralized state agencies and elected self-government on provincial, district and local levels, was finally established in 1862 by Imperial Act No. 18 as amended in 1868 by Imperial Act No. 44.

The judiciary, imperial bureaucracy, police and army were under profound German influence. German language was used as the sole commanding language in the army and for internal administration of diplomacy, postal services and railways. In 1905, a more liberal approach was adopted in Moravia, where the system of German and Czech fractions called "*curiae*" was adopted by the so-called Moravian Pact and use of the Czech language in state administration and self-government was guaranteed.

The Fundamental Law of the State regulating the Supreme Court of the Realm was concerned with the establishment of a Constitutional Court, which was entrusted with constitutional review as well as with resolving conflicts of competences. The Fundamental Law of the State on the Judicial Branch was based on doctrines embodied in the March Constitution of 1849, such as independence of the judiciary and the fundamental principles for court proceedings, including public and oral hearings, the accusatorial principle in criminal proceedings, and a jury system for certain categories of crimes – for example, murder or crimes committed by the press.

---

179 In more details Burian, P.: *The State Language Problem in Old Austria (1848–1918)*. Rice University, 1970 (also published in *Austrian History Yearbook* No. 6–7, 1970–1971), pp. 81–103, especially p. 96 and following. See also Zeman, Z. A. B.: *The Making and Breaking of Communist Europe*. Oxford: Oxford University Press, 1991, pp. 32–36. Kann, R. A.: *A History of the Habsburg Empire 1526–1918*, appendix I., pp. 603–608.

The Constitution of December 1867 was modified in some parts by subsequent legislation. For example, in May 1868 three Imperial Laws repealed the concordat with Holy See from 1855 and introduced state supervision over the financial and possession matters of the Catholic Church. Partial separation of state and church issues, including in education, was achieved.[180]

The most important change however occurred with respect to legislative power and suffrage. Even after December 1867 the Lower House of Parliament remained elective through the Provincial Diets. The reform introduced by Austrian Prime Minister Eduard Taafe in 1873 (sometimes called the April Constitution) made the elections to the Imperial Council direct[181]; however, the right to vote remained limited in accord with property qualification (censuses), and voters were divided into four classes called *curiae*. It is estimated that despite the progress achieved, only six percent of the male population (cca 1.7 million) older than twenty-four years of age were entitled to vote.[182] In 1882 and 1896 the right to vote was awarded to a wider range of society. In 1882 the property qualification was lowered by Prime Minister Kasimir Eduard Taafe from ten to five "Golden Crowns";[183] in 1896 Prime Minister Felix Badeni (therefore "Badeni's reform") established a fifth class of voters.[184] This was comprised of all men not entitled to vote in one of the four curiae. The voters in the fifth class were not required to pay a minimum tax but had had to reside in a community in one of Austrian provinces for at least six months preceding the election. As a result the number of voters rose to 5.3 million men.

Universal and equal suffrage for men was introduced as late as January 1907 by a new electoral laws adopted for elections to the House of Deputies of the Imperial Council.[185] The reform, which included the adoption of the electoral law, is sometimes referred to as "Beck's reform", after Prime Minister Max Beck.[186] The reform abolished the class (curial) electoral system; as a result, the universal, equal and secret right to vote for all men of twenty-four years of age was constituted without any property restrictions. From

180 Bernatzik, E.: *Die österreichischen Verfassungsgesetze mit Erläuterungen*, doc. No. 142 a, b, c.
181 Imperial Acts No. 40–41/1873 Austrian RGBL. Brauneder, W.: *Quellenbuch zur österreichischen Verfassungsgeschichte*, doc. No. 23, pp. 71–73. Bernatzik, E.: *Die österreichischen Verfassungsgesetze mit Erläuterungen*, doc. No. 183–184, pp. 742–747. Krejčí, O.: *History of Elections in Bohemia and Moravia*, pp. 59–60.
182 Krejčí, O.: *History of Elections in Bohemia and Moravia*, p. 61.
183 Imperial Act No, 142/1882 RGBL, Bernatzik, E.: *Die österreichischen Verfassungsgesetze mit Erläuterungen*, doc. No. 185, p. 749, Krejčí, O.: *History of Elections in Bohemia and Moravia*, p. 60.
184 Bernatzik, E.: *Die österriechischen Verfassungsgesetze mit Erläuterungen*, doc. No. 186, pp. 750–752. Krejčí, O.: *History of Elections in Bohemia and Moravia*, pp. 61–62.
185 Acts No. 15–17/1907 Austrian RGBL. Bernatzik, E.: *Die österreichischen Verfassungsgesetze mit Erläuterungen*, Doc. No. 188 – 188 a, b, pp. 756–761. Brauneder, W.: *Quellenbuch zur österreichischen Verfassungsgeschichte*, doc. No. 24, pp. 73–74. Krejčí, O.: *History of Elections in Bohemia and Moravia*, p. 68.
186 Kann, R. A.: *The Multinational Empire, Nationalism and National reform in the Habsburg Monarchy 1848–1918*, Volume II, pp. 220–227.

a total number of five hundred sixteen members of the House of Deputies, one hundred thirty mandates were elected in Bohemia, forty-nine in Moravia and fifteen in Silesia. The right to be elected to the House of Deputies was granted to all men of thirty years of age or older. Women and members of the armed forces were still excluded from suffrage. The curial electoral system for elections to the Provincial Diets remained unchanged. After 1907, 8 nations were represented in the Vienna parliament (Germans, Czechs, Poles, Rutheniens, Romanians, Croats, Slovenes and Italians) and more than 30 political parties or political movements were represented.[187]

In 1867 Czech politicians demanded a similar position for the Czech lands as Hungary had received within the Austria-Hungarian settlement. They based their political demands on the historical rights of the Bohemian Kingdom and lands of the Czech Crown.[188] Large meetings took place in Bohemia and a proposal for an Austrian-Hungarian-Czech triad settlement was put in writing in 1871, in a document called the Fundamental Articles.[189] However, the compromise proposal was not put into practice and the Constitution remained unchanged.[190] The defeat of the political program based on the "historical rights" of the Czech kingdom gradually changed Czech politics and Czech politicians and their attitude towards Austria in the next decades. On the other hand the Czech politicians ended in 1879 their policy of boycott of the Austrian Imperial Parliament and concentrated on active encouragement of Czech political claims mainly in education, language, and promotion of industry and businesses.[191] Another turning point came in 1890–1891, after the Czech National party (so called Old Czechs) did not succeed in concluding an ill-conceived compromise with the German politicians in the Czech lands and with the Vienna Government called Punctations due to the fierce opposition of the Czech public and the Young Czech party. Punctations represented a threat to the integrity of Bohemia, because of the possible establishment of German speaking border regions and a bilingual rest of the Bohemian interior territory.[192] The subsequent elections in 1891 were won by the Young Czechs with their more realistic policy of "real progress" and the political system saw also the growth of new political parties including Social Democrats, National Socialists, Agrarians and clerical parties.[193] The struggle for Czech statehood

187 The Austrian Parliament, p. 18.
188 Cibulka, P. – Hájek, J. – Kučera, M.: The Definition of Czech National Society during the Period of Liberalism and Nationalism 1860–1914. In: Pánek, J. – Tůma, O. et al.: *A History of the Czech Lands*, pp. 331 and following.
189 Bernatzik, E.: *Die österreichischen Verfassungsgesetze mit Erläuterungen*, doc. No. 205, pp. 1097–1108.
190 Höbelt, L.: Devolution Aborted: Franz Joseph I and the Bohemian Fundamental Articles of 1871, *Parliaments, Estates and Representation.* Volume 32, Issue 1, 2012, pp. 37–52.
191 It was the case especially of newly created, so called The Young Czech Party. In more details see B. M. Carver: *The Young Czech Party 1874–1901*, especially pp. 60 and following.
192 *Ibidem.* See also Urban. O.: *Czech society 1848–1918*, pp. 210–211.
193 Krejčí, O.: *History of Elections in Bohemia and Moravia*, pp. 121 and following.

entered a new stage. The Czech–German relations caused a series of political crises and all attempts to reach a mutually acceptable solution before WWI failed.[194]

---

194 See for example Wiskemann, E.: *Czechs and Germans: a study of the struggles in the historic provinces of Bohemia and Moravia*. Royal Institute of International Affairs. Oxford University Press, 1938, especially pp. 31 and following.

/**9**/
Austrian legal development 1848–1918

The events of 1848 gradually brought important changes to the Austrian legal system, which applied to the Czech lands. In many respects, alterations were interlinked with the constitutional development of the Empire and with gradual liberalization of the society. For example, the abolition of feudal subjection in 1848 brought about fundamental changes not only in the equality of citizens before the law but subsequently also in state administration, self-government and the judiciary. State administration and the judiciary were formed for the first time as universal systems applicable to all instances and inhabitants of certain districts or provinces. The abolition of censorship and the call for the freedom of press were closely connected with the introduction of a jury system, initially in matters related to the press and later spread over the various subject-matters of cases.

Oral and public criminal proceedings, along with the so-called accusatory principle, promised by the March Constitution of 1849, led to the installation of public prosecutors, to a new approach towards the assessment of evidence, and to the potential option of choice between trial by judge or trial by jury. Most new features were repealed by the Sylvester Patents in 1851. New principles of criminal procedure were introduced in 1852–1853; however, public prosecutors and the principle of publicity of proceedings remained in force.

A new Criminal Code was enacted on 27th May 1852 (No. 117/1852 RGBL Austrian Reichsgesetzblatt).[195] In fact, its text was an extensive and deep amendment of the Criminal Code of 1803.[196] The new Code applied not only in the Austrian and Czech lands, but also in Hungary. The most important change consisted of a new division of criminal offenses into three categories: felonies (most serious offences), less grave offences and misdemeanours (petty offences). The concept of the Code was modified: the Code consisted of an introductory Patent and two Parts. The First Part dealt with felonies, and the Second Part focused on less grave offences and misdemeanours. Both Parts were subdivided into general and specific subparts. General provisions encompassed definitions of relevant terms and conditions for criminal liability to arise. New conditions were set, for example, for the criminal responsibility of juveniles and even of socially weaker strata of society.

Sentencing reform focused mainly on imprisonment. Life imprisonment was introduced to replace the death penalty in cases when the Emperor used his right to give pardon. From 1853 there were only two categories of prison. Punishment had four main aims: (a) to deter the offender and others from committing crimes; (b) to prevent the commission of further crimes; (c) to seek, on the behalf of society, revenge and retribution for the criminal acts of an individual; and (d) to reform the offender through rehabilitation, education and training. In order to fulfil those objectives, a new type of so-called provincial penitentiaries was established, these penitentiaries being at Bory (near Pilsen (Western Bohemia)), Řepy (near Prague), St. Wenceslas' Penitentiary (in Prague), Špilberk (in the Moravian capital of Brno), and Mírov (in Northern Moravia). A new provincial penitentiary was built in the Prague quarter of Pankrác in 1889, and these premises have continually served as a prison since then. Corporal punishments were regulated by the Criminal Code: beating with a stick was permitted for men (limited to 30 hits) and whipping for women and juveniles.

The Criminal Code was supplemented by a special patent, entitled the Beating Patent (*Prügelpatent*), in 1854; this Patent enabled high police officials and administrative bodies to govern more specific conditions for misdemeanours against public order and to set relevant punishment. The title "Beating Patent" was in fact a nickname derived from provisions of Article 11 of the Code, which enabled the imposition of corporal punishments. In 1855 a

195 For its interesting analyses see Henry Shelton Sanford: *Penal Codes: Being a Report on the Different Codes of Penal Law in Europe*, doc. No. 68, Washington D.C. 1854, pp. 87–97.

196 Its text in German: *Das strafgesetz über verbrechen, vergehen und uebertretungen: die strafgerichts-competenz-verordnungen und die press-ordnung vom 27. mai 1852 für das kaiserthum Oesterreich*, Aus der kaiserlich-königlichen hof- und staatsdruckerei, Wien 1852, (e-book Google).

special Military Criminal Code was enacted to regulate all categories of crime committed by members of the armed forces, and special military courts were instituted to try such crimes.[197]

There were several proposals for a new Criminal Code drafted before WWI under the influence of the Hungarian Codes of 1878 and 1879, new approaches towards criminal law which included experience gained from the application of modern European codes (e.g. the German Criminal Code of 1871) and new thoughts emerging in different schools of sociology.[198] Unfortunately, the drafts of the new Code, first discussed between the 1870s and 1890s and then resumed between 1909 and 1912, were not enacted.

Criminal law was subject to gradual changes imposed by new legislation. Important changes were linked with the constitutional development of the Empire. In 1867 corporal punishment was abolished in connection with the preparation of the December Constitution. However, some pieces of legislation led to rather contentious limitations of civil rights. The Act on Police Supervision (inspection) was enacted in 1873; it was followed in 1885 by the Act on Houses of Correction, providing for compulsory work, and the Act on Dangerous Use of Explosives. Austria, like its neighbour Germany, adopted several so-called anti-socialist laws, with the most important of these passed in 1886. The Act was enacted for only a limited period of three years; its aim was to exclude juries from proceedings for so-called political crimes.

On 23rd May 1873, a new Code on Criminal Procedure was enacted (No. 119/1873 Austrian RGBL). Julius Glaser, professor of criminal law at the University of Vienna, was the main drafter of the codification; he served as the Minister of Justice in the Auersperg's Government between 1871 and 1879.[199] In many respects, criminal procedure returned back to the codification of 1850 and the December Constitution of 1867. The Code of Criminal Procedure was amended in 1877 and, together with the Criminal Code of 1852, remained in force within the whole territory of the Austrian part of the Empire not only until the end of Austria-Hungary in 1918 but in Austria and the Czech lands also during the whole period between WWI and WWII.

Criminal procedure was built upon the accusatorial principle, oral and public proceedings, unrestricted evaluation of evidence (means of proof) and upon a trial by jury for most serious crimes against the state and against the person. When a trial by jury was ordered, jurors were to decide the issue of guilt, while the panel of three professional judges decided on the issue of

---

197 Das militär-strafgesetzbuch über verbrechen und vergehen vom 15. Jäuner 1855 für das kaiserthum Oesterreich, W. Kraumüller, Wien, 1861 (e-book Google).
198 A. Wandruszka – P. Urbanitsch (eds.): Die Habsburgermonarchie 1848–1918. Volume II. Verwaltung und Rechtswesen, Chapter IX., W. Ogris, Die Rechtsentwicklung in Cisleithanien 1848–1918, p. 568.
199 Wahlberg, W.: Julius Glaser als Strafrechtslehrer und Justizminister, Wien 1886.

law, i.e. they imposed a relevant penalty. Permitted means of proof were specifically evidence by witness, documentary evidence, and real evidence. This brought more discretionary powers to the judge or the panel of judges. Preliminary (pre-trial) proceedings were held by an investigative (examining) judge. The records of judicial pre-trial investigation were permitted to be used in evidence during a trial. For the first time the Criminal Procedure Code fully applied the so-called presumption of innocence, which meant that all people accused of a crime were legally presumed to be innocent until they were proven guilty by the court.

Criminal justice was essentially built upon three instances. It allowed not only for an ordinary appeal to the Provincial High Court, but also for filing a cassation appeal with the Supreme Court in Vienna. Criminal procedure legislation set more detailed provisions regarding the position of the public prosecutor, the defendant, and his or her counsel in the course of proceedings. The institution of bail was introduced. However, criminal proceedings remained rather complex, lengthy and quite costly. It should be noted that the provisions of the Criminal Procedure Code in fact created practical obstacles for members of the socially disadvantageous layers of society to reach justice.

The speedy development of industry required business law to effectively respond to its needs and achievements. This requirement was understood even during the period of neo-absolutism, associated with the name of Alexander Bach, when the economy came to be supported by a limited freedom of association, regulated by the already mentioned special Imperial Act of 1852. The medieval concept of guilds for crafts was finally abandoned in 1859, and new provisions for individual businesses were adopted in the form of the "Order for Manufacturers and Individual Proprietorship", which dealt with crafts, retail, services and trades of individual proprietors.

This period of rapid industrial development was crowned by the enactment of the General Commercial Code in 1863. The Austrian Commercial Code in fact created a substantial part of the codification project drafted for business law by the Committee of the German Union (*Deutsche Bund*) in 1861, which was applied in Germany as *Allgemeines Deutsches Handelsgesetzbuch* (ADHGB). It was enacted in Austria in December 1862 and entered into force as the General Commercial Code (Imperial Act. No. 1/1863 RGBL) on 1st July 1863. The Code was composed of General Provisions and 4 Books, subdivided into four hundred thirty-one articles.[200] Book One defined the basic concepts and terms relevant to business activities, company law and business entities, and commercial registers or accounting books. Book Two enacted provisions regulating the basic types of company, namely: the unlimited liability company, the limited partnership company, and the joint stock company. The Book

---

200 See for example *International Encyclopedia of Comparative Law*. Volume VIII, Chapter II, Civil law and Commercial law (by Denis Talon), Martinus Nijhoff Publishers, 1972, pp. 12–13.

set conditions for their memoranda of association and by-laws, and for bodies to be established as a business entity. Book Three dealt with dormant partners. Book Four governed obligations applicable to, and arising from, various commercial activities. Popular private companies with limited liability were not included in the Commercial Code; in practice such companies were constituted under the vague provisions of the Act on Associations of 1852, representing quite an infirm legal foundation for their establishment. A special law on limited liability companies was not enacted until 1906. Beginning in 1873 another form of a business entity was introduced, namely a cooperative, which became popular not only in agriculture, but also in retail, and among small and medium size savings associations.

The Code was limited in scope and failed to cover the entire system of business law. Such institutions as payment orders, procedures concerning securities, dissolution of business entities, their liquidation or bankruptcy were omitted. It should be noted that Article 1 of the Commercial Code allowed for customary law to apply in cases were no relevant provisions were laid down by the Code or by any subsequent legislation. Commercial usage was another source of unwritten law used in business; this became an important part of the law of contracts. Therefore Austrian business law was regarded as more flexible than civil law, should the two branches be compared. The Commercial Code was a special code with respect to its relation to the Austrian General Civil Code; this position allowed for the application of provisions of civil law where no relevant provisions of the Commercial Code existed. In addition, the Commercial Code provided for the application of the principles of natural law.

The above mentioned reforms of Criminal Proceedings as well as German codification of civil proceedings influenced also the reform of civil proceedings in Austria. The new Acts were prepared in the years 1891–1895 under the supervision of Franz Klein.[201] The Austrian Government urged the reform of the proceedings in order to be more flexible, faster and cheaper. The proposal was laid down before the both houses of Parliament as a whole with a possibility either to enact it as a whole, or to reject it. Counter proposals of the deputies were therefore forbidden, as to ease the legislative process. Four individual Imperial Acts were enacted on August 1, 1895 and came into effect from January 1, 1898. The reform was based on the so called Imperial Acts of Jurisdiction No 110 and 111/1895 Austrian RGBL, Civil Order No 112/1895 and No 113/1895 Austrian RGBL.[202] The civil proceedings was based on three

---

201 For his personality see Hofmeister, H. (ed.), *Forschungsband Franz Klein (1854–1926). Leben und Wirken.* Wien, Manz, 1988, especially study by W. Kralik, Die Verwirklichung der Ideen Franz Kleins in der Zivilprozessordnung von 1895, pp. 88–89.
202 Caenegem, R. C.: *International Encyclopedia of Comparative Law.* Volume XVI, Chapter 2, History of European Civil Procedure, pp. 96–97.

instances and special provisions on appeals and so called revision applied. The proceedings before the first two instances were oral and public, while the third instance acted on the basis of submitted written documents. The new principles of "mastery of parties" (i.e. parties, not the court, are masters of their pleadings), material truths and equality of the parties were introduced. According to F. Klein the whole reform had an important "social function". In 1876 the Order on Executions followed.

The year 1848 represented a turning point not only in the development of law in general but also in legal education in the Czech lands. It was the beginning of a new era in the history of both Prague University and the Law Faculty, relating closely to the development of Czech public life and Czech politics.[203] The first lectures in the Czech language were delivered at the Law Faculty. A private associate professor, Josef Frič, started reading lectures on judicial proceedings in Czech, and Vendelín Grunwald delivered lectures on civil law in Czech. Other lectures were also read in Czech, such as those by J. N. Schnabel on the philosophy of law, and those by E. Jonák on national economy and statistics. However, the Czech language was suppressed again, and from 1855 only J. Frič taught in Czech. Czech legal scholarship began its revival after the restoration of the constitutional system in Austria after 1860. This revival was linked primarily with the achievements of Antonín Knight Randa, an outstanding professor of civil law, who combined his academic and political careers. Criminal law was read in the Czech language by extraordinary professor Josef Slavíček. At the same time, the number of Czech students of law was rising. Although the legislation was of Austrian origin, the Law Faculty contributed to the establishment of an independent Czech legal science and modern Czech legal terminology.

In 1882, Emperor Franz Joseph II issued a decree dividing Prague University into two parts – the Czech University and the German University.[204] The Law Faculty, fostering the Czech national identity and promoting Czech science, became one of the cornerstones of the new institution. Lawyer Antonín Knight Randa became the second Rector of the Czech University. The holding of a rectorship by a member of the Law Faculty became quite frequent until the 1950s, when the term of office lasted only one year. The Law Faculty was proud of its prominent teachers: such as Antonín Knight Randa, mentioned earlier, or his younger colleague, Josef Stupecký, Emil Ott, expert in procedural law (both Stupecký and Ott served as Rectors of the University), Karel Hermann Otavský, specialist in commercial law, Leopold Heyrovský, specialist in Roman law, legal historians Jaromír Čelakovský and Bohuslav Rieger, Jiří

203 Kuklík, J. et al.: *Faculty of Law of Charles University in Prague*, pp. 20–22.
204 Havránek, J.: *Characteristics of Charles University in years 1882–1918 and its faculties*, Czech university. In: *A History of Charles University*. Vol. II (1802–1990), pp. 123–131. Odložilík, O.: *The Caroline University*, 1348–1948, pp. 72–74.

Pražák, expert in administrative law, and economists (as well as prominent politicians) Albín Bráf and Josef Kaizl. Criminal law was represented by Alois Zucker and Fratišek Štorch. And in finance and statistics Matouš Talíř should be particularly mentioned.

/10/

The break-up of the Habsburg Empire and the establishment of Czechoslovakia

World War One found Austria-Hungary taking an almost universal orientation towards cooperation with the aggressive policy of Germany, which led to tensions and friction inside the multi-national Empire.[205] Parliament was suspended, the press was heavily censored, public meetings were forbidden, and those suspected of anti-Austrian activities and disloyalty, such as the leading Czech politicians Karel Kramář and Alois Rašín, were imprisoned.[206] Moreover, German politicians representing Bohemia and Moravia proposed a so-called Easter Program in 1916, which would break up the historical entity of the Czech lands, cutting it along the lines of prevailing language and nation affiliation.[207] However, Austria-Hungary lost the war, and the Empire broke up. New national states were established on their pre-war territories. An independent Czechoslovakia was one of them; in it historical Czech lands were

205 Still valuable account is in Jasci, O.: *The Dissolution of the Habsburg Monarchy*. Chicago: The University of Chicago Press, 1929, especially part I, pp. 6–23, and part VI, p. 379 and following. Okey, R.: *The Habsburg Monarchy c. 1765–1918*, pp. 369–400.
206 Harna, J.: The Czech Lands during the First World War 1914–1918. In: Pánek, J. – Tůma, O. et al.: *A History of the Czech Lands*, pp. 385–389.
207 Beneš, Z. – Kural, V. (eds.): *Facing history: the evolution of Czech-German relations in the Czech provinces, 1848–1948*, p. 37.

united together with Slovakia. The idea of an independent Czechoslovakia was not an original concept considered by Czech politicians at the beginning of WWI; it had been conceived by a small group of radical politicians and those representatives who had gone into exile. A leading role among Czech representatives in exile was played by Professor Tomáš Masaryk.[208] After 1915 Masaryk joined together with other collaborators, such as Edvard Beneš (the second Czechoslovak President) and Milan Rastislav Štefánik (a Slovak politician and officer) established the Czechoslovak National Council. They gradually gained support from the Allied Powers for the idea of an independent Czech state. They managed to form Czechoslovak military units ("legions"), composed of Czech soldiers who had deserted the Austria-Hungarian army. The legions joined the Allies in France, Italy and in Russia, where they played an important part in intervening against the new Bolshevik regime. The cooperative movement of Czech and Slovak fellow countrymen in Western Europe and the United States also played an important role, particularly in gaining political support for a united Czech-Slovak state and in raising funds for this initiative. A political union between the Czechs and the Slovaks was declared, with Masaryk's presence, in the United States on 31st May 1918; the declaration became known as the Pittsburgh Convention.[209]

In 1918 the National Council was transformed into the Czechoslovak Provisional Government in Exile. The Czechoslovak state was recognized by the Allied Powers as being conceived even before it had been solemnly proclaimed, and even before it was clear what its form and territorial borders would be. The Czechoslovak Provisional Government issued its constitutional program for an independent Czechoslovakia, entitled the Proclamation of Independence of the Czechoslovak Nation (or the so-called Washington Declaration).[210]

Czech politics at home was represented by the Czechoslovak National Committee, which was transformed at the beginning of 1918 and which encompassed all major Czech political parties, as based on the results of elections to the Austrian Imperial Council in 1911. The Committee was headed by Karel Kramář, a Czech National Democrat and a symbol of Czech anti-Habsburg resistance during WWI. The Committee proposed that the Czech lands and Slovakia should unite. Slovak politicians were represented by Vavro

---

208 For his personality and policy during WWI see Winters, S. B. (ed.): *T. G. Masaryk (1850–1937). Vol. 1., Thinker and politician.* Macmillan in association with the School of Slavonic and East European Studies, University of London. Zeman, Z. A. B.: *The Masaryks. The Making of Czechoslovakia.* Tauris, 1990, esp. pp. 65–79.
209 For the text in English see Mikuš, J. A.: *Slovakia: a political and constitutional history: with documents.* Slovak Academic Press, 1995 doc. No. 20, pp. 156–157.
210 For its text in English see *Declaration of independence of the Czechoslovak nation by its Provisional Government,* 18 October 1918, Printed for the Czechoslovak Arts Club by the Marchbanks Press, New York, 1918. Kovtun, G. J.: *The Czechoslovak Declaration of Independence: A History of the Document.* Washington D.C., 1985.

Šrobár, a member of the Committee. A special platform of socialist parties, the so-called Socialist Council, was established within the Committee to emphasize the importance of not only national, but also social aspects of the policy.

The Czechoslovak state was solemnly proclaimed in Prague on 28th October 1918 by the Czechoslovak National Committee.[211] The National Committee issued the first Czechoslovak Act on the Establishment of the Independent Czechoslovak State, which was published as Act No. 11 of a new Czechoslovak Collection of Laws. The Act proclaimed, "for the time being", juridical continuity with Austrian imperial laws and provincial laws valid on the territory of the newly established Czechoslovak state. The bodies of state administration remained operative. Juridical continuity also applied to Slovakia, where Hungarian laws remained in force. There were exceptions to the principle of juridical continuity: Czechoslovak law did not receive those Austrian laws which contradicted the fact of Czechoslovak independence. In the case of a dispute the Czechoslovak Supreme Court or the Supreme Administrative Court were to decide and to issue a judgment whether an individual Act was, or was not, part of the Czechoslovak legal system. This so-called Reception Act signified that Czechoslovak law during the period between the First and the Second World Wars was closely linked with the previous Austrian and Hungarian legal traditions; as a result, a dual legal system within Czechoslovakia was established.

A decision on a republican form of government was postponed until negotiations with the Czechoslovak politicians in exile took place in Switzerland. The Czechoslovak National Council was transformed into the Provisional Government in exile and recognized as such by the Allied Powers. The delegation of the Provisional Government, headed by Edvard Beneš, reached an agreement with the representatives of the National Committee, headed by Kramář, on an independent Czechoslovakia.[212] On 30th October 1918 the existence of the common Czechoslovak state was confirmed by the leaders of the Slovak political parties through the Slovak National Council in Slovakia.[213]

The Czechoslovak National Committee took complete control of the state and took over its supreme legislative and executive powers. The first laws enacted by the National Committee dealt with the establishment of an independent Czechoslovak Supreme Court, the Supreme Administrative Court, and twelve central administrative bodies, Ministries. On 5th November 1918,

211 In more details Mamatey, V. S.: The Establishment of the Republic. In: Mamatey, V. S., Luža, R. (eds.): *A History of the Czechoslovak Republic 1918–1948.* New Jersey: Princeton University Press, 1973, pp. 22–27. Harna, J.: *First Czechoslovak Republic 1918–1938.* In: Pánek, J. – Tůma, O. et. al.: *A History of the Czech Lands*, pp. 395–396.
212 Zeman, Z. with Klimek, A.: *The Life of Edvard Beneš 1884–1948. Czechoslovakia in Peace and War.* Oxford: Clarendon Press, pp. 34–35.
213 Krajčovičová, N.: Slovakia in Czechoslovakia 1918–1938. In: Teich, M. – Kováč, D. – Brown, M. D.: *Slovakia in History.* Cambridge University Press, 2011, p. 137–139. Text in English see Mikuš, J. A.: *Slovakia: a political and constitutional history*, doc. No. 23, p. 161.

the National Committee announced an amnesty for certain cases of "injustice" by Austrian courts against Czech patriots resulting from wartime conditions.

Independence was proclaimed by the Czechoslovak National Committee as a revolutionary step against Austrian influence and common statehood. Both these contentious issues had dominated the orientation of Czech politics for decades and even centuries. Yet, in achieving its independence, Czechoslovakia was in reality left with many remnants of the old regime: many politicians, state officials and judges remained in office and had adhered strictly to guidelines from Vienna until the end of WWI. As a result, the events of 1918 were a compromise between the idea of independence as the principle of "revolution" and the need for a certain degree of continuity, if only for the sake of stability. One should take into account the potential weaknesses of the new emerging states in the historical context of Central Europe finding itself, on the one hand, under the influence of the revolutionary ideas of the Russian Bolsheviks and, on the other hand, under the pressure of the radical leftist movement and the serious economic conditions caused by the war.[214]

Moreover, the new Czechoslovak state was weakened by yet another important factor; the representatives of the German minority in the newly born Czechoslovakia – Austrian citizens of German nationality, later merging with Sudeten Germans, did not intend to stay in Czechoslovakia. On the contrary, they formed four provinces in the border regions of Bohemia and Moravia and asked for the unification of these with the newly established Austria, represented by the Austrian Provisional National Assembly. Some German politicians planned to establish a wider Austro-German Central European entity.[215]

The Czechoslovak representative bodies had to assert Czechoslovak sovereignty over the whole territory of the newly established Czechoslovakia, i.e. the Czech lands within their historical borders and in Slovakia. They used political, economic, and military means as well. The secessionist movement of the four German provinces was defeated by the end of 1918, and the territory of the historical Czech lands was secured for the Czechoslovak state by the preliminary decision of the Allied Powers. In March 1919, when the inaugural session of the Austrian Parliament was called, the final round of protests against Czechoslovak rule in the border regions of Czechoslovakia was held. Some fifty people were shot dead. The decision on the territorial integrity of Czechoslovakia remained unchanged.

---

214 In more details Zeman, Z. A. B.: *The Making and Breaking of Communist Europe*, pp. 85–97.
215 Beneš, Z. – Kural, V. (eds.): *Facing history: the evolution of Czech-German relations in the Czech provinces, 1848–1948*, pp. 56–57. Brügell, J. W.: The Germans in pre-war Czechoslovakia. In: Mamatey, V. S. – Luža, R. (eds.): *A History of the Czechoslovak Republic 1918–1948*, pp. 167–186, or Wiskemann, E.: *Czechs and Germans: a study of the struggles in the historic provinces of Bohemia and Moravia*, pp. 51 and following.

The frontiers of the new state were defined and internationally recognized in individual steps taken during the Paris Peace Conference in 1919–1920.[216] The frontiers with Germany were outlined by the Versailles Peace Treaty, while the frontiers with Austria were set by the Saint Germain Peace Treaty. In 1919, the territory of so-called Subcarpathian Ruthenia was added to the Czechoslovak state by decision of the Paris Peace Conference. According to a special treaty concluded between Czechoslovakia and the Allied Great Powers, the so-called Minority Treaty of St. Germain, Subcarpathian Ruthenia had an autonomous status within the Czechoslovak Republic.[217]

The frontiers with Hungary became a pretext for open military conflict, particularly when the Slovak Communist Republic of the Soviets was established in the Eastern Slovak town of Prešov on 16th June 1919 with the assistance of the Hungarian communist regime of Béla Khun.[218] The Slovak territory was secured by the Czechoslovak armed forces in July 1919. The frontiers with Hungary were finally determined in 1920 by Article 27 of the so-called Trianon Peace Treaty.[219] There were also territorial disputes between Czechoslovakia and Poland after WWI concerning the Teschen (*Těšín*) territory in Silesia. This dispute was resolved by a compromise sponsored by the Allied Powers, and the territory was divided between the two neighbouring states.

216 In more details *Perman, D.: The Shaping of the Czechoslovak State. Diplomatic History of the Boundaries of Czechoslovakia, 1914–1920*. Leiden, 1962.
217 For its English translation see Beneš, Z. – Kural, V. (eds.): *Facing history: the evolution of Czech-German relations in the Czech provinces, 1848–1948*, document No. 1, pp. 295–296.
218 Hronský, M.: *The Struggle for Slovakia and the Treaty of Trianon 1918–1920*. Bratislava: Veda, 2001, pp.114–153.
219 *Ibidem*, pp. 154 and following.

/11/

Continuities and discontinuities in the initial period of Czechoslovak legal development

The Reception Act of 1918 caused the Czechoslovak legal system to remain under the influence of Austrian and Hungarian law and Central European legal culture until the 1950s. Before 1918 the Czech lands were part of Austria, whereas Slovakia was part of Hungary within the Austria-Hungary Empire; therefore there were different legal systems in the Czech lands and in Slovakia respectively. The state of affairs where different laws existed and applied in various parts of the newly established Czechoslovak state was called legal dualism. However, both source legal systems were adapted to the needs of Czechoslovak sovereignty, and they were substantially amended and modernized by subsequent Czechoslovak legislation. In addition, it was necessary to unify the Czechoslovak legal system by enacting new Czechoslovak laws applicable within the territory of the whole state. The enactment of new Czechoslovak laws in various branches proceeded at quite a low speed. Moreover, attempts to enact new Czechoslovak codes for criminal law, civil law (both substantive and procedural) and business law were suspended by the Munich Agreement in 1938 and the following Second World War. Partial success in removing differences between the Czech lands and Slovakia could be seen in the unification of state administration, in constitutional law, family law, the land reform, and in some branches of criminal law.

The most important changes were introduced in constitutional law. The Czechoslovak National Committee had been regarded as the body with supreme legislative and executive powers for the interim period, i.e. until the Czechoslovak constitutional bodies were established. As has already been mentioned, new Czechoslovak ministries, the Supreme Court and the Supreme Administrative Courts were established by the first laws passed by the National Committee. The National Committee established a committee to draft a Provisional Constitution; the committee was headed by Alfred Meissner, a lawyer and a Social Democratic politician. The Provisional Constitution adopted by the National Committee on 13th November 1918 as Act No. 37/1918 Sb. determined the republican form of the Czechoslovak state; it proclaimed the Habsburg dynasty to be dethroned. The Provisional (or Revolutionary) National Assembly, where only Czech and Slovak representatives were present, was regarded as the supreme authority of the state and the sole legislative body, with the exclusive right to elect and dismiss the highest executive body, the Government. The Provisional National Assembly had the right to vote the Government out of office by a simple majority of at least half of the Deputies as a demonstration of the lack of confidence. The Provisional National Assembly was not elected; its composition was based on the division of seats among Czech political parties, based on their (last) election results in 1911, with some seats reserved for the Slovaks.

Executive power was divided between the Government and the President of the Republic. The first Czechoslovak President, Professor T. G. Masaryk, was elected unanimously by the Provisional National Assembly. The President was the head of state and had relatively limited powers. He appointed and received diplomatic representatives, appointed judges, state officials and military officers of certain ranks, and granted pardons. The President had the right to veto passed legislation.

National minorities, i.e. the Sudeten Germans, the Poles and the Hungarians, were represented neither in the Provisional National Assembly, nor in the Government. There were no special provisions for civil rights and liberties in the Provisional Constitution; in practice, Austrian laws were used in this field. The democratic and republican character of the Czechoslovak state was strengthened by special Act No. 61/1918 Sb. of 10th December 1918, abolishing the orders and titles of the nobility. Similarly to the law adopted in the new Austrian Republic, the Act enforced the principle of equality of citizens before the law and stipulated that members of former aristocratic families were not allowed to use their titles and other attributes.

The original text of the Constitution was amended twice in 1919. The first amendment increased the number of Slovak representatives in the Provisional National Assembly; the second amendment, drafted at Masaryk's direct request and passed on 23rd May 1919, transformed the powers of the President of the Republic and the Government *vis a vis* Parliament. The latter amendment was an important move towards parliamentary democracy built upon the theory of division of powers. The President was assigned a new competence to appoint and dismiss the Prime Minister and Government ministers, along with a right to determine their number and posts. The President was awarded the right to report to the National Assembly on the state of the Republic and to appoint university professors. The Government was accountable to the National Assembly. The Assembly had the right to take a vote of confidence, as well as of no confidence.

When Czechoslovakia was established in 1918, Social Democrats, National Socialists and other left-wing political parties, together with Trade Unions, demanded a radical land reform and large scale socialization of industry, particularly heavy industry and coal mines.[220] The land reform was backed by the Agrarian Party. As a result, the first Czechoslovak Government, headed by Karel Kramář, reached an agreement that both socialization and land reform would be incorporated into the Government Program. The whole process was in fact started by the Czechoslovak Declaration of Independence, issued by the Provisional Exile Government on 18th October 1918, which declared: "… the Czechoslovak nation will carry out far-reaching social and economic reforms. The largest estates will be redeemed for home colonization."

In the beginning, ownership of real property by large owners was frozen, and the land reform was debated within the Government and Parliament.[221] A rough estimate suggests that, by the end of WWI, one third of all agricultural land and forests in Czechoslovakia was owned by a relatively small number of aristocratic families and large proprietors, many of whom were of German or Hungarian origin, and by the Catholic Church. In Bohemia less than 2 per cent of landowners owned more than 25 per cent of the land; about 40 per cent of landowners owned land smaller than one-half hectare in size. The proportion was similar in Moravia, and even worse in Slovakia. Moreover, land reforms were already in progress, or being seriously debated, in Romania, the future Yugoslavia, Bulgaria, Poland and the Baltic states. The Coalition Government of Social Democrats and Agrarians was formed after the first elections to local self-government; subsequently, the land reform was agreed and gradually carried out. It represented a relatively moderate land reform with the aim of strengthening small and medium sized private owners; expro-

---

220 See Kuklík, J. *Znárodněné Československo (Nationalized Czechoslovakia): od znárodnění k privatizaci – státní zásahy do vlastnických a dalších majetkových práv v Československu a jinde v Evropě.* Prague: Auditorium, 2010, English summary, pp. 421–426.
221 For Czechoslovak land reform see Textor, L. E.: *Land Reform in Czechoslovakia.* London: Allen and Unwin, 1923, esp. p. 29 and following. Beneš, V.: Democracy and its problems 1918–1938. In: Mamatey, V. S. – Luža, R. (eds.): *A History of the Czechoslovak Republic 1918–1948*, pp. 89–92.

priation was for adequate compensation in most cases. The land reform had, however, a strong anti-German (in Slovakia anti-Hungarian), anti-Church and anti-feudal focus; there were historical memories going back to the Battle of White Mountain in 1620. On the other hand, some politicians, historians and lawyers from the conservative end of the political spectrum pointed to a possible danger threatening future development, which consisted in the undermining of the social order and ownership rights. The land reform and its results were subject to criticism by minorities; they claimed that they were being discriminated against, while the Czech and Slovak farmers allegedly gained more and were treated more favourably.

A preparatory stage of the reform was the enactment of a law providing for the limitation of disposition rights to large real (landed) property on 9th November 1918. Such property, recorded in the Land Register, could not be alienated or mortgaged except with the consent of the Department of Agriculture. The legal framework for the land reform was enacted by Act No. 215/1919 Sb., governing the seizure of large real property, passed on 16th April 1919. The Act entrusted the Czechoslovak state with the right to expropriate agricultural (arable) land exceeding 150 hectares (about 370 acres) and all other types of land exceeding 250 hectares (about 617 acres), and to redistribute the expropriated land. Redistribution, i.e. the process by which the expropriated land was made available to small holders for very low payments and with specially guaranteed loans, was stipulated by a special law ensuring land for farmers and was enacted on 27th May 1919. The Governmental Land Office was established in June 1919 to carry out the land reform. According to another law passed on 8th April 1920, the state paid compensation for expropriated land. However, there were different assessments based on the size of the expropriated property; for example, the Habsburg dynasty was not paid any compensation at all, and their property was simply confiscated.

In reality, the right of the state to expropriate was not exercised in all potential cases; many big owners, including the Catholic Church, managed to retain a large portion of their property. A new layer of holders of so-called "residuary farms", i.e. farms which were expropriated but whose property was not redistributed, promoted features of capitalism in agriculture and maintained the Agrarian Party politically. The land reform was brought to an end in 1936 and its results did not correspond with its original intentions. Some 650,000 small farmers still possessed an average of one hectare of land per allotment.

Debates over the land reform and socialization had an impact upon the constitutional framework, which was built on grounds similar to the German Constitution of Wiemar. The Czechoslovak Constitution provided that private ownership could be restricted only on the basis of the law. As a result, expropriation on a statutory basis and in the interest of the general public was allowed.[222] As a rule, expropriation was performed for adequate compensation; however, it was possible to expropriate even without any compensation if this was provided for by an Act of Parliament. The Constitution opened a way not only to the land reform but also to the future socialisation (nationalisation) of industry.

The socialisation of industry was discussed for two years after WWI. With the post war revolutionary wave fading away, the idea was abandoned, but with a notable exception in the establishment of workers' councils possessing limited powers, particularly in the mining industry. Instead of socialisation workers were promised that changes in labour law and social security would be introduced; as early as in December 1918, an eight hour working day was guaranteed by law, with more protection given to women and juveniles, and in 1924 changes in social security in cases of sickness, disability and pension insurance of employees followed (Act No. 221/1924 Sb.).

The establishment of the Czechoslovak Communist Party in 1921 meant that the Soviet style of nationalisation without compensation, socialist types of ownership (state and cooperative), and the idea of central planning were brought into the Czechoslovak political debate. An overall view on the Czechoslovak development between 1918 and 1920 could be compared with the development in Austria and Germany, as all these three countries were based on similar ideological and political concepts, and the outcome of debates and legislation was very close.

Although the concept of private ownership in interwar Czechoslovakia was based on the Austrian General Civil Code of 1811, WWI and subsequent discussions on socialisation and the land reform brought about fundamental changes. Czechoslovakia between the two World Wars had a relatively strong state sector operating in the mining industry, production of electricity, transport and forestry. However, state-owned companies and their activities between the wars represented not a socialist, but a "state capitalist" approach to economy and legal thinking, as the concept of state ownership was not connected only with socialist or communist views. In Czechoslovakia there were so-called mixed companies of private, municipal and state capital in such sectors as the production and distribution of electricity. Such companies served both the private interest and public needs.

---

222 *Constitution of the Czechoslovak Republic with Introduction by J. Hoetzel and V. Joachim.* Prague: Politika 1920, article 109. This view was supported by several important decisions of the Supreme Court and the Supreme Administrative Court.

/12/

Constitutional development of the First Czechoslovak Republic

The final version of the Constitution for the new Czechoslovak state was adopted in February 1920 and designated as the Constitutional Charter, with the Introductory Act.[223] The first Czechoslovak Constitution was influenced mainly by the French Constitution of the Third Republic, the Constitution of the United States and by the Austrian constitutional tradition. It was based on the classical theory of the division of powers between the legislative branch (vested in a two-chamber Parliament), the executive branch (vested in the President of the Republic together with the Government) and the judicial branch.[224] The Preamble emphasized the concept of the Czechoslovak people (nation) and their desire to fulfil the principle of self-determination and to become a member of the Family of Nations as a cultured, peace-loving, democratic and progressive nation. Such phrasing, inspired by the American constitutional tradition, became a pretext for criticism by German and Hungarian politicians. This criticism was nurtured by the fact that the Constitution

223 For the text of the Constitution in English see *Constitution of the Czechoslovak Republic with Introduction by J. Hoetzel and V. Joachim.*
224 For the analysis of the Czechoslovak Constitution in English see Táborský, E.: *Czechoslovak Democracy at Work.* London: Allen and Unwin, 1944.

was adopted by an appointed Parliament, which was without representatives of minorities in its membership.

The Constitutional Charter was divided into six titles: Title One introduced general provisions; Title Two dealt with the legislative branch of government; Title Three focused on the executive branch; Title Four regulated the judicial branch; Title Five defined civil rights and liberties; Title Six dealt with the rights of minorities.

The Constitution explicitly stipulated that Czechoslovakia was a democratic republic, and the people of the Republic were proclaimed the sole source of all state power. Czechoslovakia was declared a unitary state, with the exception of autonomy being guaranteed for Subcarpathian Ruthenia (later called also Transcarpathian Ukraine), which became part of Czechoslovakia in 1919 due to the decision of the Allied Powers during the Paris Peace Conference as embodied in the Minority Treaty of St. Germains. Its legislative autonomy lay primarily with language, educational and religious matters and with the administration of the territory being headed by the Governor. However, in practise its autonomy remained unachieved until 1938, when autonomy was finally guaranteed after the Munich Agreement.

State citizenship was single and uniform in the Czechoslovak Republic; the Constitution stipulated that a citizen of a foreign state should not be simultaneously a citizen of Czechoslovakia. In 1920 a special constitutional law on Czechoslovak state citizenship was adopted, dealing with details of acquiring and losing state citizenship as well as with the rights and duties of Czechoslovak state citizens. The issue of state citizenship was closely connected with the protection of national minorities under the condition that the members of the minorities lived on the territory of the Czechoslovak state and had not opted for the state citizenship of neighbouring countries. The details were set by international treaties concluded with Austria and Germany in the 1920s.

The legislative powers of the previous Provincial Diets of Bohemia, Moravia and Silesia were abolished. Laws passed by the Czechoslovak Parliament became applicable and binding throughout the whole territory of the Czechoslovak Republic, unless their provisions provided otherwise. The National Assembly consisted of two Chambers – the Chamber of Deputies and the Senate. The Chamber of Deputies was composed of 300 members. The Constitution was based on general, equal, direct and secret suffrage. If compared with Austria, Czechoslovakia brought in important changes to the voting rights. When Masaryk and the Czechoslovak Government in Exile issued the previously mentioned Washington Declaration in 1918, women were promised equality with men with respect to their political rights, including their suffrage in voting for Parliament. For the first time in Czech history women were allowed to vote and to stand as candidates in elections to local councils in 1919. The 1920 Constitution and the Act governing elections to the Chamber of Deputies, enacted on 29th February 1920 (Act No. 123/ 1920 Sb.), guaranteed the voting right for women with respect to elections to Parliament.[225] The same Act stipulated general and direct suffrage for every citizen who had reached twenty-one years of age and was entered in the List of Voters. The right to stand as a candidate to the House of Deputies was based on the minimum age limit of thirty years. Members of the lower House were elected for a term of six years.

There were no property qualifications for the right to vote, and a secret ballot was guaranteed. The duty to cast a vote in elections was stipulated by the law; however, some exceptions with respect to age (e.g. being over seventy years old), sickness, or other reasonable excuses were permitted. The electoral system was based on the system of proportional representation; this was very closely related to the political system since political parties submitted their official lists of candidates (ballot papers) to electoral committees in individual constituencies.

The right to vote for the Senate – the upper Chamber, consisting of one hundred fifty Senators, differed in certain criteria: the right to vote for the Senate was possessed by citizens of twenty-six years or older, and the right to stand as a candidate for the Senate was set for all citizens of forty-five years of age or older. Senators were elected for a term of eight years. In practice, differences in elections did not result in a different political composition for the Senate as compared with the House of Deputies. The reason was that the system was built upon the principle of proportional representation, which resulted in almost identical results in the elections to both Chambers.

Each Chamber elected its own Chairman and other officials. The sittings of Parliament were open to the public; so-called "sessions *in camera*" closed to the public were regulated by special rules of parliamentary procedures, which were adopted for both Chambers.

Elections to Parliament were under the judicial control of a special court set by the Constitution and Act of 29th February 1920 (Act No. 125/1920 Sb.). The Electoral Court dealt with appeals against the decisions of committees on the permanent List of Voters and on elections in general; the Court examined and confirmed the validity of the elections of individual members of Parliament and local councils; and it had to decide whether a member of Parliament had forfeited his or her seat due to the lack of their right to be elected or due to the termination of their membership in the political party whose candidate they were. The Electoral Court was composed of a President and twelve members. The President of the Electoral Court was always the President of the Supreme Administrative Court.

Members of both Chambers enjoyed parliamentary immunities: they were exempt from criminal prosecution for the performance of their mandate. The statements they made in the Chamber were subject to accountability in

225 In more details Krejčí, O.: *History of Elections in Bohemia and Moravia*, pp. 160–68.

accordance with the disciplinary rules of the Chamber. The consent of the Chamber was needed should its member become liable for a civil wrong or suspected of a crime (with the exception of one who was an editor-in-chief of printed mass media). If this consent was not granted, prosecution was ruled out forever.

The President of the Republic summoned, prorogued, terminated and dissolved the Parliament. The Constitution set strict limits to these prerogatives, and it was possible to summon a Parliament even without the consent of the President. The President was bound to summon the regular sitting of Parliament at least twice a year (Spring and Autumn sessions); in addition, he could summon Parliament for extraordinary sessions.

Draft laws were proposed either by the Government or by members of either Chamber. Drafts tabled by Deputies or Senators included a mandatory part, specifying the calculation of financial costs to be incurred if the draft were to become a law. Government bills on the State Budget and military bills had to be presented to the Chamber of Deputies first. A constitutional law required a qualified majority and came into force only with the consent of both Chambers; in all other cases the Chamber of Deputies could override the Senate.

The President had the right to veto any piece of legislation. He was entitled to return any law passed by the National Assembly, adding his observations and comments. The National Assembly could reverse the veto by an absolute majority of both houses. The Constitution provided for the possibility of the Government to hold a referendum on a bill proposed by the Government and rejected by the Parliament; however this provision was never used in practice.

Bills became laws after their publication in the Collection of Laws and Decrees (*Sbírka zákonů a nařízení* in Czech). Laws were promulgated by the following formula: "The Parliament of the Czechoslovak Republic has resolved upon the following law." Each law specified which member of the Government was responsible for its performance and enforcement. The law was associated with signatures attached to it by the President, the Prime Minister and the Minister in charge.

Legislative power was closely related to the Constitutional Court set by the Czechoslovak Constitution of 1920 since the Constitutional Court was entrusted with constitutional review.[226] Only the Constitutional Court could decide whether Czechoslovak laws, orders of Standing Committees of the National Assembly and the laws of the Ruthenian Diet were in compliance with the Czechoslovak Constitution and other laws amending the Constitution.

---

226 In more details see excerpt from the book by Langášek T.: Ústavní soud Československé republiky a jeho osudy v letech 1920–1948 (Constitutional Court of the Czechoslovak Republic and its fortunes in years 1920–1948). Plzeň: Aleš Čeněk, 2011; www.usoud.cz/en/

The Constitutional Court was composed of seven justices, three of whom were nominated by the President of the Republic, including the President of the Court. Two of the remaining four were taken from the ranks of the judges of the Supreme Court, and the other two from the Supreme Administrative Court. The application for a constitutional review in individual cases was reserved to the Supreme Court, the Supreme Administrative Court, the Electoral Court and to both Chambers of the National Assembly. There was a time-limit for filing the application: it was possible to review an individual Act within a period of three years after it had been promulgated.

However, the Constitutional Court was not functioning properly within the Czechoslovak constitutional system between the World Wars. Soon after its first members were appointed, serious political obstacles to its activities became clearly visible, and the Court was not fully operative for most of its first term. There were practically no proposals to start proceedings before the Court regarding constitutional review of the Acts of Parliament.

There was an attempt to promote the significance of the Constitutional Court between 1937 and 1938, when the Czechoslovak Government was seeking a certain *modus vivendi* regarding national minorities.[227] It was proposed by the Government headed by Milan Hodža (within the draft of the Statutes of National Minorities) that the Constitutional Court would serve as a guarantor of minority rights, i.e. the Constitutional Court would deal with petitions in individual cases.[228]

Should Parliament not sit, both Chambers elected a specific "Permanent Committee" consisting of twenty-four members, sixteen of whom were from the Chamber of Deputies. This Committee was entrusted with passing legislation in the form of emergency provisions proposed by the Government and approved by the President. There were certain limits: for example, it was forbidden within such a regime to alter or amend the Constitution, and adopted provisions must have been approved by a subsequent full Parliament.

The Constitutional Charter stipulated that Government decrees (or by-laws) would be issued only under the law and within its limits and provisions. However in practice, particularly in the 1930s, the legislative power of Parliament was bypassed through the introduction of so-called "entrusted" or delegated legislation. This type of legislation was used for the first time in the 1920s, when the democratic character of the state was endangered by the radical Communist left, and, subsequently, in the beginning of the 1930s in order to cope with economic problems of the Great Depression and political

227 See especially *Policy Statement of the Czechoslovak Government on its Nationality Policies,* February 20, 1937, Beneš, Z. – Kural, V. (eds.): *Facing history: the evolution of Czech-German relations in the Czech provinces,* 1848–1948, document No. 3, pp. 298–299.
228 Kuklík, J. – Němeček, J.: *Od* národnostního státu ke státu národností? *Národnostní statut a snahy o řešení menšinové otázky v Československu v roce 1938.* Prague: Nakladatelství Karolinum, 2013, pp. 48 and 315.

threats from Nazi ideology. Despite these legislative "concessions", Czechoslovakia was the only nation in the region retaining its democratic character and parliamentary democracy during the whole period between WWI and WWII.

The executive power was divided between the President of the Republic and the Government. The President was elected by both Chambers of the National Assembly for a term of seven years, with one re-election permitted by the Constitution. However, Tomáš Masaryk was re-elected four times, since he was seen as a key figure of independent Czechoslovakia. Powers granted by the Constitution enabled the President to significantly influence the politics of the state. The President was not legally responsible for his political acts; the only exception was impeachment for high treason, with this action being filed by the House of Deputies and the proceedings being carried out by the Senate.

The President was the head of state; he represented the state in its foreign relations, possessing the right to negotiate and ratify international treaties. Presidential prerogatives included receiving and appointing diplomatic representatives, declaring a state of war (together with the Parliament), reporting to the National Assembly on the state of the Republic, appointing university professors, judges, state officials and military officers of certain ranks and granting amnesties and pardons.

The Constitution contained important provisions regulating mutual relations between the President and the Government. The President had the right to appoint and dismiss the Prime Minister and Government Ministers, including the right to decide on the number of the latter. He had the right to preside over Government meetings, if present. On the other hand, the Government was responsible for implementing decisions and performing the administrative acts of the President. Each administrative act of the President was to bear the signature of a member of the Government who was responsible for its execution.

The Government was answerable to the Chamber of Deputies, which could take a vote of no confidence. The motion had to be signed by a minimum of one hundred Deputies, and it was necessary to reach a simple majority of those Deputies present, providing that more than one hundred fifty members of the House were present. However, this procedure was never used during the interwar period, because the Government was usually dismissed by the President during political crises; in such cases, the President appointed a caretaker or semi-political Government for the interim period.

Due to the system of proportional representation applicable during the interwar period, the Czechoslovak Government was always formed by a coalition of the main Czechoslovak political parties. After 1920 the coalition was agreed by the Republican Party of Peasants (the Agrarian Party), the Czechoslovak Social Democratic Party (without the Communists who left in 1920 and established their own party), the Czechoslovak National Socialist Party, the Czechoslovak People's Party (the Catholic Party) and the Czechoslovak National Democratic Party. The leading representatives of these parties met before Government meetings and resolved on key problems. Such gatherings were known as "the Five". Decisions of the Five went smoothly through the Government and Parliament. The system was abandoned in 1925: Sudeten German politicians decided to cooperate with the Czechoslovak Government and the German civil parties took part in the Government; as a result the Czechoslovak socialist parties were excluded. This was the moment when the Sudeten Germans gave up, for the first time, their negativism towards the Czechoslovak Republic and started to participate actively in public life.

Title Four of the Constitution governed the judicial branch. Basic principles were guaranteed, including the independent judicial system, built essentially upon public proceedings and ordinary courts. The Constitution stipulated an important principle that no one should be tried by a judge other than that assigned by law.

A single Supreme Court of Justice was established for the whole territory of the Czechoslovak Republic, with a special department for Slovakia to reflect the dual legal system. Judicial power in all courts was to be separated from administrative power; however, this principle was not fully applied in practice as courts were in many respects, e.g. in financial, personal and administrative matters, responsible to the Ministry of Justice, and the Austrian Act on Administration of Courts, from 1896, remained in force and applicable. Moreover, presidents of individual courts had wide disciplinary powers over the judges of their respective courts.

The Constitution stipulated that judges were independent and only bound by the law in their decision-making. They were appointed for life by the President of the Republic and could not be transferred, dismissed or retired against their will. However, amendments to the original Austrian laws on the judiciary set exceptions. Judges could be transferred should a new judicial organization be introduced. Their dismissal was permitted on the grounds of disciplinary proceedings, and there was also an age limit for retirement. Judges were not allowed to perform other paid functions.

Judgments were delivered in the name of the Czechoslovak Republic, with proceedings being oral and open to the public. Judgments in criminal matters were always declared in public. The Constitution set some other principles for court proceedings, including the basic principles for trial by jury.

The Constitution of 1920, in Title Five, which was called "Rights, Liberties and Duties of the Citizens", guaranteed a wide range of civil rights and freedoms. The leading principle was the principle of equality before the law, irrespective of one's origin, nation and language affiliation, race or religion. Privileges based on gender, birth or occupation were not recognized. This provision was closely connected with new democratic tendencies of the

Czechoslovak Republic, which had abolished the titles and privileges of nobility as early as 1918.

The Czechoslovak Constitution proclaimed and guaranteed rights and freedoms, such as personal freedom, liberty at one's home, the right of free association and assembly, the right of inviolability of domestic rights, the freedom of the press, the right of private ownership, the right of petition, postal secrecy, liberty of instruction and teaching, the freedom of speech and scientific research and the freedom of conscience and religious creed, religion or faith. In their details and implementation most of these rights and liberties were based on the Austrian laws assumed by the Czechoslovak legal order. However certain new Acts were adopted, particularly those regarding the freedom of association, the freedom of the press and the freedom to assemble. Religious matters, which were based on the equality of all confessions, were influenced by international negotiations with the Holy See, finally concluded in 1927 – which brought in a so-called *modus vivendi* with the Catholic Church.

Debates were held over explicitly guaranteeing social rights in the Constitution; however, in the end, only marriage and family were proclaimed to be under the special protection of the law. The only duty stipulated by the Constitution for citizens was military service; specifying provisions in this respect were laid down by a special constitutional law.

/13/
Legal aspects of national minorities

The most important political and legal issue between the two world wars was the position of national minorities. The Czechoslovak Republic had to accommodate considerably large minorities that found themselves located within the borders of the Czechoslovak state newly established in 1918. According to the 1921 census the population of the Czechoslovak Republic was roughly ten million, of which over three million were Germans (the largest minority in any country in Europe at that time), 110,000 were Polish, 470,000 were Russians (Ruthenians) and 760,000 were Magyars.[229] The Jewish minority (approximately 200,000 people) represented a special case.[230]

The Czechs and Slovaks were regarded as a single political nation, although it was noticeable that historically, culturally and linguistically they represent two independent nations. Reasons for such an approach, designated as the theory of Czechoslovakism, were mainly political, as it appeared beneficial to

---

229 Beneš, Z. – Kural, V. (eds.): *Facing history: the evolution of Czech-German relations in the Czech provinces, 1848–1948*, table prepared by V. Kural, p. 57.
230 In more details see Rabinowicz, A.: The Jewish Minority, Legal Position. In: *The Jews of Czechoslovakia, Historical Studies and Surveys*. New York: Society for History of Czechoslovak Jews, 1968, Vol. I, pp. 155 and following.

combine the Czech and Slovak forces, especially with respect to the national composition of the Czechoslovak state. From a long-term perspective, this theory and approach brought in latent instability due to the Slovak national revival and the rapid development of the Slovak society.[231]

The issues of minorities in Czechoslovakia gave rise to the question of how to reconcile various historical, political, cultural, economic and social traditions of each of those minorities into a functional state structure. It is obvious that the problems of political, social, culture and economic relations between the Czechs and Germans in that territory which constituted Czechoslovakia in 1918 was one which had existed for many centuries. Throughout the period between World War I and World War II a number of methods were employed in an attempt to offer those minorities within the Czechoslovak borders not only formal protection but also cooperation and inclusion. This was attempted even during this period of radical changes and the deteriorating of the international environment. The most significant steps taken by the Czechoslovak Republic to ensure the status of minorities and their protection can be classified in four categories: (a) obligations under international law, (b) constitutional measures, (c) implementation and protection of minority rights, and (d) political, economic and social inclusion guaranteed by Czechoslovak law.

The Peace Treaties concluded in Paris during the Paris Peace Conference contained provisions concerning minorities; their protection was stipulated as an obligation for all successor states of the Austro-Hungarian Empire. According to Article 57 of the Peace Treaty with Austria, the Czechoslovak Republic promised to sign an agreement regarding its obligations with respect to minorities. During the Paris Peace Conference in September 1919, Czechoslovakia signed the Treaty for the Protection of Minorities as a treaty between the Principal Allied and Associated Powers and Czechoslovakia, under which its linguistic, racial and religious minorities were guaranteed Czechoslovak state citizenship and placed under the protection of the League of Nations.[232] All citizens, including national minorities, were equal before the law and fully enjoyed civil rights and freedoms irrespective of their language, race or religion. The treaty ensured the freedom to use any language in private life. However, there were special minority language rights regarding the public sphere. It was necessary to ensure the possibility to use minority languages before courts and administrative bodies. The Czechoslovak language (i.e. the Czech language and the Slovak language) was proclaimed an official language; in addition, there were so-called minority languages. What language was deemed to be a minority language was to be set by Czechoslovak legislation; besides, Czechoslovakia was obliged to respect the language

---

231 Krajčovičová, N.: Slovakia in Czechoslovakia 1918–1938. In: Teich, M. – Kováč, D. – Brown, M. D.: *Slovakia in History*, pp. 139 and following.
232 Beneš, Z. – Kural, V. (eds.): *Facing history: the evolution of Czech-German relations in the Czech provinces, 1848–1948*, document No. 1, pp. 295–296.

rights of other language communities where they represented a "substantial percentage" within individual districts. According to the Minorities Treaty, minorities were entitled to establish and control, at their own expense, religious and social institutions, schools and other educational establishments, and to freely use their language therein. The Czechoslovak Republic was obliged to observe that no law, regulation or official action would conflict or interfere with the stipulations of the Treaty, nor would any law, regulation or official action prevail over them.

The 1920 Constitution fulfilled the obligations placed upon the Czechoslovak Republic by the Minority Protection Treaty of Saint-Germain. In its Title Six the Constitution guaranteed the protection of national (language), religious and racial minorities. It established full equality for all Czechoslovak citizens before the law and in their exercising civil and political rights, equal rights to join civil service and equal access to all trades and professions. National minorities were free to use their own language in private and business intercourse, in the press, in publications and in public assemblies as well as in religious matters. If a national minority represented twenty per cent of the population within a particular court district, their members were entitled to have schools with instruction in their own language subsidized by the state. In those districts the respective minority languages were permitted for use in dealings with the Czechoslovak state authorities and before courts. The respective body of state administration and higher courts usually issued their decisions in both languages – Czechoslovak and that of the minority at issue. Actual figures for particular minority districts were determined by censuses. There were two of them held in the interwar period – in 1921 and 1930. Minority districts were established for German, Hungarian, Ruthenian, and Polish minorities. The Jewish minority was recognized not only as a religious but also as a national minority, but without special language rights. Forcible denationalization was forbidden, and minorities were protected by special provisions of criminal law. Provisions regarding the use of minority languages were enacted not by the Constitution itself but in a special Language Act (Act No. 122/1920 Sb.), promulgated on the same date as the Constitutional Charter.[233]

Members of minority groups were entitled to lodge complaints with the League of Nations against violations of the Treaty. The complaint was made in the form of a petition. The Secretariat of the Council commenced proceedings against the state in question upon receiving a petition. The Council of the League of Nations and its Minority Committee were entitled to consider the violation of the Treaty and to demand remedy. They could submit the case to the Permanent Court of International Justice or order sanctions. The complaint

---

233 For its English translation see Beneš, Z. – Kural, V. (eds.): *Facing history: the evolution of Czech-German relations in the Czech provinces, 1848–1948*, document No. 2, pp. 296–298.

was usually heard by a panel of three experts of the Minority Committee. However, it became apparent that the League of Nations was reluctant to pursue actions against allegedly violating states.[234] Allegations were negotiated at the diplomatic level and resulted in mediation and compromise. Despite a large number of petitions submitted against the Czechoslovak Republic, particularly by German and Hungarian minorities,[235] the majority of them were unsuccessful. A greater part of them claimed breaches of the Minority Treaty in connection with the Czechoslovak Constitution, the language law, the land reform, the proportion of state officials or social security laws. In 1934 an important petition was submitted on behalf of Ruthenia; it dealt with alleged breaches of language rights and rights of minority schools. In the 1930s individual cases, such as discrimination in social security, employment, etc., prevailed. The only example of a successful petition against the Czechoslovak state was decided in 1936; this dealt with so-called Machník's decree, which, according to the petitioners, brought discrimination against German companies in the construction of Czechoslovak fortifications.

Reluctance to take actions against violating states signified the highly political nature of the whole system. The situation worsened in the 1930s, as Poland refused to yield to international pressure, and Nazi Germany started to misuse the minority question for its own aggressive policy. A similar approach was taken by Italy. It should be noted that some petitions against Czechoslovak minority policies in Ruthenia were addressed directly to Mussolini. In 1937 it was apparent that it was primarily the Great Powers who preferred a different approach to solving minority disputes.

Minority rights within Czechoslovak legislation were primarily protected by the Supreme Administrative Court. A special procedure was applied by the Supreme Administrative Court, where findings on so-called minority matters were delivered in both the Czech and German languages. The findings of the Supreme Administrative Court not only dealt with individual cases (ordering effective remedies in many of them), but they served as precedents and played an important role in the interpretation of minority legislation, relating in particular to language rights.

Although the standard of minority protection in Czechoslovakia, especially with respect to language and cultural rights, was higher than in many other European states at that time (with the notable exception of Switzerland),

---

234 See Azcárate, P. de: *League of Nations and National Minorities: An Experiment*, Washington D.C., Carnegie Endowment 1945; for Czechoslovakia pp. 35 and following.
235 For the Hungarian minority in Czechoslovakia see in more details Šutaj, Š. – Gajdoš, M. et. al.: Ethnic minorities and their culture in Slovakian the context of historical development of the twentieth century. In: Kováč, D. (ed.): *Slovak contributions to 19th International Congress of Historical Science*. Bratislava: Veda, 2000, pp. 135–149.

there were some shortcomings and imperfections concerning both the implementation of law in practice and the political environment.[236]

From a legal perspective, the original wording of the Language Act was fully implemented in practice as late as after 1926, when a Government Order was enacted. The delay was partly connected with long lasting debates over the reform of state administration.

There were attempts to reconcile the Germans and the Czechs through their active participation in governing the country. Such moves were resisted by German political parties for some time; however in 1925, the first German ministers sat in the Czechoslovak Government. The so-called activist policy (connected particularly with German Agrarians, Christian Democrats and Social Democrats) replaced the negative approach applied during the initial period. The German parties took part in Czechoslovak coalition governments until 1938.[237]

Traditional national minorities, i.e. Germans, Hungarians and Poles, enjoyed support from neighbouring states; however, some ethnic groups regarded as minorities today, such as the Gypsy population, received no such protection from any source. On the contrary, the Gypsies were differentiated by the law on the grounds of their behaviour (resentment to permanent settlement), and subsequently prosecuted under criminal and administrative law. For example, a special law was enacted in 1927 (Act No. 117/1927 Sb.) to prosecute Gypsy vagabonds and wanderers.

---

236 For more details see Brügel, J. W.: *Czechoslovakia before Munich. The German minority problem and British appeasement policy.* Cambridge: Cambridge University Press, 1973, pp. 136–149. See also Chapter 25.

237 *Ibidem*, especially pp. 68–76. Beneš, Z. – Kural, V. (eds.): *Facing history: the evolution of Czech-German relations in the Czech provinces, 1848–1948*, pp. 295–296.

/14/

<u>Changes in Czechoslovak law 1918–1938</u>

Between 1918 and 1938 the Czechoslovak Republic tried to implement new Czechoslovak laws to resolve the problematic issues of the dual legal system. The Reception Act caused the Austrian Criminal Code of 1852, the Military Criminal Code of 1855 and the Criminal Procedure Code of 1873 to remain in force and apply in the Czech lands; whereas in Slovakia and Subcarpathian Ruthenia, the Hungarian Criminal Code of 1878 and the Code on Petty Offences of 1879 were retained. Other relevant statutes and regulations supplementing and amending the codes applied accordingly.

The new Czechoslovak state intended to unify law for its whole territory by preparing a new Criminal Code. However, only partial reforms were carried out. For example, in 1919 an Act governing suspended sentences and releases on parole was introduced to represent modern and liberal tendencies in criminology and penology; in 1931 an Act regulating criminal proceedings against juveniles was passed, introducing, for the first time in Czech history, special provisions for such types of trial, along with establishing so-called youth courts.

The existence of a new sovereign state brought about changes in substantive criminal law, particularly those relating to the protection of the state, independence, the democratic order and civil rights. In 1919 a special law on the protection of the state was enacted; it stipulated that the Austrian and Hungarian laws, which had become part of the Czechoslovak legal system by reception, expressly applied to the protection of the Czechoslovak state and its constitutional bodies.

In 1923, a young Communist radical shot the Czechoslovak Finance Minister, Alois Rašín, who died in hospital several weeks after the attack. The Czechoslovak Government used the opportunity to prepare and quickly enact a special law on the protection of the Republic, its representatives, independence, territorial unity and the democratic order, which was applicable to the whole territory of the state (Act No. 50/1923 Sb.). A specialized State Court was introduced for criminal procedure. In 1936, the Defence of the State Act (Act No. 131/1936 Sb.) was passed. It provided for measures to be taken at the outbreak of a war or during emergency situations; the Act allowed the Government to declare martial law in areas where the state, or its democratic or republican nature, was threatened. During such situations the Government was entrusted with the power to enact by-laws having the force of Acts of Parliament, and to restrict civil rights and liberties.

The dual legal system was apparent also in civil law: the Austrian Civil Code applied in the Czech lands, whereas various sources of Hungarian civil law applied in Slovakia. Unfortunately, an attempt to prepare a new Czechoslovak Civil Code to unify the law for the whole territory of the state failed. Although the Government agreed (in 1937) on the draft of a code built upon an idea to modernize and partially amend the Austrian General Civil Code, the Munich Agreement and subsequent events prevented the enactment of the Code by the National Assembly.

As a result, only partial reforms were introduced in civil law through new Czechoslovak laws. In addition to the land reform, the most important were changes in family law. In the beginning, different rules on the law of marriage applied in the Czech lands and in Slovakia. For example, in Slovakia the Hungarian law of 1894 stipulating a civil marriage as obligatory applied, whereas the ecclesiastic marriage concluded before the Church was most common in the Czech lands. There was a different legal status regarding the property of spouses. Act No. 320/1919 Sb. provided for uniform rules for the whole state to apply to the conclusion and dissolution of marriage and to marital impediments. The civil form of marriage was optional, as was the conclusion of marriage before the Church. Divorce was, for the first time in Czech history, available also for Catholics.

The dual system applied also to state administration; its operation in the Czech lands and Slovakia was based on different legislation, bodies and traditions. The first step towards its unification was taken in 1919, when a uniform Czechoslovak law on self-government at the communal level was enacted. A year later, the reform of state administration was proposed as part of the debates regarding a new Czechoslovak constitution. The reform attempted to abolish traditional lands; regions (called župy) were to serve as a uniform level of state administration within the whole territory.[238] However, the proposed reform was rejected by the majority of the Czech political parties; as a result, its limited scope applied only to Slovakia. The reform of state administration was not successfully completed until 1927. It strengthened the centralized form of the Czechoslovak state; and, as such, it was opposed not only by national minorities, but also by Slovaks, among whom autonomous tendencies were growing. The territory of Czechoslovakia was divided into four provinces – Czech, Moravian, Slovak and Subcarpathian lands; each land was subdivided into districts. Lands were headed by Governors (called Presidents); the principle of self-government was symbolized by elections to Land Assemblies. State administration was accompanied by limited self-government: at the level of Provincial Diets one third of the assembly members were appointed by the Government and only two thirds were elected.

The establishment of an independent Czechoslovakia on 28th October 1918 represented a new stimulus for legal education and legal professions. A special law, named "Lex Mareš" after its sponsor, renamed the Czech University as Charles University; Charles University was declared to be the successor of the university founded by Charles IV in the 14th century.[239] Many teachers from the Law Faculty participated in the substantial legislative work during the pre-WWII Republic; many were appointed or elected into prominent political or executive positions. For example, professor of civil law Jan Krčmář was a leading representative of the commission preparing a new civil code; he served twice as the Minister of Education. Jiří Hoetzel, teacher of administrative law, was the main expert of the Government for the Czechoslovak Constitution of 1920; Minister of Finance Karel Engliš became a member of the Law Faculty later, on 15th March 1939. Another Minister of Education, Jan Kapras, taught Czech legal history and was famous for his scholarly seminars, forming future prominent representatives of this branch. Prominent positions were hold also by Vilém Funk and Josef Drachovský, specialists in financial law. Cyril Horáček Senior, Josef Gruber and Vilibald Mildschuh represented a younger generation of national economists at the Law Faculty. Cyril Horáček Junior specialised in statistics.

It should be noted that the Law Faculty of Charles University and its teachers took part in forming other law faculties within Czechoslovakia – in Brno and Bratislava, although relations between these later became less than positive: in particular, the relationship between Prague and Brno developed into a strong rivalry reflected in the legal and theoretical discourse between legal positivists and normativists (the latter represented by Professor František

---

238 Harna, J.: The First Czechoslovak Republic 1918–1938. In: Pánek, J. – Tůma, O. et al.: *A History of the Czech Lands*, p. 397.
239 For the documents see Krčmář, J.: *The Prague Universities*. Compiled according to the sources and records. Ministry of Education. Prague: Orbis, 1934, especially pp. 25–31.

Weyr, collaborator with father of the Austrian Constitution Hans Kelsen), as well as in disputes over the reform of legal education.

The impacts of original Austrian law can be traced within legal education during the First Republic (1918–1938) due to significant and strong interlinks between original Austrian law and continuing development of Czechoslovak law. Despite attempts to reform legal education, the earlier system of three blocks of study, each terminating with a state examination, was only slightly improved. A wide range of subjects focusing on typical judicial issues as well as branches of public law, national economy, finance and statistics enabled law graduates to engage in many professions, ranging from those which were typically legal to public administration or private business. However, the necessity to expand the practical orientation of legal education was emphasized, with some lawyers pointing out that new skills, such as typewriting, should also be acquired.

In 1918 the Law Faculty in Prague, in addition to the Faculty of Arts and the Faculty of Medicine, opened its door to women to become regular students.[240] The number of female students was rather low at the beginning – some 5–7% of the student body. The first woman to be awarded the university law degree was Anděla Kozáková-Jírová, in 1923, which symbolized the commencement of the complicated journey of women to establish themselves in traditionally male-occupied legal professions. Ms Kozáková became the first Czechoslovak notary, and a colleague of hers, Matylda Mocová-Wíchová, was registered with the Bar as the first female lawyer. Jarmila Veselá, specializing in criminal law, was the first female teacher awarded the academic title of associate professor. The number of law students increased during the First Republic, and the Law Faculty became one of the largest faculties of Charles University. Whilst 2,154 students of law were enrolled in the academic year of 1913–1914, the number reached 4,495 (10% females) in 1930–1931, and more than 5,000 law students were registered two years later.

Completion of legal education, terminating with the three state exams, was a necessary qualification for the traditional legal professions of judges, state prosecutors, attorneys at law (called advocates) and notaries. Legislation concerning legal professions was adopted by reception from Austria-Hungary; however, national independence brought about certain changes, for example the requirement of Czechoslovak state citizenship.

The extensive curriculum of legal education in the period between WWI and WWII caused the Law Faculties to be the principal source of future experts also in finances and national economy. Many lawyers joined various levels of state administration and self-government. Courses of international law were relevant and suitable for the careers of diplomats serving the newly created Czechoslovak foreign policy.

240 Kuklík, J. et al.: *Faculty of Law of Charles University in Prague*, pp. 24–25.

/15/

The Munich Agreement and the Protectorate of Bohemia & Moravia

Growing tensions between Czechs and Slovaks as well as between the Czechoslovak state and its national minorities worsened at the beginning of the 1930s due to international crises in Central Europe. As part of its expansive policy, Nazi Germany, headed by Hitler, demanded fundamental changes in the position of the German minority.[241]

The internal causes for the crises were closely connected with developments within the Sudeten German society and policy, which led to the establishment of the Sudeten German Party chaired by Konrad Henlein. This party, with support from Nazi Germany, gradually became the leading political representation of the German minority in Czechoslovakia.[242] The party misused not only the declining economic situation during the Great Depression but also some flaws and misconceptions in Czechoslovak minority policies.[243]

241 See for example Beneš, Z. – Kural, V. (eds.): *Facing history: the evolution of Czech-German relations in the Czech provinces, 1848–1948*, pp. 103–109.
242 Brügel, J. W.: *Czechoslovakia before Munich, The German minority problem and British appeasement policy*, pp. 120–122.
243 Brügell, J. W.: *The Germans in pre-war Czechoslovakia*. In: Mamatey, V. S., Luža, R. (eds.): *A History of the Czechoslovak Republic 1918–1948*, pp. 182–187. See also an interesting analyses in

During 1938 the Sudeten German Party presented far reaching proposals for self-determination, initially in the form of autonomy. The most severe conditions for Czechoslovakia to accept were set in the so-called Karlsbad Programme of April 1938. The Czechoslovak Government tried to react and prepared the Statute for National Minorities, the Language Bill and the Administrative Reform Bill.[244] The proposed legislation was very liberal, and, if put into practice, it could lead to the transformation of Czechoslovakia from a national state with minorities into a state of national minorities close to the Swiss model. The Czechoslovak Government was prepared to accept mediation offered by the British Government in the form of a mission by Lord Runciman.[245] Runciman arrived in Czechoslovakia at the beginning of August 1938, and his activity led to a report addressed to British Prime Minister Chamberlain on 21st September advocating a plebiscite and transfer of a part of the Czechoslovak territory to Germany.

The international circumstances which led to the Munich Agreement could be characterized as being due to the violent and aggressive nature of the international policy of Nazi Germany. The aim of this policy was to crush Czechoslovakia and to see the Czech lands as a sphere of vital German interests. This was followed by changes in the French policy towards Central Europe. The French were, from the very beginning of its existence, the main allies of the Czechoslovak state. In 1935 their alliance was declared by the French-Soviet and Soviet-Czechoslovak Treaties on mutual assistance in the event of an unprovoked attack by third parties. After the Anschluss of Austria and after the fall of the last Government of the Popular Front, the French Government, headed by Eduard Daladier, became more and more dependent on British policy. The policy maintained by British Prime Minister Chamberlain is usually depicted as a policy of appeasement.[246] Although there might be lengthy debates about the reasons for such a policy, it should be noted that, as a result of this policy, the Czechoslovak Government was forced at

---

Wiskemann, E.: *Czechs and Germans: a study of the struggles in the historic provinces of Bohemia and Moravia*, especially pp. 254 and following.

244 In more details Kuklík, J. – Němeček, J.: *Od národnostního státu ke státu národností? Národnostní statut a snahy o řešení menšinové otázky v Československu v roce 1938*, (text of the documents published as an appendix, pp. 293–433). See also Principles of the Statute of Nationalities prepared for the British and French Governments. Beneš, Z. – Kural, V. (eds.): *Facing history: the evolution of Czech-German relations in the Czech provinces, 1848–1948*, document No. 4, pp. 299–300.

245 For Runciman mission including his report for the British Government see recently Vyšný, P.: *The Runciman Mission to Czechoslovakia. Prelude to Munich.* Basingstoke Palgrave Macmillan, 2003.

246 From vast literature on the British policy leading towards the Munich see for example recent excellent book by Parker, R. A. C.: *Chamberlain and Appeasement: British Policy and the Coming of the Second World War.* London: Macmillan, 1993. See also Robbins, K.: *Britain and Munich Reconsidered: A Personal Historical Journey.* In: Evans, R. – Cornwall, M. (eds.): *Czechoslovakia in a Nationalist and Fascist Europe 1918–1948.* Oxford, 2007, pp. 231 and following.

first to yield to pressure from the Sudeten German party and then from Hitler in September 1938.

The atmosphere on the international scene deteriorated even more during September 1938 as a result of Hitler's threats to launch war against Czechoslovakia. The need to solve Czechoslovak minority issues, especially the problem of the Sudeten German minority, served as an excuse for his threats. As early as 19th September 1938, France and Great Britain demanded that Czechoslovakia transfer to Germany that part of its territory settled by a majority German population.[247] Negotiations between Hitler and Chamberlain in Berchtesgaden and Godesberg, followed by a mission of Chamberlain's aide, Horace Wilson, formed the prologue to an international conference to officially solve the issue.[248]

On 29th September 1938 the international conference was called in the Bavarian capital of Munich to settle the so-called Czechoslovak crisis and to save European peace. Czechoslovakia was not invited to take part in the conference. The Munich Agreement, concluded on 30th September 1938 by Germany (Adolf Hitler), Italy (Benito Mussolini), Great Britain (Neville Chamberlain) and France (Eduard Daladier), forced Czechoslovakia to cede almost one third of its territory, inhabited by a numerous German minority, to Nazi Germany; the territory has been known as the "Sudetenland" section of Czechoslovakia.[249]

According to the Agreement, there were four zones, which were gradually occupied by Germany; the final boundaries were to be decided by an international committee formed by the representatives of the four parties to the Agreement and one from Czechoslovakia. The Munich Agreement included an immediate guarantee to preserve the remaining Czechoslovak territory by two of the four signatory powers (Great Britain and France), and a promise of guarantee by the other two signatories (Germany and Italy) contingent upon the fulfilment of Polish and Hungarian demands concerning their minorities and their parts of the Czechoslovak territory.

The Czechoslovak Government and President Beneš accepted the Munich Agreement with protest, because the settlement was made "without and against Czechoslovakia". Therefore Czechs have usually depicted the Agreement as the "Munich Dictate". Germany occupied all zones of the territory granted to them by the Munich Agreement despite stipulations in the agreement providing for plebiscites in certain zones vitally important for Czechoslovakia. Even those boundaries were exceeded, and further protests of the Czechoslovak government were disregarded. The final settlement of the Czechoslovak-German frontiers was even more in Germany's favour than

247 See for example Eubank, K.: *Munich*. In: Mamatey, V. S – Luža, R. (eds.): *A History of the Czechoslovak Republic 1918–1948*, pp. 248–249.
248 See especially *Documents on British Foreign Policy*, III. Series, vol. II, London, 1949.
249 For Munich Agreement in English see *Ibidem*, doc. No. 1225, pp. 627–629.

the initial Hitler's proposals in September 1938. The Czechoslovak Government was not given the guarantees promised of its new post-Munich frontiers and found itself defenceless in the "sphere of the most basic interests of the Reich".[250]

The Munich Agreement dealt with the position of other national minorities in Czechoslovakia, and, as a direct consequence of the Agreement, a part of the Czechoslovak territory was ceded to Poland and to Hungary in November 1938.

The acceptance of the Agreement caused great changes not only in Czechoslovak foreign policy and its new orientation towards Germany but also in the pre-Munich liberal democratic political system. The post-Munich Czechoslovak state adopted far reaching changes to its democratic Constitution of 1920. In the Czech lands only two political parties were allowed to exist. The Government and President were given full powers to legislate instead of Parliament for a period of two years. The so-called Second Republic (Czecho-Slovakia, as the country was known from October to March 1939)[251] meant autonomy for Slovakia and Sub-Carpathian Ruthenia.[252] The Munich Agreement caused severe economic losses and social problems.

Czechoslovakia was promised economic assistance by Great Britain and France to sweeten the bitter pill of Munich.[253] Not much remained of the original British promises concerning economic assistance, which had been made by the British Prime Minister in the House of Commons immediately after Czechoslovakia had been forced to accept the Munich Agreement. Following complicated negotiations, a proposed loan was agreed as a part of the trilateral Czechoslovak-British-French agreement of 27th January 1939. However, it did not fulfil its original purpose, namely to provide Czecho-Slovakia, crippled by Munich, with funds for the reconstruction of its stricken economy and for a solution to the complicated problems stemming, in particular, from the inflow of refugees from the surrendered areas of Czechoslovakia into the remainder of its territory. The negotiations on the provision of the loan demonstrated that according to some British and French diplomats the Second Republic was moving irrevocably towards the German sphere of influence, and to strengthen Germany economically was not in the interests of Western democracies. This fact, along with Hitler's military gains in the form of fortifying Czecho-

---

250 Smetana, V.: *In the Shadow of Munich. British Policy towards Czechoslovakia from the Endorsement to the Renunciation of the Munich Agreement (1938–1942)*. Prague: Karolinum Press, 2008, especially pp. 69–73.

251 In more details Prochazka, T.: *The Second Republic: The Disintegration of Post-Munich Czechoslovakia (October 1938–March 1939)*. New York, 1981 and Prochazka, T.: *The Second Republic 1938–1939*. In: Mamatey, V. S., Luža, R. (eds.): *A History of the Czechoslovak Republic 1918–1948*, pp. 255 and following.

252 Bystrický, V.: *Slovakia from the Munich Conference to the declaration of Independence*. In: Teich, M. – Kováč, D. – Brown, M. D.: *Slovakia in History*, esp. pp. 157–160.

253 In more details Kuklík, J.: Do *poslední pence (To the last penny)*. Prague: Nakladatelství Karolinum, 2007, English abstract, pp. 447–450. See also Smetana V.: *In the Shadow of Munich*, pp. 81–82.

slovakia, clearly raised questions about the strategic value of Chamberlain's appeasement policy.

In January 1939 Czechoslovakia was given a £8 million loan, the main purpose of which was to create conditions for solving the plight of refugees from the surrendered areas. Only the remainder of the loan was allowed to be used for reconstruction of the transport infrastructure in Czecho-Slovakia. The loan was supplemented from the British side with a "grant" of £4 million, the purpose of which was to provide, under strictly stipulated conditions, assistance to those refugees from the areas surrendered after the Munich Agreement who decided to leave Czechoslovakia.

What is even more important is that the Munich Dictate represents the most important step leading towards the complete break-up of Czechoslovakia in March 1939, when the German occupation began and German troops marched into the rump Czecho-Slovakia. The Munich Agreement is therefore viewed from the Czechoslovak (and especially Czech) perspective not only as an unjust solution to a disputed minority question, but also as one of the most tragic and fateful moments of Czechoslovak history, which ended a democratic period, caused a fatal blow to liberal democracy and paved the way to the Nazi, and later Communist, dictatorship. It should be emphasized that this dimension is sometimes underestimated outside the Czech Republic. According to Václav Havel the Munich Agreement was Hitler's "final test to democracy and its ability to defend itself."[254] For Czechoslovakia and the present Czech Republic the Munich Agreement represents a theme with a deep moral and emotional background. It is also a question which was reflected on several times from a philosophical point of view and widely resonated in Czech poetry and literature. According to many Czech intellectuals, writers or historians, there is still a latent presence of the syndrome of the Munich Agreement within Czech society.[255] While it may have directly affected only that generation whose lives were directly touched, the experience of being forced to accept the loss of sovereignty and national identity has come to hold a place in the social consciousness of later generations.

It was Hitler who decided that the crippled, post-Munich Czechoslovakia had no right to exist as an independent entity. On 14th March 1939 he asked Slovak representatives to formally proclaim an independent Slovak state under the direct influence of Germany;[256] on 15th March Hácha, President of

---

254 Vaclav Havel's speech given on 17th February 1995 at Charles University, Prague as a part of series "Czechs and Germans on their way to a Good Neighborhood", Official Press Release of the Press Department of the Office of the Czech President.

255 See for example Kosík, K.: *The crisis of modernity: essays and observations from the 1968 era.* Rowman & Littlefield, 1995, pp. 169 and following. The idea was developed mainly by Czech historian Jan Tesař and also by I. Sviták. Sviták, I.: *The unbearable burden of history: the Sovietization of Czechoslovakia,* vol. I. Prague: Academia, 1990, pp. 8–19.

256 Bystrický, V: *Slovakia from the Munich Conference to the declaration of Independence.* In: Teich, M. – Kováč, D. – Brown, M. D.: *Slovakia in History,* pp. 173–174. For the wartime Slovakia

the Second Czecho-Slovak Republic declared in Berlin that he "entrusted with entire confidence the destiny of the Czech people and Czech country to the hands of Führer of the German Reich".[257] On 16th March 1939 the German Protectorate of Bohemia and Moravia was established by Hitler's decree.[258] The Czechoslovak state ceased to exist de facto. The Protectorate became a part of the German Empire, but for international and propaganda reasons it was given an insignificant degree of autonomy. Hitler appointed Konstantin von Neurath as "Reichsprotektor", the highest representative of the German Empire in the Protectorate and Hitler's personal deputy. The Protector was entitled to issue special laws for the Protectorate and supervise the decisions of the Protectorate bodies. In addition, there were German bodies at the local level, called "High Land Councilors" (Oberlandrat), supervising several Czech administrative units. The German police operated in the Protectorate, including the fearful State Police, the Gestapo.

The President of the Second Czecho-Slovak Republic, Emil Hácha, was appointed as State President, i.e. the formal head of the autonomous Protectorate entity. There was the Government of the Protectorate and autonomous state administration at regional and local levels. The Parliament and all other forms of self-government were abolished. All Czech political parties ceased to exist, and the only political organization, the National Alliance, supplanted the non-existent political system.

Three categories of citizens were classified in the Protectorate, with different law applying to each of them. These were:
a) German citizens, with privileged position, their own law and administrative and judicial bodies;
b) Protectorate citizens of Czech nationality, with a disadvantaged position;
c) Jewish and Roma (Gypsy) populations, for which even more punitive and discriminatory provisions applied.

This approach, closely connected with the Nazi philosophy, again brought the system of personality into the legal system. In the Protectorate Germans tried to control all spheres of life of the Czech nation. Initially Germans concentrated their attention on the Jewish population; after freezing and confiscating virtually all Jewish property (so called aryanisation), they started transporting Jews to the Ghetto in Terezín in 1941, and later to extermination camps.[259]

---

see Kamenec, I: The Slovak State 1939–1945. In: Teich, M. – Kováč, D. – Brown, M. D.: Slovakia in History, pp. 175–192.

[257] For its English translation see Beneš, Z. – Kural, V. (eds.): Facing history: the evolution of Czech-German relations in the Czech provinces, 1848–1948, document No. 5, p. 300.

[258] Ibidem, doc. No. 6, pp. 300–302. See also Grant Duff, S.: A German Protectorate. The Czechs under Nazi Rule. London: Macmillan, 1942, pp. 55–57.

[259] For the fate of Jewish population in Protectorate see in more details Rothkirchen, L: The Jews of Bohemia and Moravia: Facing the Holocaust. University of Nebraska Press, 2006, pp. 98–187, and Láníček, J.: Czechs, Slovaks and the Jews, 1938–48: Beyond Idealisation and Condemnation. Palgrave Macmillan, 2013, especially pp. 76 and following.

Jewish natural persons and legal entities were at first limited in the free usage of their property through the imposition of the Nuremberg laws on the territory of the Protectorate in June 1939; it was possible to identify a corporation as Jewish which was only under the "Jewish influence", or if just one member of the Board was of Jewish origin. As early as March 1939, the first confiscations began to be pursued by special Gestapo commandos. The first period, until the end of 1940, was connected with the promotion of Jewish emigration in accord with the Austrian model. Those Jews who were given permission to leave the Protectorate were forced to transfer all their valuable property to the Nazis. This approach is therefore sometimes referred to as "the collection of ransom for life". In 1940, the first series of laws adopted by the Protectorate Government on German order banned Jewish citizens from holding various professions and occupations, and the Jewish population was subjected to many other prohibitions and persecution measures.

When the possibility to move from the Protectorate ceased in 1940, the Jewish population was stripped of their property through a complicated system of German laws, especially with respect to real property, financial means, gold and other precious metals, objects of art, residential premises, insurance policies, etc.[260] Various forms of curtailment, removal from positions of authority, forced sales, aryanisation and confiscation went along with mass deportations. Aryanisation of small and medium sized Jewish property was done in the Protectorate with the help of loans given by the German financial institution *Kreditanstalt* der *Deutschen*.[261]

The Nazi system of directed war economy was introduced in the Protectorate.[262] For example, the Reich German Walter Bertsch was introduced as the Minister of Economy of the Protectorate Government and, on 8th March 1941, he clearly announced Hitler's decision to adapt the economy of the state to the needs of the Reich with respect to the war and to exploit it for this purpose.

German occupation bodies tried to change the concept of labour law and social security in accordance with Nazi ideology. They pressed the Protectorate Government to introduce compulsory labour and a special system of Labour Offices through two Governmental Ordinances, No. 190/1939 and No. 195/1939 Sb. (published in the Collection of Laws). At first, compulsory work was limited to young people between 16 and 25 years of age, and special conditions were applied to compulsory work in agriculture. Even more far reaching changes were enacted between January and August 1941. Compulsory work

---

260 See especially Milotová, J. – Kubů, E. – Jančík, J. – Kuklík, J. – Šouša, J.: The *Jewish Gold and Other Precious Metals, Precious Stones, and Objects Made of Such Materials – Situation in the Czech Lands in the Years 1939 to 1945*. Prague: Sefer, 2011 and Teichová,A.: The Protectorate of Bohemia and Moravia. In: Teich, M. (ed.): *Bohemia in History*, pp. 289–290.

261 See in more details Jančík, D. – Kubů, E. – Šouša, J.: *Arisierungsgewinnler. Die Rolle der deutschen Banken bei der "Arisierung" und Konfiskation jüdischer Vermögen im Protektorat Böhmen und Mähren 1939–1945*. Wiesbaden, 2011.

262 Teichová, A.: *The Protectorate of Bohemia and Moravia*, especially pp. 279–286.

was decreed for all able inhabitants between 18–50 years of age; in 1942, Ordinance No. 154/1942 Sb. provided that compulsory work applied not only within the Protectorate but also on the territory of the German Reich. Some 400,000 Czech workers were sent to Germany to work in coal mines, iron works and other industries important for Nazi Germany. Again special provisions were enacted for the forced labour of the Jewish population. Germans used a system of slave labour within their concentration and extermination camps, which applied also to Jews from Czechoslovakia.

There were other changes to labour law and social security, like the limits on freedom to conclude labour contracts, an increase in working hours, or limits on trade union rights. Moreover, the whole trade union movement was unified in order to be subject to Nazi control and influence. On the other hand, workers especially were corrupted by the introduction of more social advantages for them in comparison with other strata of society. The system of the war economy led to the introduction of strict rationing, and it was part of Nazi policy, especially during the rule of Heydrich, to give more rations to workers (together with planned holidays, etc.)

The first wave of persecutions of the Czech population came soon after the establishment of the Protectorate when Germans sent selected groups of former or presumed political opponents to jail and concentration camps.[263] After mass protests connected with the anniversary of the funeral of the Czech 19th century Romantic poet K.H. Mácha and the 21st anniversary of the Republic on 28th October 1939, there were disturbances and bloodshed. After the shooting to death of Jan Opletal, a university student attending the demonstration, another anti-German protest was called at his funeral; subsequently the Nazis decided to close down the Czech universities. Student leaders were executed and 1,200 students were deported to concentration camps.[264]

The German occupation bodies limited civic rights and freedoms for the Czech population; they introduced tough censorship, and Czech national cultural and sports associations were persecuted. The Nazis extended persecution to the Catholic Church and other religious groups.

In September 1941, the Head of the Protectorate, Konstantin von Neurath, was replaced by Reinhard Heydrich, who was appointed Deputy Reichsprotektor.[265] Immediately after his arrival in Prague, Heydrich proclaimed a state of emergency and martial law, and hundreds of Czech participants in the

---

263 Luža, R.: *The Czech Resistance Movement.* In: Mamatey, V. S. – Luža, R.: *A History of the Czechoslovak Republic,* pp. 150–151. See also still valuable account, although not based on Czech archive sources in Mastný, V.: *The Czechs Under Nazi Rule: The Failure of National Resistance, 1939–1942.* Columbia University Press, 1971, especially pp. 65 and following.
264 See especially *The 17th November: the Resistance of Czechoslovak Students: Almanac about the Resistance of Czechoslovak Students in the Years, 1939–1945.* Prague: Orbis, National Union of Czechoslovak Students, 1945, especially pp. 48–52.
265 For his personality see recently Bryant, Ch. C.: *Prague in Black: Nazi Rule and Czech Nationalism.* Harvard University Press, 2007, pp. 141–142.

resistance movement, members of intelligentsia or those who committed "economic crimes" against the war economy were sentenced to death by special courts operated by the German State Police ("Gestapo" in German) and executed.[266] Within the first 105 days of his brutal rule, 394 people were sentenced to death and 1,134 handed over to the Gestapo and usually sent to concentration camps. The former Prime Minister of the Protectorate Government, General Alois Eliáš, who maintained close links with the Czechoslovak Exile Government and President Beneš in London, was imprisoned and sentenced to death in extraordinary court proceedings by a German People's Court. The Sokol sports association, which took part in the national resistance, was dissolved and most of its members imprisoned. Heydrich prepared plans for the liquidation of most of the Czech people after an assumed victorious war and combined with the Germanization and resettlement of the remainder of the population. The Czech lands were planned to become an integral part of the German Empire.[267]

Moreover, Heydrich proposed changes in the administration of the Protectorate to curtail its autonomy and to impose more effective forms of exploitation of the Czech labour force, industry and agriculture for German war needs. At the beginning of 1942, he appointed a new Protectorate Government headed by Jaroslav Krejčí. The symbol of Czech collaboration with Germans, Minister of Education Emanuel Moravec, and the German politician Walter Bertsch, as the wartime Minister of Labour and Economy, held the strongest positions within the Protectorate Government. During Heydrich's rule in the Protectorate the forms of persecutions tightened. In addition to forced labour, various forms of confiscation and transfer of property from Czech and Jewish hands into German ownership were implemented. Germans applied the Nazi interpretation of criminal law against both genuine and potential opponents of Nazi occupation, including changes in criminal proceedings and misuse of already valid laws.

The peak of German persecution came after the successful assassination of Heydrich by two Czechoslovak soldiers sent to the Protectorate under a combined operation of the Czechoslovak military resistance and the British Special Operations Executive (SOE), known under its code name Operation Anthropoid.[268] Heydrich's deputy, K. H. Frank, immediately announced a second martial law in the Protectorate, and a new series of executions began. The German revenge against Czech civilians had their most brutal expression

---

266 For the imposition of martial law see the publication by the Czechoslovak Government in Exile, *On the Rule of Terror under the Regime of Reinhard Heydrich*. London: Czechoslovak Ministry of Foreign Affairs, Department of information, 1941, especially pp. 18–24.

267 Bryant, Ch. C.: *Prague in Black: Nazi Rule and Czech Nationalism*, pp. 139–144.

268 A standard work in English is MacDonald, C. A.: *The Killing of SS Obergruppenführer Reinhard Heydrich*, New York: The Free Press, 1989. From the Czech authors see most recently in English Burian, M.: *Assassination: Operation Anthropoid 1941–1942*. Prague: Ministry of Defence of the Czech Republic, 2011.

in the fate of the villages Lidice and Ležáky. In June 1942 Lidice, as a result of false allegations that its inhabitants took part in the assassination of Heydrich, were eradicated from the map, all men found in the village were shot on the spot, and women and children sent to concentration camps, where the majority of children were killed. Ležáky followed the same destiny several weeks later. Between 28th May and 3rd July 1942 there were at least 1,288 executions; 653 more followed between July and December 1942.

The following years of the war witnessed more brutal ways of persecution by German judicial and police authorities headed by the German state police, the Gestapo. For example, between 1943 and 1945, on the basis of adjudication by German courts, the guillotine in the Pankrác prison in Prague decapitated 1,075 Czech civilians.

In 1943 an important change to the German occupation bodies in the Protectorate was introduced. In August Wilhelm Frick was appointed as the new Protector, but K. H. Frank became the German State Minister for the Protectorate (Der deutsche Staatsminister für Böhmen und Mähren) and the head of a ministry established for the administration of German interests on the occupied Czech territory. He was entrusted especially with the implementation of the so-called "total war" announced by Joseph Goebbels, German Minister of Propaganda.

/16/

Re-establishment of Czechoslovakia in pre-Munich borders

The German occupation was opposed by active forms of the resistance movement organized both at home and abroad. The Czechoslovak resistance movement set as its aim re-establishing an independent Czechoslovakia as the common and national state of Czechs and Slovaks. Those Czechoslovak politicians who went into exile after the break-up of Czechoslovakia considered the Munich Agreement void and not binding on Czechoslovakia from the very beginning because it was imposed upon Czechoslovakia under the threat of launching an aggressive war and because it represented other serious violations of international law.[269] The establishment of the Protectorate was invalid under international law as well. The leading role in the struggle to re-establish Czechoslovakia was played by the Second Czechoslovak President, Edvard Beneš, who resigned under German pressure after Munich on 5th October 1938. Following the establishment of the Protectorate Beneš

---

[269] First arguments in this respect were published by professor Quincy Wright, *The Munich Settlement and International Law*, The American Journal of International Law, vol. 33, 1939, pp. 12–32. See also Táborský, E: *The Czechoslovak Cause. An Account of the Problems of International Law in Relation to Czechoslovakia*. London: Witherby, 1944, especially pp. 5–25.

prepared a series of official protests, which were sent to the representatives of France, Great Britain, the United States and the Soviet Union. Beneš urged them not to recognize the Protectorate. A special protest was sent to the League of Nations. Beneš proclaimed the beginning of the Czechoslovak exile movement for the re-establishment of independent Czechoslovakia.[270] Beneš developed the political theory of the continuity of the Czechoslovak Republic. According to Beneš the Czechoslovak Republic never ceased to exist as an independent legal entity despite the Munich Agreement and the events of March 1939. He especially emphasized that the Czechoslovak Government accepted the Munich Agreement only under the duress expressed by Nazi Germany, and that Hitler himself breached the Agreement when he occupied the rest of Czechoslovakia in March 1939. The goal of the Czechoslovak exile movement was thus to re-establish Czechoslovakia in its pre-Munich borders.

The position of the Czechoslovak state after March 1939 was very uncertain and difficult from the perspective of international law, particularly due to the existence of independent Slovakia and the Protectorate Bohemia and Moravia. The only symbols of existence of the Czechoslovak state were the Czechoslovak envoys to France, Great Britain, the United States and the Soviet Union, because the western democracies and the USSR refused to recognize the establishment of the Protectorate by Nazi Germany.[271]

After the outbreak of WWII Beneš and his followers were trying to establish a Czechoslovak Government-in-Exile. The main aim of such a Government was not only to represent the existence of an independent Czechoslovakia but also to start a political struggle to repudiate the Munich Agreement. France and Great Britain were unwilling to support such schemes for Central Europe, and they allowed only for the establishment of Czechoslovak military units in France and a political body, the Czechoslovak National Committee.[272]

This transitional period ended when Winston Churchill became the Prime Minister and after the military collapse of France. In July 1940 the Provisional Czechoslovak Government in Exile was recognized by Great Britain. On 21st June 1940 Beneš presented the memorandum entitled "The Constitution of the Czechoslovak Government" to the Foreign Office and asked for British recognition of the Provisional State Apparatus in Great Britain, consisting of Dr. Edvard Beneš as the President, the Exile Government and the State Council.[273]

---

270 *Memoirs of Dr. Eduard Beneš, From Munich to New War and New Victory*, Houghton Mifflin, 1954, pp. 65–68. For the standpoint of Great Powers see The Czechoslovak Yearbook of International law, pp. 226–229.

271 For the Soviet stand see Degras, J. (ed.): *Soviet Documents on Foreign Policy, vol. III, 1933–1941.* New York: Octagon Books, 1978, pp, 322–324.

272 For the establishment of the Czechoslovak military units in France see the Czechoslovak-French Agreement of 2nd October 1939. *Czechoslovak Yearbook of International Law.* London, 1942, pp. 232–235.

273 Brügel, J. W.: *The Recognition of the Czechoslovak Government in London.* In: Kosmas – Journal of Czechoslovak and Central European Studies, vol. II, No. 1, 1984, pp. 2–4.

The Czechoslovak Provisional Government-in-Exile was recognized by Great Britain on that same day. During its recognition of the Czechoslovak Exile Government the British Government made certain reservations concerning the juridical continuity of the Czechoslovak state, its future frontiers and the authority of the Czechoslovak Government over Czechoslovaks and their property in Britain. It was quite clear that the British attitude towards the Munich Agreement was behind such reservations.[274]

The most important legal questions related to the activities of the Czechoslovak Government in Exile were focussed on the struggle for repudiation of the Munich Agreement, the international status of the Czechoslovak Government in Exile, the re-establishment of independent Czechoslovakia, and the transfer or expulsion of the German minority after the war.

The British official view was that the Munich Agreement represented an international treaty dealing with the Czechoslovak minority question which was valid until 15th March 1939, when the Agreement was violated by Hitler. Moreover in the years 1938–1940 the British Government claimed that cession of Czechoslovak territory with a substantial proportion of German population was a solution made only when the system of protection under the auspices of the League of Nations had collapsed. The first change in the British attitude towards Munich emerged in 1940 following recognition of the Czechoslovak Provisional Government-in-Exile.

On the occasion of the second anniversary of the adoption of the Munich Agreement, on 30th September 1940, Winston Churchill stated in the BBC Czechoslovak programme that the date of signature of the Munich Agreement was "a date which the world will always remember for the tragic sacrifice made by the Czechoslovak people in the interest of European peace. The hopes which this agreement stirred in the heart of civilized mankind have been frustrated. Within six months the solemn pledges given by the unscrupulous men who control the destiny of Germany were broken and the agreement destroyed with a ruthlessness which unmasked the true nature of their reckless ambitions to the whole world." In addition, Churchill stressed that on 15th March 1939 Hitler had brought Czechoslovakia "nothing but moral and material devastation" and that the Czechoslovaks "are being persecuted with a deliberate cruelty which has few parallels in modern history". Churchill therefore refused "to recognize any of the brutal conquests of Germany in Central Europe and elsewhere" and stressed that the British Government "have welcomed the Czechoslovak Provisional Government in this country, and that

---

274 Kuklík, J.: *The Recognition of Czechoslovak Government in Exile and its International Status 1939–1941*. In: Prague Papers on History of International Relations, vol. 1. Prague: Faculty of Arts, Charles University1997, pp. 180–185.

we have made the restoration of Czechoslovak liberties one of our principal war aims...."[275]

The British Government nevertheless did not wish to commit themselves to recognize or support the establishment of any particular frontiers in Central Europe, and this covered the Munich line. On 11th November 1940 the Foreign Office sent a letter to Beneš to inform him that "in declining to commit themselves to the restoration of any particular frontiers in Central Europe", the British attitude naturally applied "to all and any frontiers, including of course the frontiers drawn as a result of the Munich Conference...". The British decision regarding the Czechoslovak frontiers was thus postponed until the end of the war. Great Britain, for other reasons (e.g. the status of national minorities, position of Slovakia, position of other states in the region), did not intend to simply return the region to the status quo ante Munich.

Beneš tried to change the British attitude when he asked for *de jure* recognition of the Czechoslovak Government-in-Exile in Spring 1941.[276] In the document handed to the Foreign Office entitled "Political and Juridical Relationship of the Czechoslovak Republic to Great Britain" the Czechoslovak Government in London, acting in the name of the whole Czechoslovak nation, adopted the standpoint that the Czechoslovak Republic continued to exist just as it had existed before 19th September 1938. The Anglo-French plan of that date demanding the cession of the Czechoslovak territory to Germany was forced upon Czechoslovakia by the French threat that, if it had been rejected by Czechoslovakia and if it had led to a German invasion and war, France would have regarded Czechoslovakia as responsible for the war and therefore would have not participated in it. The Munich Agreement, however, was not an application of the Anglo-French plan, whose scope was far exceeded. The Czechoslovak Government was neither consulted regarding the Munich decision nor even admitted to the negotiations concerning it.

The occupation of Czechoslovakia by Germany on 15th March 1939 was designated by Beneš as "an infringement of the Munich Agreement". Under these circumstances the only acceptable conclusion for the Czechoslovak people and the Czechoslovak Government-in-Exile was that, as far as international law was concerned, nothing that happened from September 1938 onwards could be recognized, and that the Czechoslovak Republic legally continued to exist just as it had existed before the September crisis".

According to the British Foreign Office the Czechoslovak position differed from that of the other Allies because there were separate governments both in the Protectorate and in Slovakia. The US Government as well as the

---

275 Beneš, E. – Hauner, M. (eds.): *The Fall and Rise of a Nation: Czechoslovakia 1938–1941.* New York: East European Monographs, 2004, pp. 104–105.
276 *Memoirs of Dr. Eduard Beneš*, pp. 124–125. See also Táborský, E.: *Politics in Exile 1939–1945.* In: Mamatey, V. S. – Luža, R. (eds.): *A History of the Czechoslovak Republic 1918–1948*, pp. 326–327.

Dominions of the British Empire and the Polish Government opposed further recognition.

The Czechoslovak position was strengthened after the German attack upon the USSR. The Soviet Union immediately changed its relationship towards the "Czechoslovak case" and was prepared not only to recognize Beneš and his Exile Government in London but also to conclude an agreement on cooperation in military matters. The Soviet recognition of the Czechoslovak Exile Government in July 1941 implied the re-establishment of Czechoslovakia in its pre-Munich borders. Britain accorded *de jure* recognition to the Czechoslovak Exile Government on 18th July 1941 but was not prepared to withdraw its principal objections concerning the Czechoslovak frontiers.[277]

From January 1942 on Beneš and the Czechoslovak Government-in-Exile drew a linkage between the non-validity of the Munich Agreement and the final settlement of the Czechoslovak frontiers.[278] Simultaneously they suggested the transfer of a substantial part of the German minority from Czechoslovakia together with the cession of a limited part of the Czechoslovak territory.

The actual negotiations on the repudiation of the Munich Agreement began at the end of January 1942. Beneš, upon British request, prepared a formula to resolve the issue of Munich as an acceptable compromise between the Czechoslovak and British positions. The Czechoslovak standpoint was as follows: a) any decisions regarding Czechoslovakia since September 1938 were not valid under international law because they were imposed on Czechoslovakia under the threat of force or through violation of international treaties and Czechoslovak law; and b) the pre-Munich legal status of Czechoslovakia should be restored and confirmed by the victorious allied countries during official negotiations concerning the post-war organization.

For the British Foreign Office the question of "repudiation" of Munich was not only closely connected with the transfer of German minorities from Central and Eastern Europe but also with the proposed Central European Confederation, based mainly on cooperation between Czechoslovakia and Poland. The British Government was prepared to repudiate Munich on condition that a compromise be found on the relationship between Czechoslovakia and the democratic representatives of its German minority.

The situation changed dramatically after the assassination of Heydrich and especially after the unprecedented German retaliations against Czech civilians symbolized by the fate of the Lidice village.[279] The Czechoslovak position in this respect was also strengthened again with the help of Soviet diploma-

277 Táborský, E.: *Politics in Exile 1939–1945*, p.328. *Memoirs of Dr. Eduard Beneš*, pp. 125–157.
278 See *Memoirs of Dr. Eduard Beneš*, pp. 197 and following. See also Smetana, V.: *In the Shadow of Munich*, pp. 262 and following.
279 Recently in Stehlík, E.: *Lidice – The Story of a Czech Village*. Prague: Ráj for Lidice Memorial, 2004, especially pp. 60 and following.

cy. The re-establishment of a "strong and independent" Czechoslovakia in its pre-Munich borders was expressly confirmed by Bogomolov, Soviet Ambassador to the Czechoslovak Government-in-Exile, and by the Soviet Minister of Foreign Affairs Molotov on 9th July 1942. This opened the way for a diplomatic compromise with broader political consequences.

The compromise was based on the separation of controversial points. The British were ready to denounce the Munich Agreement provided their different view concerning the initial validity of the agreement was not challenged. The British Government was not ready to acknowledge confirmation of the post-war Czechoslovak frontiers. The British Secretary of State for Foreign Affairs, Anthony Eden, informed the British War Cabinet about the negotiations with the Czechoslovaks. At this point the question of the validity of the Munich Agreement was directly connected with the proposals for the solution of the minority issues by transfer.[280]

On 5th August 1942 Eden handed a diplomatic note to the Czechoslovak Minister of Foreign Affairs, Jan Masaryk. According to Eden, the statement made by Winston Churchill on 30th September 1940 represented "the attitude of His Majesty's Government in regard to the arrangements reached in Munich", i.e. that "the Munich Agreement had been repudiated by the Germans". The British Government maintained its reservation concerning the final Czechoslovak frontiers but stated that, "in order to avoid any possible misunderstanding", the frontiers should be decided by the end of the war and "they will not be influenced by any changes effected in and since 1938". The British Government stated that the position of the Czechoslovak Government-in-Exile was the same as the position of other Allied Governments-in-Exile in London.

That same day Masaryk sent a reply to Eden in which he regarded the British note "as a practical solution of the questions and difficulties ... maintaining of course our political and juridical position with regard to the Munich Agreement and the events which followed it..." Masaryk's letter ended with the following symbolic words: "Between our two countries the Munich Agreement can now be considered dead."

Another party to the Munich Agreement, France, took a different approach towards the repudiation of Munich during WWII.[281] In September 1942 the French National Committee headed by Charles de Gaulle reached an agreement with the Czechoslovak Government-in-Exile on the issue of the non-validity of Munich.[282] The negotiations were not easy, but in the end

---

280 Kuklík, J. – Němeček, J. – Šebek, J.: *Dlouhé stíny Mnichova (Lasting Shadows of Munich): Mnichovská dohoda očima signatářů a její dopady na Československo.* Prague: Auditorium, 2011, English resume, pp. 367–369.

281 Kuklík, J. – Němeček, J.: *Repudiation of the Munich Agreement during the Second World War as seen from Czechoslovak Perspective.* In: Voráček, E. (ed.): *The disintegration of Czechoslovakia in the end of 1930s: policy in the Central Europe.* Prague: Institute of History, 2009, pp. 117–119.

282 *Memoirs of Dr. Eduard Beneš,* p. 232.

the French National Committee proclaimed the Munich Agreement to be null and void from the very beginning. The French proclamation on Munich led to severe protests by the Polish Government-in-Exile and opened up the question of the Czechoslovak-Polish frontiers.

The importance of the French proclamation on Munich was weakened by the attitude of the Polish Exile Government until the Summer of 1944. When the French Provisional Government was established, the Czechoslovak Government was among the first Allied Governments to recognize it in June 1944. The Czechoslovak exile representatives planned to use this friendly step in the issue of repudiation of Munich. The French attitude towards the Munich Agreement was re-opened, and on 17th August 1944 the French Provisional Government repeated its proclamation on the non-validity of the Munich Agreement from the very beginning.

Italy was the last party to the Munich Agreement to change its attitude towards the Munich Agreement during WWII. However, this was only after the Mussolini fascist leadership had been replaced, when the Italian Government proclaimed the Munich Agreement to be null and void from the very beginning. On 26th September 1944 the Italian Minister for Foreign Affairs, Count Sforza, announced the unanimously reached decision of the Italian Government to the Czechoslovak representative, Vladimír Vaněk. Under the pressure of the Allied conditions of armistice with Italy in September 1943 the Italian Government took the most favourable stand towards the Czechoslovak view of the Munich Agreement and proclaimed the territorial changes between Slovakia and Hungary to be null and void as a direct consequence of Munich. The Italian proclamation on the Munich Agreement had wider consequences. It influenced Czechoslovak relations with the Holy See and was used as a precedent for the Peace Treaty with Hungary after the end of WWII.[283]

The issue of the transfer of the German minority from Czechoslovakia in association with the repudiation of the Munich Agreement has been mentioned. The idea of the transfer of members of the German minority from Czechoslovakia can be traced back to the beginning of the home resistance movement, with the most radical support for the idea coming from the military segment of the resistance.[284] Beneš originally combined the principle of transfer with a possible cession of part of the Czechoslovak border territory; and this linkage was to persist in his proposals to various degrees until the

283 *Ibidem*, pp. 335–341. See also Kuklík, J. – Němeček, J.: *Repudiation of the* Munich *Agreement during the Second World War as seen from Czechoslovak Perspective*, pp. 120–121.
284 The best book on transfer was written by Brandes, D.: *Der Weg zur Vertreibung 1938–1945: Pläne und Entscheidungen zum "Transfer" der Deutschen aus der Tschechoslowakei und aus Polen*, Munich: Oldenbourg, 2005, especially pp. 79 and following, In English see Beneš, Z. – Kural, V. (eds.): *Facing history: the evolution of Czech-German relations in the Czech provinces, 1848–1948*, especially pp. 226 and following. For critical views with objective approach see recently Douglas, R. M.: *Orderly and Humane, The Expulsion of the Germans after the Second World War*. Yale University Press, 2012, pp. 7–38.

very end of the war.[285] The cession of the territory was supposed to not only reduce the numbers of German population in the Czechoslovak Republic but also to justify the transfer of those leaders of the German minority who had committed the worst offences against the Czechoslovak Republic.[286] On 6th January 1942 Beneš drew up a "Memorandum on the Question of the Borders of the Czechoslovak Republic". He ruled out the possibility of simply returning back to the concept of the "minority policy of the First Republic".[287] Essentially, he demanded the restoration of the pre-Munich frontiers while conceding "modifications of the former historic frontiers of the Republic in such a way as to cede to Germany a more substantial piece of the Czechoslovak territory in return for a significantly smaller piece of the German territory, an exchange that would automatically reduce the overall number of Germans in Czechoslovakia by a significant percentage in a peaceful way and without further sacrifices and sufferings for the population". According to Beneš, the number of Germans could be reduced in this way by 600–700,000. He intended to make the exchange of territory subject to the proviso "that approximately another 1,200,000 – 1,400,000 German-speaking inhabitants will be moved out of Czechoslovakia by transferring them to Germany and Austria." In support of this solution he referred to the transfer of inhabitants from Turkey to Greece in 1922. In overall figures, his proposal meant that 2,100,000 Germans would be resettled in Germany and that about 1 million German inhabitants would remain in Czechoslovakia. The transfer would be carried out in an organized way, with financial aid for the departing population, and would be internationally approved. Beneš also envisaged that the property of persons included in the transfer would, to a significant extent, satisfy the main Czechoslovak demands for reparations for "all the looting and robbing of the Republic during the long German occupation". However, Beneš's proposals for the cession of a part of the territory, just like his proposal for Sudeten German "self-government" within the Czechoslovak Republic, met with opposition not only in the home resistance but also in the Government-in-Exile, with which he discussed his transfer plans both officially and unofficially.[288]

The great powers, the so-called "Big Three", had been considering the option of transfer throughout the Second World War and confirmed "in principle" their approval of its future implementation to the Czechoslovak (and also Polish) side, even though they certainly differed in their conception of the goals which the transfer would achieve and in their reasons for finally expressing agreement to the measure as a component of Allied policy towards Germany. The question is far from being simple and must be seen in terms of

285 Táborský, E.: *Politics in Exile 1939–1945*, pp. 334–335.
286 Bryant, Ch. C.: *Prague in Black: Nazi Rule and Czech Nationalism*, pp. 209–212.
287 Kuklík, J. – Němeček, J.: *Repudiation of the* Munich *Agreement during the Second World War as seen from Czechoslovak Perspective*, p. 113.
288 See for example Luža, R: *The transfer of the Sudeten Germans*, pp. 229 and following.

a developing line of the policy, progressively responding to a whole series of international political factors, from the Atlantic Charter to the conferences of representatives of the Big Three in Teheran, Yalta and Potsdam between 1943 and 1945.[289]

At a meeting of the War Cabinet the British Government declared its agreement to the "general principles of the transfer of German minorities" from the countries of Central and South-Eastern Europe after the war on the basis of a memorandum of Anthony Eden entitled "Anglo-Czechoslovak Relations" of 2nd July 1942.[290] This was at a time when, as suggested earlier, the Czechoslovak and British sides were seeking a compromise formula for the repudiation of the Munich Agreement, and the memorandum explicitly confirmed the linkage.[291] On 7th July 1942 Eden informed Beneš that the British War Cabinet approved in principle the post-war transfer of the German national minorities from the states of Central and South-East Europe. During May and June 1943, the USA and the USSR confirmed that the policy of transferring the German minority should apply in the Czechoslovak and Polish cases after the war. The USSR in particular supported the Czechoslovak claims, including the transfer, as part of their expansion to Central Europe; the Soviet support of the pre-Munich Czechoslovak frontiers and the transfer of the German minority was confirmed to Beneš by the Soviet representatives during Beneš's visit to Moscow in December 1943.

In Moscow Beneš also concluded the Treaty of Alliance, Friendship and Mutual Aid between the USSR and Czechoslovakia on 12th December 1943.[292] Its Article 4 stipulated that "both contracting parties shall act in accordance with the principles of mutual respect of their independence and sovereignty and of non-interference with the internal affairs of the other party". Beneš believed that this would protect Czechoslovakia from any future German expansion as well as from interference of the Soviets into Czechoslovak internal politics. However, the USSR disregarded the Treaty on several occasions, and this proved to be a decisive turnabout in the orientation of the Czechoslovak state towards the East.

Towards the end of 1943 the Czechoslovak Government-in-Exile started preparations for a post-war Peace Conference. The large proportion of Czechoslovak claims were based mainly on the Czechoslovak view regarding the non-validity of the Munich Agreement as connected with the transfer of the German minority. On 25th July 1944 the European Advisory Commission asked the Czechoslovak Government to present the Czechoslovak conditions

289 In more details Brandes, D.: *Der Weg zur Vertreibung 1938–1945*, pp. 271 and following,
290 The document is now available online, CAB 66/26/10, nationalarchives.gov.uk.
291 Kuklík, J. – Němeček, J.: *Repudiation of the* Munich *Agreement during the Second World War as seen from Czechoslovak Perspective*, p. 115.
292 For the historical context see Táborský, E.: *President Edvard Benes. Between East and West 1938–1948*. Stanford: Hoover Institution Press, 1981. For the content Táborský, E.: *The Czechoslovak Cause*, pp. 152–154.

for armistice with Germany. The Czechoslovak Government agreed with the proposal on 24th August 1944.[293] The Czechoslovak Government especially demanded that Germany (and also Hungary) should "without prejudice to her responsibility, as defined in the armistice terms recognize ….: a) nullity of the Munich Agreement of 29th September 1938, and the so-called Vienna Arbitrary Award of 2nd November 1938, as well as all enactments arising from these Agreements and enactments, or others connected with them…; b) nullity of enactments regarding the establishment of the Protectorate of Bohemia and Moravia…; c) sovereignty of the Czechoslovak Republic over territory within the frontiers before 29th September 1938, ensuing from the preceding points, and all other consequences ensuing from them". The minority question was proposed to be settled by transfer not only of the German but also the Hungarian minority.

The Czechoslovak arguments were not officially confirmed, and the final solution was left until post-war negotiations. On 11th January 1945 the European Advisory Commission presented to the Czechoslovak Government its proposal for the unconditional surrender of Germany, which spoke about the German frontiers as they had existed before 31st December 1937.

293 Luža, R.: *The transfer of the Sudeten Germans*, p. 246.

/17/
Presidential decrees (so-called Beneš decrees)

The second interesting legal problem connected with the period of WWII and the Czechoslovak provisional state apparatus abroad was the issue of emergency legislation. In the Czechoslovak case this was implemented in the form of presidential decrees. Presidential decrees were an expression of the extraordinary constitutional situation of the Czechoslovak state and legal order after the Munich Agreement and after 15th March 1939, when the Czechoslovak Republic ceased to exist *de facto*, with the Protectorate of Bohemia and Moravia and the Slovak Republic being established. The Decrees of the President of the Republic, initially published in exile in London and later in the liberated Czechoslovak territory, could in no case be identified solely with the person of Dr. Edvard Beneš, President of the Republic; they were the product neither of Beneš's arbitrary will, nor of an authoritarian regime. Under the terms of Constitutional Decree No. 2/1940 of the Official Czechoslovak Journal "on the interim exercise of legislative power", both constitutional decrees and ordinary decrees were published on the basis of government drafts with signatures attached by the Prime Minister and ministers entrusted with their execution.[294] The Government-in-Exile was initially only provisionally recognized, but in 1941–1943 recognition *de jure* was awarded not only by Great Britain, the USSR, and the USA but also by other states of the anti-Hitler coalition.

Beneš's status as President and head of the whole system of the Provisional State Apparatus was based on the argument that his resignation of 5th October 1938 had been made under the pressure of the German side and under the threat of force against the post-Munich Czechoslovakia. As a result, the resignation was invalid in the same way as the acceptance of the Munich agreement was invalid for Czechoslovakia. Beneš linked his theory regarding the continuity of his presidential function with the theory of the continuity of the Czechoslovak state. This claim was confirmed by both the Government-in-Exile (in the form of the Government Resolution of December 1942), and by the Provisional National Assembly after the war. A legal fiction was created in this way, presuming the uninterrupted existence of the office of the President of the Czechoslovak Republic from the election in 1935 to the re-elections in 1945 and 1946.

From 1942, the State Council, as the third body of the interim State Constitution-in-Exile was involved in the passage of decrees. Known as an exile "quasi-parliament", it was an advisory body to the President and Government; from 1941 it was composed of the representatives of all major political groupings in exile. Draft decrees were submitted to the State Council by the Government for an advisory report, thus broadening political responsibility for the Presidential Decrees.

The drafting of decrees was put on a more expert footing in 1942 with the formation of the so called Legal Board. The Legal Board was conceived as an expert legal body before which complaints of Czechoslovak citizens against decisions of the Ministries and administrative bodies of the interim state authority could be brought. It was the responsibility of the Legal Board to scrutinise decrees from an expert legal perspective and report to the Government and President accordingly.

During the period of the Provisional State Apparatus of the Czechoslovak Republic in London in exile the Decrees of the President of the Republic dealt mainly with issues related to the reestablishment of a pre-Munich Czechoslovak state. In this respect they symbolize the ongoing and uninterrupted existence of the Czechoslovak Republic. In 1944–1945 the Decrees of the President of the Republic served in order to prepare not only the constitutional and legal restoration of Czechoslovakia but also its economic and social reconstruction. The restoration of Czechoslovakia prepared in London was based mainly on the ideological and political views of Edvard Beneš; however,

294 For its English translation see Beneš, Z. – Kural, V. (eds.): *Facing history: the evolution of Czech–German relations in the Czech provinces, 1848–1948,* document No. 8, p. 301.

after the Slovak National Uprising in the second half of 1944 one was confronted with a different situation on the liberated territories of pre-Munich Czechoslovakia.

The system of the Provisional Czechoslovak State Apparatus in exile was composed of President Edvard Beneš, the Government, headed by Msgr. Jan Šrámek, and the State Council, as the advisory quasi-parliamentary body. In 1942 the Czechoslovak Government-in-Exile started to establish military units in the Soviet Union to supplement the already existing Czechoslovak army in Great Britain and the Middle East. The improvement of the status of the Czechoslovak Government-in-Exile was in striking contrast to the weakening position of the Protectorate Government.[295]

The Czechoslovak Government-in-Exile and President Beneš took advantage of the improvement of the legal status of the Czechoslovak exile bodies to adopt a more active role in inter-allied negotiations over the post-war development as well as over the punishment of war criminals. On 1st January 1942 twenty-six states signed a Joint Inter-Allied Declaration on the Common Fight against Nazi Germany and its Allies in Washington D.C., with no option of concluding a separate peace.[296] Twelve days later (13th January), the Czechoslovak and Polish Governments-in-Exile in London agreed together with the representatives of Great Britain, the USSR and the USA in St. James's Palace to adopt a declaration on the principles concerning the punishment of war crimes committed by Nazi Germany against occupied nations. The declaration was presented as a joint proposal of the Czechoslovak and Polish Governments-in-Exile.[297]

The international policy of the Czechoslovak Government-in-Exile focused, until 1942, on the idea of Czechoslovak-Polish post-war collaboration. On 11th November 1940 the Czechoslovak and Polish exile representatives issued a joint declaration on a Czechoslovak-Polish confederation.[298] The Governments declared their intention "to create a political and economic association, which could form the basis for a new order in Central Europe and safeguard its stability". Other states of the region were welcome to join the confederation. In the beginning of 1941 actual negotiations began, but the idea of a confederation or federation in Central Europe was endangered from the very beginning by numerous historical, economic and social differences between

---

295 For more details see documents and introductory study *Czechoslovak government in Exile 1942* by J. Kuklik and J. Němeček in: Němeček, J. et al. (eds.): *Zápisy ze schůzí československé vlády v Londýně II.* (1942). Prague: Institute of T. G. Masaryk, 2012.
296 For the text of declaration see Public Papers of the Presidents of the United States: F. D. Roosevelt, 1942, Vol. 11, 1950, pp. 3–5.
297 See *Punishment for War Crimes*, United Nations Information Office, London 1943 Part I, pp. 4 and following.
298 The Inter-Allied Review: Documentary supplement covering the period from the outbreak of war to January 1, 1941, United Nations Information Office, 1944, pp. 7–8.

the two countries. Moreover, varying attitudes towards cooperation with the Soviet Union played an important role.

However, on 18th January 1942 the principles of confederation were published in the form of a protocol.[299] The protocol stipulated that the proposed confederation was open to other states in the region. It dealt with political, economic, financial, military, social and cultural affairs as well as with the structure and competences of the union. For Czechoslovak diplomacy it was important to ensure cooperation between the Czechoslovak-Polish confederation and Yugoslavia and Greece, because potential Balkan and Central European federations played an important role in British foreign policy. However, the Czechoslovak Government urged the Polish Government to maintain friendly relations with the Soviet Union as a *conditio sine qua non* of Czechoslovak-Polish cooperation in the project. On 15th July 1942 the Soviet Ambassador, A. J. Bogomolov, openly told the Czechoslovak Minister of Foreign Affairs, Jan Masaryk, that the Soviet Government was officially against such a confederation. Hence the Czechoslovak Government told the Polish Government to stop the negotiations for the time being.[300]

The Czechoslovak Government-in-Exile in London was forced to cooperate with the Czechoslovak Communists, who had their exile centre in Moscow.[301] In 1943 Czechoslovakia not only concluded an Alliance Agreement with the Soviet Union, but London exile representatives also came to terms with Moscow Czechoslovak communists on the programme for the post war reconstruction of the Czechoslovak state. It was a programme of profound economic, social and political changes, described as a "national and democratic revolution". Far reaching nationalization of industry, land reform, and confiscation of property of war criminals, home traitors, and also of Germans and Hungarians were proposed.

In May 1945, by the end of WWII, Czechoslovakia was re-established in its pre-Munich borders but with the notable exception of Sub-Carpathian Ruthenia (after 1945 called Trans-Carpathian Ukraine). Czechoslovakia was re-established as a national state of Czechs and Slovaks, i.e. Slavonic nations. The majority of members of the German minority was either expelled or transferred to Germany and the rest deprived of virtually all civic rights and freedoms. This could be regarded as a delayed Czechoslovak response to the unjust solution of Munich. Moreover the shadow of Munich heavily influenced Czechoslovak-British relations; together with distrust of the Western Allies, which was wide and common especially within Czech society, it represented

---

299 See Wandycz, P.: *Czechoslovak Polish Confederation and the Great Powers, 1940–1943*. Bloomington, 1956, pp. 67–70.
300 Táborský, E.: *Politics in exile 1939–1945*, pp. 338–339.
301 In more details documents and Introductory study *Czechoslovak government in Exile 1943* by J. Kuklík and J. Němeček in: Němeček, J. et. al. (eds.): *Zápisy ze schůzí československé vlády v Londýně III.1* (1943). Prague: Institute of T. G. Masaryk, 2013.

an important reason for the Czechoslovak orientation towards the Soviet Union (which was not a party to the Munich Agreement) during and after WWII.

Czechoslovakia was not re-established in its pre-Munich arrangement because of the situation in Slovakia. The Communist and non-Communist underground groups in Slovakia concluded a so called Christmas Agreement in 1943 to establish the Slovak National Council as a centre of unified resistance endeavours.[302] During the Slovak National Uprising against the Germans in Autumn 1944 the Slovak National Council proclaimed itself to be the supreme body of the executive and legislative powers in Slovakia and assumed the right to issue its regulations for the Slovak territory, important for the success of the anti-Nazi fight.[303] It proclaimed different principles regarding the continuity of the laws from the Second Republic and the war time Slovak Republic, which remained in force on the Slovak territory on a larger scale than envisaged by the Czechoslovak Government-in-Exile in London.

The Slovak National Council continued to issue its regulations on the liberated territory. The relationship between the Slovak National Council and the Czechoslovak Government-in-Exile was one of the points subject to debates over the post-war Government. It was clearly visible that the theory of one political Czechoslovak nation was unattainable, and the search for the solution of a stable constitutional relationship between Czechs and Slovaks began.[304]

---

302 Document published in English by Lettrich. J.: *History of Modern Slovakia*. New York, 1955, pp. 303–304. Doc. No. 26. In more details Prečan, V.: *The Slovak National Uprising: the most dramatic moment in the nation's history* : In: Teich, M. – Kováč, D. – Brown, M. D.: *Slovakia in History*, pp. 206–228.
303 Lettrich. J.: *History of Modern Slovakia*, p. 306, Doc. No. 28.
304 See also Skalnik Leff, C.: *National Conflict in Czechoslovakia. The Making and Remaking of a State, 1918–1987*. Princeton University Press, 1988, pp. 213 and following.

/18/
The Third Czechoslovak Republic 1945–1948

In May 1945 the overwhelming part of Czechoslovakia was liberated by the Red Army; the U.S. troops only released Western Bohemia from German occupation. The period of the Third Republic lasted for only two years, until February 1948. It was a period of a limited democratic system, as well as a period of clashes between democratic parties and communists.

The first major change in post-war Czechoslovakia was connected with national minorities. The transfer of German minorities to Germany was finally agreed in the Potsdam Conference in August 1945.[305] Unfortunately, immediately after the end of WWII many Czechs were not willing to wait until organized transfers were officially agreed and took part in "wild expulsions", during which 600,000 Germans were expelled from the Czech lands.[306] In 1946 the officially organized transfers to the occupation zones in Germany

---

[305] See Final protocol of August 2, 1945. *Documents on British Policy Overseas*. Series I, vol. I. The Conference of Potsdam July–August 1945, (ed. R. Butler), London, 1984, p. 1275 and FRUS, Diplomatic Papers, 1945. The Conference of Berlin (Potsdam Conference), Washington, 1960. Vol. II, pp. 1511–1551.

[306] Douglas, R. M.: *Orderly and Humane. The Expulsion of the Germans after the Second World War*, pp. 93 and following.

began, and by the end of 1947 2,700,000 Germans left Czechoslovakia. Paris Peace Conference in 1946 did not approve a similar solution proposed by the Czechoslovak Government for the Hungarian minority[307] and the Treaty on mutual exchange of population with Hungary from 27th February 1946, applied in practice. However only 76,000 people were actually affected.[308]

The second major change applied to the political system. A new Czechoslovak Government, in 1945, was composed of Communists, Social Democrats, National Socialists and the catholic People's Party. In Slovakia, the Slovak National Council was established and another two political parties organized – the Slovak Communists and the Democratic Party. The new system was called a "people's democracy" to make it distinct from the interwar period. It was based on a so-called National Front, a political organization of existing governmental political parties. Other parties were not even allowed to exist. This move particularly affected the strongest Czech political party of the interwar period, the Agrarian Party; it helped the Communists to strengthen their position among the peasants. The National Front was placed above the Parliament in the political hierarchy and beyond any democratic control.

The State and Legal Councils established in London during WWII were dissolved as soon as the Government and President departed London; as a result, they took no part in the subsequent formulation of decrees on the liberated territory. This did not change the basic constitutional procedure, since the later decrees were first drawn up by the relevant ministries and then debated and approved by the first post-war Government of the National Front, before being submitted to the President of the Republic for signature. These decrees were primarily instruments for carrying into effect the Government Programme announced on 5th April 1945 in Košice (the so-called Košice Governmental Programme).[309] This Programme promulgated profound changes in the Czechoslovak political, social and economic system. The decrees thus mainly symbolized "revolutionary changes".[310]

The draft of the Košice Programme had been prepared by the Communist Party, and the Communists reserved a key position for themselves in the new government. Zdeněk Fierlinger, left wing oriented social democrat (some

307 *Foreign Relations of the United States* (FRUS) 1946, vol IV: Paris Peace Conference, Washington, 1970, pp. 727 and following.
308 Šutaj, J.: *Slovakia and Hungarian minority between 1945 and 1948*. In: Key issues of Slovak and Hungarian History, a view of Slovak Historians. Prešov: Universum-EU, pp. 227 and following.
309 The program was published in English as a separate volume of the Czechoslovak Newsletter and distributed to the foreign mission to the Czechoslovak Government in the second half of April 1945.
310 In more details see, Gsovski, V. – Grzybowski, K. (eds.): *Government Law and Courts in the Soviet Union and Eastern Europe*. London: Atlantic Books, 1959, vol. I, Chapter 8, Czechoslovakia, pp. 228–229.

historians called him even "crypto communist")[311] and ardent collaborator with Soviets, became the Prime Minister.

According to Ján Lettrich, Slovak Democrat, who took part in the negotiations on the Programme of the post-war Government, the discussions "took place in the shadow of Kremlin, while the advancing Soviet Armies were about to take control of the Western parts of Czechoslovakia as well as the Eastern". He disclosed the aims of the democrats in dealing with the Communists. They opted for a lesser evil, to return home and continue the relentless fight and the disadvantage was that they were not united.[312] The Programme was a compromise and reflected the belief of democratic leaders that their acquiesce regarding some of Communist demands would induce the latter to refrain from immediate revolutionary action and, in the meantime, it would permit the democratic parties to secure a working parliamentary majority. That is why not only Czechoslovak democrats, but also the British ambassador to Czechoslovakia Philipp Nichols paid such a big attention to the parliamentary elections. Such hopes proved to be too optimistic as early as in the following year of 1946.

The Programme of the new Czechoslovak government brought important changes to Czechoslovak foreign policy. It secured a strong orientation of the Czechoslovak military and of foreign policy towards the Soviet Union, which was later continually misused by Communist propaganda. As a counter-balance, friendly relations with the West (the USA, Britain and France) were mentioned. The USSR asked its price for assistance during WWII; as a result, the territory of Sub-Carpathian Ruthenia (Ukraine) was ceded to the Soviet Union. [313]What was extremely unfortunate for the democratic parties in post-war Czechoslovakia and for the position of Western democracies in Central Europe was the fact that the US Army had not been allowed to liberate more than the Western part of Bohemia. President Beneš was only successful in his requirement that the Red Army, holding approximately nine/tenths of the Czechoslovak territory, should withdraw from the country by December 1945, along with the American troops.

The main areas affected by the Government Programme implemented by the Presidential Decrees covered the changes in the Constitution (in particular the Czech-Slovak relationship), the question of German[314] and

---

311 See for example Lukeš, I.: *On the Edge of the Cold War: American Diplomats and Spies in Postwar Prague.* Oxford University Press, 2012, pp. 53–54 or from foreign authors; Massimo. S.: *The Rise of Modern Communism: A Brief History of the Communist Movement in the Twentieth Century.* London: Forgotten Books, 2013, pp. 68–69.
312 Lettrich, J.: *History of Modern Slovakia*, p. 233.
313 Gsovski, V. – Grzybowski, K. (eds.): *Government Law and Courts in the Soviet Union and Eastern Europe.* Vol. I, Chapter 8, Czechoslovakia, pp. 233–234.
314 In more details see Beneš, Z. – Kural, V. (eds.): *Facing history: the evolution of Czech-German relations in the Czech provinces, 1848-1948*, pp. 237–238.

Hungarian[315] minorities (primarily the confiscation of their property and deprivation of Czechoslovak state citizenship), the introduction of a new type of public administration in the form of so called "national committees", the nationalization of major types of industry or banks, and the punishment of war criminals and traitors (retribution). In all of these areas, the Presidential Decrees brought in fundamental changes to the pre-Munich Czechoslovak legal order and can be regarded as the beginning of political, legal and social changes which resulted in the Communist takeover in February 1948.

The Government Programme confirmed the position of the Slovak National Council as the Slovak National Legislative and Executive Authority. The Programme proclaimed the principle of two equal Slavic nations, Czechs and Slovaks. Nevertheless the implementation of this principle was found in an asymmetrical division of powers. The division of competences and the relationship between the Slovak bodies and the Czechoslovak Government was dealt with in a special decree by the Slovak National Council, No. 32/1945, which stipulated the possibility for the President of the Republic to issue decrees applicable to the whole Czechoslovak territory only with explicit consent of the Slovak National Council. The issue was partly resolved later by the First and Second Prague Agreements of June 1945 and 1946.[316]

At that time the Slovak bodies, not only the Slovak National Council but also national committees on regional and local levels, already had in reality vast competence in everyday administration, the recovery and reconstruction of the Slovak territory, the implementation of land reform, national administration, education, culture and punishment of war criminals; the most important matters became the responsibility of the Czechoslovak Government only gradually.

People's "national committees" were in many respects a replica of the Soviets of the Russian Bolshevik revolution and represented the administrative foundation of the local, regional and provincial government. They replaced the existing system of state administration as well as self-government. First, national committees were not elected but were formed under the sponsorship of the advancing Soviet Army; in most cases they became influenced by local communist receivers (administrators) and trade union members. The composition of national committees on the liberated territory was agreed politically as an equal division of seats among all parties of the National Front.

The transfer (or rather "expulsion") of the Sudeten German population was used for radical land reform as well as for far-reaching confiscations of "enemy" property. The confiscated land vacated by the expellees was used for

---

315 For Hungarian minority in Czechoslovakia after 1945 see Šutaj, J.: *Slovakia and Hungarian minority between 1945 and 1948*, pp. 227–243.
316 See for example Rychlík, J.: *From Autonomy to Federation*. In: Musil, J. (ed.): *The End of Czechoslovakia*, Central European University Press. 2nd edition, 1997, pp. 191–193.

resettlement of the border regions.[317] During the first stage of the land reform medium-sized agricultural farms of Czech and Slovak owners, who were justifiably, or sometimes mistakenly, accused of collaboration with Germans, were confiscated. The whole process was under the auspices of the Ministry of Agriculture, controlled by the Communists and the local and regional national committees.

The Košice Programme provided for the nationalization of mines, key industrial enterprises and banks; but for tactical reasons it spoke of the "subjection of the entire monetary and credit system, key industrial enterprises, banks, insurance companies, national sources and sources of energies to the general direction of the state."

The foundation of a new social and economic system was initially created through the confiscation of the land and other property of Germans, Hungarians, home traitors and war criminals. Next followed the nationalization of mines, heavy industry, food industry, banks and insurance companies.[318]

During WWII the national resistance movement both at home and abroad demanded far reaching political, social and economic reforms be carried out in the re-established Czechoslovakia. The nationalization connected with economic planning was seen as an obvious result of victory in the War. In addition, the nationalization had a very strong "national", anti-German content, as most of Czech industry was in German hands during WWII.

There was an important intention within the Czechoslovak resistance movement period to punish most of the Czech capitalists for their collaboration with Germans. The nationalization was advocated not only by the political left but also by most other politicians and economists who took part in the resistance movement at home or abroad.

The nationalization was planned as an integral part of other important social and economic reforms. It was connected with the imposition of the so-called national administration (the freezing of property) and confiscation of "enemy" property, i.e. the property of persons of German and Hungarian ethnicity. German and Hungarian minorities in Czechoslovakia were accused of collaboration with Nazi Germany and, as enemy citizens, expelled from the country. Their property, along with the property of the German Reich, Nazi organizations and Czech collaborators, was confiscated without compensation and used to cover Czechoslovak war losses.

Far reaching nationalization of coal mines, metal industry and banks was initially advocated mainly by the Social Democrats and trade unions. When Communists saw how popular such a policy was among the people, they joined

---

317 Teichová, A.: *The Czechoslovak Economy 1918–1980.* London: Routledge, 1988, pp. 96–97.
318 Sharp, S. L.: *Nationalization of Key Industries in Eastern Europe.* Foundation of Foreign Affairs, Pamphlet Number 1. See especially Appendix Containing the Nationalization Decrees, pp. 13–21. See also Michal, J. M.: *Postwar economic development.* In: Mamatey V. S. – Luža, R. (eds.): *A History of the Czechoslovak Republic 1918–1948,* pp. 438–442.

forces with the Social Democrats and proposed the nationalization of all coal mines, electric power stations and all industrial plants with more than 500 employees even before the Provisional National Assembly was established. The Czech National Socialist Party and President Beneš were also in favour of nationalization, but they preferred a step by step strategy, so that more attention could be paid to the interests of foreign investors, particularly those from the Allied countries. Non-communist democratic parties in the National Front were unable to moderate the radical proposals of the Communists and Social Democrats for the nationalization of not only mines and industries but also the food industry, banks, and private insurance companies. There was virtually no opposition to nationalization from the Christian Democrats; some critical voices were heard only from the Slovak Democratic Party.

The nationalization was connected with economic planning and reconstruction.[319] Nationalized plants were merged, and larger units, called "state-owned national enterprises", were established.[320] These were subjected to the Two Year Plan of reconstruction in terms of the allocation of their capital and output, but enjoyed some economic liberty.[321] Between 1946 and 1948 some sixty-five to seventy per cent of all industry was in the hands of the state. Some areas, such as coal mines, banks, insurance companies, production of electricity, defence industry or film industry were nationalized completely, i.e. the Czechoslovak state was given a monopoly. There were not only economic reasons assisting nationalization; for example, the production and distribution of films was seen as an important means of propaganda. Previous owners of nationalised plants and factories were promised compensation; however, the Czechoslovak Government was ready to negotiate only with former foreign investors.

The nationalization was connected with the establishment of Factory Councils in individual enterprises, with wide competences in social, labour and economic issues. Factory Councils enabled Trade Unions and their representatives to partly control the national enterprises. The nationalization thus fulfilled the "old" programme of socialist parties.

The Czechoslovak nationalization between 1946 and 1948 can be compared with other European states in order to identify whether the Czechoslovak nationalization was closer to that in Britain or France, or whether it was closer in nature to the development in states composing the emerging Soviet bloc. There were certain common features between Czechoslovak and French nationalizations in particular both from legal and economic perspectives;

---

319 Jech, K. – Průcha, V.: *Outline of Economic Development of Czechoslovakia 1945–1948*. In: Jech, K. (ed.): *The Czechoslovak Economy 1945–1948*. Prague: State Pedagogical Publishing House, 1963, pp. 7–29.
320 For the English text of nationalization decrees see Sharp, S. L.: *Nationalization of Key Industries in Eastern Europe*, appendix, pp. 53 and following.
321 Michal, J. M.: *Postwar economic development*, pp. 442–444.

however, nationalisation in Czechoslovakia produced more far-reaching effects and had a stronger confiscatory character. Another factor distinguishing the processes in Czechoslovakia and France was the manner in which Czechoslovak Communists utilized nationalization in order to strengthen their political and economic position and create a foundation for their political takeover. This proved to be a decisive aspect in February 1948, when Czechoslovakia finally took its journey to communism.

The Government Programme of 1945 provided for retribution or, more clearly expressed, the punishment of Nazi war criminals and collaborators with the representatives of Nazi occupation.[322] There were three main Presidential Decrees on retribution – the Decree on Extraordinary People's Courts and Punishment of War Criminals, Traitors and Collaborators, the Decree on the Establishment of the National Court, and the Decree on Punishment of Petty Collaboration with Nazis.[323]

The crimes committed by Nazis were in most cases connected with the prosecution of officials of Nazi political organizations (like NSDAP and the Sudeten German Party) and members of the police or military elements of the occupational regime, like the Gestapo, SS or SA. Czechoslovak courts reviewed not only the formal position of the accused but also the intensity of their harmful activities. Most of the crimes were punishable in accord with the Czechoslovak interwar legislation, but the Presidential Decrees set more severe punishments, including the death penalty and forced labour in special camps; they established special courts with a fast-track procedure and limits on the rights of the accused. On the other hand, this was seen as an extraordinary measure for a limited period of time and for cases where facts could be proven without protracted proceedings. If a defendant was acquitted, he or she might be prosecuted again for the same offence before an ordinary court. People's Courts were extraordinary courts presided over by a professional judge and consisted of lay judges chosen usually from credible members of the domestic resistance movement.

The most important cases heard by Czechoslovak People's Courts under the category of Nazi crimes were those cases against above mentioned K. H. Frank, responsible for the disintegration of the Republic in 1938–1939 and for a wide range of Nazi persecutions in the Protectorate, including the Lidice massacre.[324] There were similar cases brought against members of the Gestapo or the Nazi Deputy Mayor of Prague, Pfitzner, which ended up with death penalties.

Prosecution of Nazi war criminals was in compliance with Articles 9, 10 and 11 of the Charter agreed in August 1945 for the International Military

---

322 See recently Frommer, B.: *National Cleansing, Retribution against Nazi Collaborators in Postwar Czechoslovakia.* Cambridge University Press, 2005 especially pp. 63 and following.
323 For their English translation see *Ibidem*, appendix 1–3, pp. 348–373.
324 *Ibidem*, pp. 233–237.

Tribunal in Nuremberg.[325] The retributory decrees had, to a certain degree, retroactive force. The punishments were severe especially in the initial phase of the retribution process and became milder in mid-1946, when lower officials were sometimes acquitted, and punishment was in many cases reversed to the transfer of these persons to the occupation zones in Germany, or convicted people were released earlier from jail and sent to Germany.

There is a paradox that retribution in later stages was more severe regarding Czechs than Germans. Czechs were usually accused of various forms of collaboration, including political and economic help rendered to the occupation forces or profiting from the persecution of Jewish or Czech compatriots. There were special regulations regarding informants and denunciators. It is surprising to find a high number of informants in the registers of Nazi organizations and the Gestapo; motives varied and ranged from personal hatred to attempts to annihilate neighbours, business competitors or even family members.

However, there was a political aspect to the retribution process as even the accused people lost their franchise in Parliamentary elections; proceedings usually taking a long time in order to prevent their participation in the 1946 elections. As a result, there were allegations of, and complaints against, the abuse of the retribution process especially by local communists and the police, controlled by the Ministry of the Interior. Political abuse was visible with regard to proceedings with the members of post-Munich governments accused not only of collaborating with Nazis but also for the "catastrophe" of post-Munich Czecho-Slovakia. Proceedings before the National Court were based on the results of preliminary examinations conducted by a special National Prosecutor; the rights of the accused were limited.

The period based on the Decrees of the President on the liberated territory lasted from 2nd April 1945 to 28th October 1945, i.e. until the convening of the Interim National Assembly. The Assembly unanimously confirmed Edvard Beneš in the office of the President of the Republic, thus providing sufficient political and legal endorsement of the theory of continuity of both the Czechoslovak state and the function of the President of the Republic. The Interim National Assembly drew up, debated and approved what was known as the constitutional endorsement or supplementary constitutional ratification of the Decrees of the President of the Republic.

The idea that the Decrees of the President were subject to the scrutiny and approval of constitutional bodies of the Czechoslovak Republic following the liberation had been accepted as early as 1940 by the Constitutional Decree "on the Interim Exercise of Legislative Power" of 15th October 1940. The fundamental principle was confirmed once again in the Constitutional Decree

---

325 See for example Kochavi, A. J.: *Prelude to Nuremberg: Allied War Crimes Policy and the Question of Punishment.* University of North Carolina Press, 1998, pp. 224–226 and 242.

"on the Restoration of Legal Order", No. 11/1944 of the Official Czechoslovak Bulletin, as amended. After a lengthy discussion and the clarification of several legal theoretical and political problems the Interim National Assembly ratified the Decrees on 28th March 1946 by passing Constitutional Act No. 57/1946, which approved the Decrees of the President and promulgated them to be the law.[326] Article 1 states that the Interim National Assembly approves and proclaims as law the Constitutional Decrees and Decrees of the President of the Republic issued on the basis of the Constitutional Decree of 15th October 1940 "on the Interim Exercise of Legislative Power", including that decree itself. Therefore all Decrees of the President were, from the date of their issue, regarded as law, and the Constitutional Decrees regarded as constitutional law. This step completed the process of incorporating Presidential Decrees into the legal order of post-war Czechoslovakia.

Post-war Czechoslovakia found its position to be very close to the Soviet sphere of influence, this fact being intensified by the internal political fight for the character of the renewed state.[327] The remnants of the democratic character of the Czechoslovak political, social and economic system were lost, and the combination of internal and international factors led to the imposition of a communist totalitarian regime of the Soviet style on Czechoslovakia.

In this context, the Czechoslovak politician and diplomat Ivo Ducháček should be quoted: "Although Czechoslovakia was known for its faith in democracy and for skilful politics and diplomacy, in the end it could serve as a very good example that a small nation living in the shadow of a Great Power could not be a real master of its own destiny. National leaders could, at the best, attempt to take part in decision-making but, in the worst case, they could end up as prisoners or puppets. A small nation living in the sphere of interest or influence of the Great Power has often only very limited choices."[328] Ducháček's words aimed at the relation of Czechoslovakia towards the Soviet Union in the 1940s; in the beginning of the 1950s they were of even more general relevance.

However, the period between 1945 and 1948 is the period of post-war reconstruction. The reconstruction was connected with the economic planning mentioned earlier.[329] The two-year plan for the reconstruction of the economy started on 1st January 1947. It was not so much an economic plan in the Soviet style as it was a plan for a mixed economy, and, for example, French

---

326 Beneš, Z. – Kural, V. (eds.): *Facing history: the evolution of Czech-German relations in the Czech provinces, 1848–1948*, p. 252.

327 In more details see for example, Luža, R.: *Czechoslovakia between democracy and communism 1945–1948*. In: Mamatey, V. S. – Luža, R. (eds.): *A History of the Czechoslovak Republic 1918–1948*, pp. 387–391 and Krejčí, J.: *Czechoslovakia at the Crossroads of European History*. London: I. B. Tauris, 1990, pp. 172–180.

328 Cited according to the unpublished Diary of Ivo Ducháček, Hoover Institution, Stanford, Ducháček Collection, Box 1.

329 Jech, K. – Průcha, V.: *Outline of Economic Development of Czechoslovakia 1945–1948*, pp. 45–66.

and Polish experience was used. On the other hand, it gave the Government and the Communist Party a greater say in economic matters. The plan was oriented towards setting production targets in the key sectors of the economy, and the Government could influence the state nationalized sector. The implementation of the plan was, with the notable exception of construction, relatively successful; but in the middle of its implementation the Communists grabbed power.

In 1946 the Communists won the Parliamentary elections and formed a coalition government headed by Klement Gottwald, Chairman of the Communist Party.[330] After the 1946 elections the Constitutional National Assembly was convened, and its main task was to prepare a new constitution. Unfortunately, at the same time the Czechoslovak Communists intensified their preparations for the seizure of all political power. Czechoslovakia was under the direct influence of the Soviet Union and Stalin's policies. The Czechoslovak Government was, for example, forced, under direct pressure from Stalin, to reject the reconstruction plan launched in June 1947 by the US Secretary of State, George Marshall.[331]

The new organization of Communist parties of the emerging Soviet Block, called the Communist Information Bureau (Comminform),[332] advocated, as early as November 1947, the necessity of a Communist takeover to finish the initial stage of the confrontation with non-Communist parties.[333] There were emerging signs of political crises, including the shift of power within the Slovak bodies in favour of the Communists (even though they lost the elections in Slovakia) and the limitation of the Slovak National Council by the so called Third Prague Agreement, the dispute over control of police forces and discussions about a new wave of nationalization and land reform.

The struggle for power culminated in February 1948. On 20th February 1948 twelve non-Communist ministers of the National Socialist Party, the People's Party and the Slovak Democratic Party resigned in protest against the Communist advances in the police forces.[334] However, the Communist Party found

---

330 Communists won in the Czech lands, where their poll 40 per cent, in Slovakia Democratic party won and the Communists came the second. For the elections and their results see Krejčí, O.: *History of Elections in Bohemia and Moravia*, Table 18a, and 18 b, pp. 196–197.

331 For other consequences of this situation for the Czechoslovak foreign policy see Korbel, J.: *The Communist Subversion of Czechoslovakia 1938–1948. The failure of coexistence.* Princeton New Jersey, 1959, pp. 181–183 and Ripka, H.: *Czechoslovakia Enslaved. The Story of the Communist Coup d'Etat.* London: Victor Gollanz, pp. 56–79.

332 For historical context see Gori, F. – Pons, S. (eds.): *The Soviet Union and the Cold War.* London: Macmillan, 1996, especially Part II, *The Comminform and the Soviet bloc*, pp. 197–221.

333 Korbel, J.: *The Communist Subversion of Czechoslovakia 1938–1948*, p. 186. See also Luža, R: *Czechoslovakia between democracy and communism, 1945–1948*, pp. 409–410.

334 For the account of the February events see Gsovski, V. – Grzybowski, K. (eds.): *Government Law and Courts in the Soviet Union and Eastern Europe.* Vol. I, Chapter 8, Czechoslovakia, pp. 241–251 and Korbel, J.: *The Communist Subversion of Czechoslovakia 1938–1948. The failure of coexistence*, pp. 198–235 and Ripka, H.: *Czechoslovakia Enslaved, The Story of the Communist Coup d'Etat*, pp. 229 and following.

collaborators within other parties and used the pressure of strikes and workers' militia controlled by the Communist Party. Workers' militia were given weapons, and mass demonstrations were organized to support the Communist strategy of maintaining the Government of the National Front. Congresses of Trade Unions and the Councils of Peasants backed the Communist proposals for nationalization and a land reform. The non-Communist ministers counted on the support of President Beneš and wanted the Social Democrats to join them. The only active move on their side was a protest by university students, who demanded the preservation of parliamentary democracy and primarily backed President Beneš. Communists were strengthened by a special mission of the Soviet Deputy Minister for Foreign Affairs, V. Zorin, who visited Prague during the crises along with Soviet generals, clearly influencing the outcome of the political struggle.[335] On 23rd February, stepping up their pressure, the Communist Party established so-called Action Committees of the National Front and Employees' Councils in all factories, enterprises, national committees, courts, public agencies and organizations. These committees started purges, house arrests and other forms of intimidation against the political opponents of the Communist Party. A day later the Central Action Committee was established as a political body to coordinate collaboration within the new Communist power and to direct local and regional national committees. An Action Committee was established within Parliament, whose session was postponed to eliminate the functioning of democratic procedures at the Parliamentary level. The purges by the Action Committees were approved *ex post facto* by a special law, No. 213/1948 Sb., which declared that steps taken by Action Committees during the coup were lawful measures even if they otherwise were not in compliance with the respective legal provisions.[336]

In the end President Beneš yielded to the Communist pressure and appointed a new government of the so-called "Reborn National Front", led by Klement Gottwald.[337] The communist or "socialist" political and legal system was thus introduced formally within the Czechoslovak constitutional framework, because Gottwald claimed that only a minority of ministers had resigned and he was able to replace them with members of the same political parties. The situation in Czechoslovakia in 1948 therefore differs if compared with other states of the emerging Soviet Block, as the Communist Party seized power (mis)using the constitutional framework of the democratic Czechoslovakia. Communists always used this argument for their own ideological purposes. However, the Czechoslovak road to socialism, which was advocated at the beginning, was soon replaced with Soviet style Stalinism.

---

335 For the importance of Zorin's presence in Prague see already Korbel, J.: *The Communist Subversion of Czechoslovakia 1938–1948*, pp. 223–224.
336 Gsovski, V. – Grzybowski, K. (eds.): *Government Law and Courts in the Soviet Union and Eastern Europe*. Vol. I, Chapter 22, Administration of justice – Czechoslovakia, p. 672.
337 Ripka, H.: *Czechoslovakia Enslaved. The Story of the Communist Coup d'Etat*, pp. 290–296.

Moreover, the pressure of the worker's militia, purges by the Action Committees and the usage of other means of intimidation of political opponents clearly show the true totalitarian foundations of the new regime. It is now well documented that the coup was a long-term, planned subversion of the democratic system. Nevertheless at the beginning it was a communist dictatorship with a semi-democratic façade, which was decorated mainly by the existence of several political parties within the continuation of the National Front as well as by proclamations in the new Constitution. Other political parties and all organizations, including the youth organization and trade unions, were nevertheless in fact controlled by Communists or by open collaborators with them.

The Constitution was in fact only a fiction and was not respected in practice. The regime soon became an open dictatorship characterized by political trials (even against the leading members of the Communist Party), harsh punishment of political opponents and the Church, the confiscation of property, further nationalization, and the introduction of the Soviet style of collective farms in the countryside (forced collectivization). The regime was officially characterized by the Communists themselves as the "dictatorship of the proletariat".

/19/

May Constitution of 1948 and the political system of the People's Democracy

The hasty preparations for new a Constitution of the "People's Democracy" led to the enactment of the Constitutional Act of 9th May 1948, officially promulgated on 9th June 1948. The Constitutional Act was formally enacted by the Constituent National Assembly, but was debated mainly by the new political leaders in the Central Committee of the Communist Party and in the bodies of the National Front. By then the main opponents of the new communist regime had been removed from Parliament.

The Constitution in some respects followed the constitutional tradition of the interwar period. Nevertheless it enacted the most important features of the new pro Soviet regime, including changes in state administration and the economic and social system.[338] However, it is necessary to look not only at the text of the Constitution but also to analyse the law in action.[339] The

---

338 For the controversy between continuity and Soviet influence see Skilling, H. G.: *The Czecho-slovak Constitutional System: The Soviet impact*. In: Political Science Quarterly, June 1952, pp. 198–224. See also in comparative perspective Skilling, H. G.: *The Governments of Communist East Europe*. New York: Thomas Y. Crowell, 1966, pp. 50–53.

339 The text in English was published already in 1948 by the new Czechoslovak Government. *Constitution of the Czechoslovak Republic, Constitutional Act of 9th May, 1948*, Prague: Czechoslovak Ministry of Education, 1948.

Czechoslovak Constitution is a classic example of the profound difference between the law as it is in books and the law in action,[340] as the Constitution was used as a fig leaf or a camouflage for the true nature of the communist regime in its initial stage.

The character of the new communist regime is clearly visible in the Preamble to the Constitution. It gives quite a lengthy account of Czech and Czechoslovak history from the Marxist and communist perspectives. Communists misused the milestones of the Czech history, including the Hussite period, and depicted them as social revolutions against feudal society. The First Czechoslovak Republic was proclaimed to be a bourgeois state directed against the people; the establishment of the independent state was seen as the result of the Russian revolution. The Munich period was portrayed as a period of the betrayal of the West, which resulted in an orientation towards the Soviet Union. The Preamble skilfully used the prevailing anti-German feelings, promulgating Czechoslovakia as a national state of Czechs and Slovaks and as a Slavic state which "had gotten rid of all hostile elements". The role of the Soviet Army and the Communist Resistance Movement was glorified; the period between 1945 and 1948 was designated as the beginning of the national and socialist revolution, leading to the establishment of a true People's Democracy.

The structure of the Constitution is very interesting from the constitutional law point of view. It consists of the Fundamental Articles and detailed provisions in individual chapters. The main principles of the Constitution, important for the interpretation of its text, were stressed in Twelve Fundamental Articles.

Chapter One addressed the rights and duties of citizens. Most of this part was based on the preceding Constitution of 1920; nevertheless it proved almost immediately that most of the civic rights were mere proclamations.[341] The proclamation of civic rights and freedoms by the Constitution was either followed by a qualifying clause frustrating the guarantee, or such a guarantee was completely denied by the law or governmental decrees intended for implementation. The Supreme Administrative Court, which represented an important judicial safeguard of civic rights, was at first reduced in its organization and powers and then abolished entirely in 1952.[342]

For example, the right of association was limited by a system of "socialist organizations", which were members of the political framework of the National Front controlled by the Communist Party. The right to convene public meetings was equally limited in practice. Personal freedom was undermined

---

340 Representing new dimension to the original idea of Roscoe Pound. See famous article by Pound: *Law in Books and Law in Action*. In: American Law Review, 44/1910, pp. 12 and following.
341 See also analyses in Gsovski, V. – Grzybowski, K. (eds.): *Government Law and Courts in the Soviet Union and Eastern Europe*. Vol. I. Chapter 8, Czechoslovakia, pp. 261–271.
342 *Ibidem*, p. 679.

particularly in the initial stage of the communist regime by various criminal and administrative punishments based on class criteria including the system of labour camps.

Act No. 184/1950 Sb., on the Press, represents a very good example of the communist concept of freedom of the press. Section 1 stipulated that the role of the press was to assist the effort of the Czechoslovak people to build their new future and the struggle for peace and socialist education. The production of films, as well as broadcasting and press institutions were solely in the hands of the state, since private ownership was not allowed even in the production of paper or the distribution of newspapers; censorship was introduced. The Ministry of Information and Education was entrusted with awarding state consent to individual publications. All journalists were forced to register as members of the Union of Czechoslovak Journalists and were under state and Communist Party control.[343]

Freedom of movement was gradually curtailed. At first, a strict system of border control was developed, and people were stripped of their passports. Those who tried to escape were prosecuted; if their escape was successful, they were sentenced *in absentia* and their property was confiscated. Later barber wire was used along the western borders to stress the existence of the Iron Curtain.

The communist regime constrained religious and academic freedoms along with its fierce attack on the freedoms of press and speech. Direction of education and research was under the supervision of the state alone. For example, church schools were dissolved, and education and all instruction should not be in contradiction with the People's Democratic Order.

For the first time the May Constitution of 1948 included provisions for social rights in order to stress the social dimension and ideological background of the new regime. The Constitution, in particular, mentioned the right to work (accompanied by the duty to work, set by labour law); this right had to be secured by the state in pursuance of a planned economy. Women were promised special work conditions, set by labour laws, in the event of pregnancy, maternity leave and child care needs.[344] Special conditions should apply also with respect to the work of youth. The right to work was supplemented with the right for fair remuneration, together with the principle of "equal remuneration for equal work for men and women", the right to leisure and recreation after work, and the right to protect life and health during work. Every citizen had the right to health care; the Constitution provided for the social security of pensioners and of those facing incapacity to work. The protection of family and the right of youth to education were paid a great deal of attention.

343 Gsovski, V. – Grzybowski, K. (eds.): *Government Law and Courts in the Soviet Union and Eastern Europe.* Vol. 1, part I, *The Regime and its origin*, pp. 266–267.
344 For the actual situation see *Women as Workers in Captive Europe,* Mid European Law Project, Library of Congress, New York, 1954.

Youth was under the special protection of the state, which undertook to apply "systematic measures in the interest of increasing the population within the nation". Large families were promised special relief and assistance. Vague proclamations of the Constitution were to be implemented by special laws.

The equality principle was included in a new way: the Constitution emphasized not only the equality of citizens before the law, but also the equality of men and women in their positions in the family and community, including equal access to all professions, offices and honours. This approach had an impact upon, and gave rise to major changes in, family and labour law. Yet, again, constitutional proclamations when applied in practice proved to be only a half-way measure.

The part of the Constitution dealing with the fundamental duties of citizens towards the state and community represented yet another novelty of the Czechoslovak constitutional development. Citizens were obliged not only to defend the state and the People's Democratic Order, to pay taxes or render other personal services demanded by public authorities, but also to be loyal to the Czechoslovak state, to uphold its Constitution and laws, and to respect the interests of the state in all their conduct and actions. In particular, it was the "patriotic duty" of every citizen "to assist in the maintenance and furtherance of national property and to guard it against any reduction or damage". Every citizen should discharge all public functions to which they were called by the People "conscientiously and honestly in the spirit of the People's Democratic Order", and to work "in accordance with one's abilities and contribute with one's work to the common wealth".

Chapters Two, Three and Four dealt with the National Assembly (Parliament), the President of the Republic, and the Government. Although the system resembled the division of powers in the Constitution of 1920, the communist system was based on different foundations. Firstly, it should be mentioned that the real centre of power was not vested in the official constitutional bodies but in the party apparatus of the Communist Party. Practically all decisions were decided on the Party level first and only then implemented through central and local state bodies.[345]

In accord with the Soviet model, major policy decisions regarding also envisaged legislation were published as common resolutions of the Central Committee of the Communist Party and the Government.[346] The state and representative bodies were thus put under the direct leadership of the Communist

---

345 See excellent study by Táborský, E.: *Communism in Czechoslovakia: 1948-1960*. Princeton University Press, 1961, pp. 22–50.
346 Korbel, P.: *The Czechoslovak Cabinet as an Indicator of Political Developments*. National Committee for a Free Europe, Research and Publications Service. Czechoslovak Section, 1952, pp. 1–7. In comparative perspective and with respect to Soviet theoretical approaches towards the sources of law see Hazard, L. N. – Shapiro, I. – Maggs, P. B.: *The Soviet Legal system. Contemporary Documentation and Historical Commentary*. New York: Dobbs Ferry, 1969, pp. 45–47.

Party.[347] A second problem was connected with legislative power, which was shifted by various means from Parliament to the Government. The Government was allowed to redefine the tasks set by the laws on economic plans, including the right to take such measures as would otherwise require an Act of Parliament. The Constitutional Act No. 47/1950 Sb. authorized the Government to create ministries and other agencies of public administration and to define their competences. The number of Governmental Orders increased rapidly, whereas the number of laws adopted by Parliament decreased. In 1951 Parliament adopted 21 Acts and the Government issued 74 Decrees; a year later the same categories were 39 to 69 respectively, and 16 to 70 in 1953.

Parliament consisted of only one chamber; the election of Deputies was based on the National Front's system, with a single list of candidates for every constituency. Candidates were nominated by the National Front and were under the control of the Communist Party. The first elections of the new regime took part in May 1948 and National Front candidates got 87.12 per cent in the Czech lands and 84.91 per cent in Slovakia. About 9 per cent of the votes were the so called "blank ballots" and the rest were invalid votes.[348] The electoral law was changed in 1954. The right to nominate candidates was reserved to the National Front, as the "union of workers, peasants and working intelligentsia" and the "combat block" of the Communist Party of Czechoslovakia, the Revolutionary Trade Union Movement, the Youth Organization, the Czechoslovak Socialist Party, the Czechoslovak People's Party, two small Slovak parties and other social organizations of the working people. There was only one nominee for one seat. Elections were manipulated through propaganda and various means of indirect coercion, for example through a directive spread by employers and communist functionaries in local communities to take part in the elections.[349] Thus the regime secured more than 90 percent in the polls. Members of Parliament were "answerable" to the people, who could recall them. In reality, this provision represented a safety measure to ensure the loyalty of MPs to the Communist Party.

Parliamentary meetings were seldom, and their sessions quite short – just to function as "voting machinery" for prepared legislative drafts. The National Assembly elected 24 members as its Presidium, which had the legislative powers of the Parliament when it was between sessions.

The Government was defined as the supreme body of governmental and executive powers. In practice, and again according to the Soviet model, the Government delegated most of its decisions to individual ministers, and the

347 See also Skilling, H. G.: *The Governments of Communist East Europe*, pp. 121–123.
348 Korbel, P.: *Parliamentary Elections in Czechoslovakia*. National Committee for a Free Europe, Research and Publications Service. Czechoslovak Section, 1952, pp. 1–21. Krejčí, O.: *History of Elections in Bohemia and Moravia*, table 20, p. 213.
349 *Ibidem*, especially pp. 214 and following. See also Gsovski, V. – Grzybowski, K. (eds.): *Government Law and Courts in the Soviet Union and Eastern Europe*. Vol. 1, part I. The Regime and its origin, pp. 254–256.

number of ministries was gradually increased to reflect the importance of atomized and centrally directed branches of industry.

The Constitution dealt with the Slovak national bodies, which remained as a residuum of Slovak autonomy. The Constitution was an attempt to return to a more centralized version of the Czechoslovak state in accordance with the third Prague Agreement, mentioned previously. The Slovak National Council was entrusted with the care and development of national culture, primary and secondary education, a part of the public health and social security system, local funds, construction of local roads and other constructions according to the uniform economic plan, maintenance and development of land, and development of trade, together with some other competences of local and minor importance. It could enact Acts, but in the period between 1951 and mid-1953 the Slovak National Council did not discuss a single draft. Slovak national bodies were in reality subject to the decisions of the Communist Party; however the semi-independent branch of the Slovak Communist Party survived such centralizing endeavours.

This part of the Constitution was replaced in July 1956 by a special Constitutional Act which enlarged the competences of the Slovak bodies.[350] The competences of the Slovak National Council in legislation were defined as "all matters of an ethnical or regional nature". However, such a broad description was limited by a proviso that the powers are granted only to the "extent that the entire economic and cultural development of Slovakia would require separate regulation". If the laws passed by the Slovak National Council were contrary to the Constitution, or if the Slovak National Council exceeded its powers, the Slovak legislation was declared void by the Presidium of the National Assembly. The executive powers in Slovakia were divided between the Czechoslovak Government and the Slovak Board of Commissioners.

Chapter Six of the May Constitution focused on national committees as the basis for public administration on local, district and regional levels.[351] The national committees were entrusted with general internal administration, administration of education, culture, planning, labour, administration of health care and social service, construction, maintenance of national property and some financial matters within their respective territories.[352] They were responsible for the "protection of the People's Democratic Order", i.e. they were given powers to punish violations under administrative law.

The old structure of provinces in the Czech lands was abolished, and a system of regional administration (called "*kraje*") introduced for the whole

350 Gsovski, V. – Grzybowski, K. (eds.): *Government Law and Courts in the Soviet Union and Eastern Europe*. Volume 1, part I. The Regime and its origin, pp. 258–260.
351 See also Gsovski, V. – Grzybowski, K. (eds.): *Government Law and Courts in the Soviet Union and Eastern Europe*. Volume 1, part I. The Regime and its origin, pp. 260–261.
352 Korbel, P.: *National Committees in Czechoslovakia*. National Committee for a Free Europe, Research and Publications Service. Czechoslovak Section, 1954, pp. 1–19.

territory of Czechoslovakia. All property of self-government was turned into state-owned property. This move strengthened the state sector even more than the second wave of nationalization. Although the Constitution provided for the election of national committees by local people, the first elections were held only as late as 1954. They lacked democratic standards, as Parliamentary elections did, and were based on a similar principle of a single list of candidates drawn up by the National Front. Members of the committees could be removed by their electors, but only on a motion by the National Front.

Chapter Seven dealt with the judicial power. The undermining of the independence of the judiciary was a key step towards the domination of the communist regime in the field of law. The Constitution laid down the framework of changes in the judiciary and stated that judges abide by laws and orders and interpret them "in the light of the Constitution and of the principles of the People's Democratic Order". The implementation of real changes was connected with the enactment of the special Act on the Popularization of Justice, No. 319/1948 Sb.[353] The term *popularization* was based on the concept of the People's Democracy laid down by the May Constitution. Popularization was seen as the opposite to *professionalism*, the alleged formalism and anti-people tendencies of the "bourgeois" lawyers. As a result, judges with legal education formed only a minority on panels and were outnumbered by lay judges, politically loyal to the communist regime and nominated by national committees.[354] Candidates had to be "devoted to the idea of the people's democracy system". Juries were abolished.[355] Lay judges were present even in the Supreme Court, to which they were nominated by the Government. This was the first step towards political control over the judiciary. Next was a gradual replacement of "old" judges by new ones educated by the Communists themselves. The Minister of Justice was authorized to endorse candidates for judicial positions even though they lacked "professional qualifications" and legal practice; a new subject was included in the judicial exam, which was called "political theory of Marxism and Leninism" and the exam was afterwards taken by judges periodically.[356]

The first period of changes in the judiciary was completed in 1952 when Constitutional Act No. 64/1952 Sb., on Courts and the Office of Public Prosecution, was enacted, followed by Acts No. 66 and 65/1952, on the organization of the courts and the prosecution offices.

Act No. 64 provided that both the professional and lay judges should be elected. It changed the life tenure for professional judges, provided for by the May

353 Gsovski, V. – Grzybowski, K. (eds.): *Government Law and Courts in the Soviet Union and Eastern Europe*, volume, I. Chapter 22, Administration of justice – Czechoslovakia, pp. 674–675.
354 Kühn, Z.: *The Judiciary in Central and Eastern Europe, Mechanical Jurisprudence in Transformation?* Leiden, Boston: Martinus Nijhoff Publishers, 2011, pp. 21–25.
355 See also Ulč, O.: *The Judge in a Communist State; A View from Within.* Ohio University Press, 1972, p. 20.
356 *Ibidem*, p. 394.

Constitution 1948. The Act of 26th July 1957 (No. 36) established the elections for judges of lower instances – district (called *"People's Courts"*) and regional. They were elected for a period of 3 years by the respective district and regional national committees. All other judges were appointed by the Government.

The Soviet model of a state prosecution system[357] was fully implemented, although it was gradually put into practice from 1950 on, and state prosecutors were assigned to the State Court for the Preparation of Political Trials as early as 1949. The office of prosecutor was an independent, monocratic and centralized body controlling the implementation of laws and other legal regulations by state bodies and citizens in all spheres of law; a state prosecutor represented the state in penal and civil proceedings. The prosecutor was entitled to lodge a protest against any act, decision or measure taken by public authorities, with the exception of the Government and the National Assembly.

Prosecution was proclaimed as a safeguard of "socialist legality", exercising direct supervision and control over the implementation and observance of the law by courts, public authorities and citizens in accordance with the socialist principles. It became a very powerful institution serving the interests of the Communist Party, which strictly controlled the personal composition of the public prosecution offices. In 1956 the law was amended and prosecutors were given the right to attend the meetings of national committees, administrative agencies, cooperatives and national enterprises in an advisory capacity. The Prosecutor General could take measures for the redress of any violation of socialist legality, regardless of who committed the violation; the Prosecutor General was to see that everyone who caused a violation was held responsible. However, in practice this wide power was used arbitrarily and according to political needs.

The communist leadership used methods similar to those in other states of the Soviet block and introduced short, non-university courses for selected cadres of working class origin and those loyal to the party. There were, for example, one year "Law Schools for the Working People", established by the Ministry of Justice in 1949. The goal of the Ministry was that the School should prepare "new lawyers linked to the people as a class and not influenced by the bourgeois understanding of the law."[358] In March 1951 Minister of Justice S. Rais openly declared that it was "necessary to give full support to the cadres of workmen and to appoint their members to the most responsible positions in the administration of justice".[359] When the experiment with the special

---

357 For the Soviet model see Hazard, L. N. – Shapiro, I. – Maggs, P. B.: *The Soviet Legal system, Contemporary Documentation and Historical Commentary*, pp. 63–65.
358 Gsovski, V. – Grzybowski, K. (eds.): *Government Law and Courts in the Soviet Union and Eastern Europe*. Volume, I. Chapter 22, Administration of justice – Czechoslovakia, pp. 672–673.
359 *Report on Czechoslovakia*, No.3/1951, National Committee for a Free Europe, Research and Information Center. New York, 1951, pp. 20–21.

School failed, distance courses at Law Faculties started to be held for special, politically selected workers.

The effects of the Communist Coup in February 1948 were detrimental to the existing Law Faculties.[360] Communists managed to reinforce their power over universities, cancel their autonomy, academic freedoms and the freedom of scientific research and teaching. Student opponents of the communist regime were excluded from study as a result of "student clearance". Many teachers, including the Rector of Charles University, Karel Engliš, were banned from teaching or forced to take early retirement; by the end of 1951 the majority of the pre-war teaching staff had been removed.[361] Some professors, like Vratislav Bušek, escaped from Czechoslovakia; Bušek, in particular, became a prominent representative of the exiled Czech legal scholars. By the end of the political clearance, 1,300 students had been expelled from the Law Faculty in Prague. Three law students, Boris Kovaříček, Karel Bacílek, and Veleslav Wahl were executed by the communist regime. In an infamous case against Dr. Milada Horáková, Zdeněk Peška, professor of constitutional law, was convicted; Otto Fischl, professor of financial law, was even sentenced to death within another political case against Rudolf Stránský.[362]

There were changes in the law curriculum to correspond with the Soviet model. For example, in Prague in 1949 new subjects were introduced in accord with the model of Lomonosov University in Moscow. Future lawyers had to take compulsory lectures and seminars in new subjects like Essentials of Marxism-Leninism, Marxist Philosophy, Political Economy, Economic Planning, History of the Soviet Union and the Soviet Communist Party, History of the Workers Movements, and History of the Czechoslovak Communist Party. Students had to learn Soviet law, and Russian language was made an obligatory subject.[363]

The Faculty was directly supervised by the Law Commission of the Central Committee of the Communist Party. A negative impact could be seen in international relations as well as in legal scholarship.[364] A new university law was adopted in 1950 abolishing the autonomy of universities. Universities were governed directly by the Ministry of Education. The Ministry not only appointed representatives of universities but also dictated the number and political profile of students to be admitted. Following the Soviet pattern, departments were established as a collective of teachers engaged in the same branches of law. Until 1955 legal studies had taken four years; they were then extended

---

360 Broader context see in Connelly, J. – Grüttner, M.: *Universities Under Dictatorship*. Pennsylvania State University Press, 2005, pp. 170–176.
361 In more details, Pousta, Z.: *Law faculty*. In: *A History of Charles University*. Vol. 2 (1802–1990), pp. 313–316 and Kuklík, J. et al.: *The Faculty of Law of Charles University in Prague*, pp. 30–32.
362 Kaplan, K.: *Report on the Murder of the General Secretary*. London: I. B. Tauris, 1990, pp. 227.
363 Pousta, Z.: *Law faculty*, pp. 314–316.
364 In more details see Kühn, Z.: *The Judiciary in Central and Eastern Europe. Mechanical Jurisprudence in Transformation?*, pp. 129–136.

to five years. In 1977 a reduction to four years was reintroduced. Education faced many experimental activities: such as abolishing the traditional title of JUDr. and replacing it with the title of "graduated lawyer" (although only for a limited period of time); students had to work in industry for a certain period of time during their legal studies; and they had to serve in the army as part of compulsory military service.

Entrance exams and the whole study programme were under the close scrutiny of the Communist Party bodies to ensure that the new generation of lawyers would be educated in a "new style". However, the goal to establish a student population predominantly from the working class or peasants was not fully achieved in Czechoslovakia, especially when compared with a more successful approach taken by the East German Communist Party.[365]

New lawyers, step by step, took over the positions within the judiciary and public prosecution offices. Purges among attorneys at law followed only shortly afterwards. The legal framework for the purges was set by Act No 322/1948 Sb., on Legal Professions. Traditional autonomous Bar Chambers, based on the Austrian law tradition, were abolished and regional Bar Associations under the direct auspices of Ministry of Justice introduced; only lawyers "loyal to the Government and devoted to the system of People's Democracy" were allowed to practice law.[366] Loyalty to the regime was embodied in a new oath, which was compulsory to take at the beginning of practicing law. The attorneys at law were expected to put the interests of society above the interests of their clients.[367] The regional bars exercised control over the profession, but also redistributed money to abolish the alleged "capitalist" nature of attorneys.

Another traditional and self-governed legal profession of public notaries, entrusted by courts with probate proceedings, drawing up instruments of public nature, protesting delinquent bills and notes or notarizing declarations and signatures, were changed into state controlled notaries appointed by the Minister of Justice and subordinated to the People's Democratic Order.[368]

Chapter Eight addressed the economic foundations of the communist regime. The main categories of means of production were either national (state) property, or the property of the people's cooperatives. Private property was limited only to small enterprises with fewer than 50 employees and only to certain branches of industry. Immediately after the February Coup of 1948 the Communists carried out a second wave of nationalization of industry combined with a far reaching land reform and confiscation of the property of

365 Connelly, J.: *Captive University: The Sovietization of East German, Czech, and Polish Higher Education 1945–1956.* The University of North Carolina Press, 2000, pp. 34 and following.
366 On the "sovietization" of the Bar Chambers in Czechoslovakia see Gsovski, V. – Grzybowski, K. (eds.): *Government Law and Courts in the Soviet Union and Eastern Europe.* Volume 1, pp. 697–706.
367 Táborský, E.: *Communism in Czechoslovakia: 1948–1960,* pp. 293–294.
368 Gsovski, V. – Grzybowski, K. (eds.): *Government Law and Courts in the Soviet Union and Eastern Europe.* Volume, I. Chapter 22, Administration of justice – Czechoslovakia, pp. 695–696.

political opponents.[369] State property was administered by the state either directly or through national enterprises. Private property was gradually limited only to small holders of land (up to 50 hectares) or small private business; and all leading branches of industry were almost completely nationalized between 1948 and 1950. Nationalization in Czechoslovakia was more rapid and extensive than in the German Democratic Republic, Poland, Hungary or Romania. No compensation was paid to Czechoslovak citizens, and nationalization in the end became confiscation. The land reform was a first step towards the collectivization of agriculture.

The Constitution mentioned the possibility of communal property in connection with enterprises owned by national committees; however, this form of ownership ceased to exist in 1949, when the property of national committees was transferred to state ownership. In order to make a distinction between private ownership of a capitalist nature and the private belongings of individuals based on their work, a new type of ownership was introduced by the Constitution called "individual ownership".

These changes in the form of ownership were linked with the introduction of "scientific" economic planning of the Soviet style.[370] The economy was centralized and planned in the form of Five-Year Plans.[371] Economic plans were based on special laws, which were implemented in detail by Government orders every year.

Chapter Nine dealt with general provisions connected with state citizenship, frontiers, the capital city of Prague and state symbols; Chapter Ten contained final and transitional provisions. The final provision dealt with the promulgation of the Constitution. Czechoslovak President Edvard Beneš refused to sign it, and the Constitution became effective only after his resignation, when the Constitution was symbolically signed by the new President and leader of the Communist Party, Klement Gottwald, on 9th June 1948. On this day the Constitution of 1920 ceased to be formally valid.

369 Jech, K. – Průcha, V.: *Outline of Economic Development of Czechoslovakia 1945–1948*, pp. 67 and following.
370 Skilling, H. G.: *The Governments of Communist East Europe*, pp. 189–190.
371 Teichová, A.: *The Czechoslovak Economy 1918–1980*, pp. 134–140.

/20/
Changes in the Czechoslovak legal system 1948–1960

There were new features of socialist law introduced to the Czechoslovak legal system after 1948. The first important characteristic is that the law was very much based on ideology. [372] Marxist-Leninist theory designates the first period after communist accession to power as the dictatorship of the proletariat. Lenin's works on the role of the state in the initial period after the communist takeover, as readdressed and simplified by Stalin (and also Vyshinski for Legal Theory and Criminal Law),[373] worked as an official ideology in the form of the socialist theory of the state and law in Czechoslovakia as well. Its primary role was to legitimize the existing communist power in the form of a totalitarian system. The Czechoslovak environment was quickly determined by Soviet doctrine, even though it initially took the form of a simplified and scientifically low level set of guidelines.[374] Concepts such as the dictatorship of the working

---

372 The Marxist legal theory claimed to be in the first instance "scientific" and that it is derived from the whole Marxist philosophy. Kelsen, H.: *The Communist Theory of Law*. New York, F. A. Praeger 1955, especially preface and chapter I. For changes during Lenin's period see pp. 51 and following.

373 *Ibidem*, pp. 116–132.

374 In more details see Slapnicka, H.: *Soviet Law as Model: The People's Democracies in the Succession States*; Natural Law Forum. Notherdam Law School 1963, Paper 97, pp. 109–121, and

class, the class approach and socialist legality were applied. On the other hand, it should be noted that the doctrine changed in accord with changes made both in the Soviet Union (particularly after the death of Stalin) and the whole Soviet Bloc, which resulted in a more liberal period in the second half of the 1950s and the 1960s.[375] Perception of the atmosphere in the society significantly declined from an "optimistic" and very active attitude towards the class approach at the beginning of the 1950s to a later more "pessimistic" and, in many ways, formalistic approach, culminating in the period of so-called "normalization" after 1969, based upon the concept of the "law of real, existing socialism."[376] It is necessary to look at the real life of the law, which could escape unnoticed behind the facade of formal law and which was very often in direct contradiction to the wording of the laws. The known contradiction between law in the books and law in action acquired yet another dimension in the socialist law of Czechoslovakia.

The first wave of changes was connected with the two-year "legal plan" of codification. After the idea had been discussed by political bodies of the Communist Party, the Ministry of Justice was entrusted, in September 1948, to prepare a series of new "socialist" codes to change the existing legal system according to the new political and ideological needs. The deadline was set for September 1950, i.e. in two years. That is why the re-codification process is known as a two-year legal plan, to terminologically approximate it with the two-year economic plan of reconstruction. The main outline of codification was set during a special congress of "progressive" lawyers, where the new ideology, together with its adherence to the Soviet model, were discussed. The Communists attacked the formalistic, apolitical and impartial "old" legal system; they also attacked the continuity of the Austrian legal system, emphasizing its backward and feudal nature dating back to Maria Theresa. They preferred that the new law assist the ideology, the working class and the establishment of a socialist society. The "new law" was seen as a mere tool for political and ideological aims, and, as Klement Gottwald put it, "the law serves us to transform the society".[377] As proclaimed several times by leading Communist politicians, the law had to express the will of the working class.

Skilling, H. G.: *The Soviet Impact on the Czechoslovak Legal Revolution.* Soviet Studies Volume 6/ 4, 1955, pp. 361–381. See also Táborský, E.: *Communism in Czechoslovakia: 1948–1960*, pp. 175–176. Táborský speaks about the "transplants from the East".

375 For theoretical aspects of an attempt to introduce gradually modern aspects of civic society, rule of law and socialist democracy into the socialist society see Kusin, V. V.: *The Intellectual origins of the Prague Spring. The Development of reformist ideas in Czechoslovakia 1956–1967.* Cambridge University Press, 1971, especially Chapter 3, Legal re-thinking, pp. 28 and following.

376 For judiciary see excellent study by Kühn, Z.: *The Judiciary in Central and Eastern Europe, Mechanical Jurisprudence in Transformation?*, especially pp. 21–45 and 67–124.

377 Cited according to Gottwald, K.: *Právo v lidové demokracii* (Law in People's Democracy). In: *O kultuře a úkolech inteligence v budování socialismu.* Prague: Státní nakladatelství politické literatury, 1954, pp. 30–31.

The traditional division of law into public and private had to be abolished and replaced by a universal legal system. This was another example of the intention to introduce the Soviet legal principles as soon as possible. Another goal was to simplify the legal system. The assumption was that abridged law would be more understandable for people. This approach was accompanied with the changes in interpretation of existing "old laws" with the aim to "fill them with new, socialist spirit" before they were abolished and replaced by new laws.[378]

The result of the two-year legal plan was a very rapid and efficient change, especially in civil and criminal law. Another aim of the codification was to unify the law applicable to the Czech lands and Slovakia. Various outcomes of codification endeavours from the interwar period were used to speed up the preparation. Communists misused and presented them as another example of the effectiveness of people's democracy, in comparison with the unsuccessful twenty years of bourgeois interwar democracy.

Two main commissions were set up in the beginning of the codification process. One commission was in charge of civil law, with sections dealing with substantive law and procedure, and this same model applied to criminal law.

A new family law in accord with the Soviet pattern was introduced in 1949.[379] The concept of family law as a new branch of law was the first example of the fragmenting of civil law. The Czechoslovak codification commission cooperated closely with their Polish colleagues; they proposed a common Czechoslovak-Polish Civil Code. The proposal did not assume material form, with the notable exception of the Czechoslovak Family Act in December 1949, which was heavily influenced by the Polish "People's Democratic" model. Thus the Soviet view of the separate existence of family law under the special curatorship of the state prevailed, and the concept of the law of persons, known from the Austrian Civil Code (ABGB), abandoned. Family law was thus excluded for decades from the Civil Code. On the other hand, the new Family Act was the first example of the successful unification of Czech and Slovak law. The Act implemented the provisions of the May Constitution of 1948 regarding the equality of men and women, both as parties to marriage and as parents towards their children, as well as the special protection of family and children by the state.

The Family Act (No. 265/1949 Sb.) prohibited the conclusion of a marriage before the Church; the only valid form was a marriage concluded before national committees, which were in charge of all personal status records (compulsory civil marriage). Religious celebrations were allowed, but could take place only after the marriage was concluded before the civil authority.

---

378 From comparative perspective see Gsovski, V. – Grzybowski, K. (eds.): *Government Law and Courts in the Soviet Union and Eastern Europe.* Vol. 1, part I. Continuity of law, pp. 495–496.
379 Hikl, M.: *The Civil Codes in Communist Czechoslovakia.* Toronto: The Czechoslovak Foreign Institute in Exile, 1959, pp. 23–27.

Both parties to marriage were equal; they had an obligation to live together, to be faithful and mutually assist each other morally and materially. The power of the father of the family was abolished, and both parents had equal rights towards their children. They were responsible for the physical and mental development of their children, for their alimentation, property and education. Differences between legitimate and illegitimate children were abolished.

The Family Act unified the property rights of spouses and introduced an obligatory type of community property between spouses. Community property covered all property acquired during the existence of the marriage; however, there was still the individual property of each spouse, what he or she owned prior to marriage or acquired by inheritance.

A spouse could seek termination of marriage through a judicial decision; the term "divorce" was used to define general reasons for the court to grant a divorce "if deep and lasting breakdown developed between the spouses for serious reasons". However, the discretion of courts was limited by specific provisions protecting minor children; another provision stated that that spouse who alone was guilty of causing the serious and deep breakdown could not file the petition for divorce, unless the other, innocent, spouse consented to it. In 1955 an amendment of the Family Act emphasized the interests of society as an important condition for the decision of courts on divorce; for example, the court was examining whether or not the marriage "was fulfilling its social functions". The Family Act dealt also with tutorship. In practice also family law was influenced by new "socialist ideology" and for example Czechoslovak (and also East German) courts in the 1950s in several cases favoured guardianship of special state social welfare institutions to those parents (especially during divorce or as a result of criminal proceedings) who "failed to educate their children in socialist way".[380]

The new Czechoslovak Civil Code was adopted in 1950 (Act No. 141/1950 Sb.).[381] To a certain extent it rejected the Roman law tradition in private law; civil law was misused for the purposes of the communist ideology.[382] This was particularly visible in the concept of ownership, which in fact followed the principles already set by the May Constitution of 1948. National property and the property of people's cooperatives was proclaimed to be a socialist type of ownership and, as such, given priority. On the other hand, private ownership, ideologically related to capitalist exploitation and limited to small enterprises, houses or land not exceeding 50 hectares, was

380 See cases cited by Gsovski, V. – Grzybowski, K. (eds.): *Government Law and Courts in the Soviet Union and Eastern Europe.* Vol. 1, part I., pp. 505–506.

381 For its detailed analyses in English see Falada, D.: *Codification of private law in the Czech Republic.* In: Fundamina: A Journal of Legal History (South Africa), Vol. 15, Issue 1, 2009, pp. 58–61 and Hikl, M.: *The Civil Codes in Communist Czechoslovakia*, pp. 6–22.

382 Gsovski, V. – Grzybowski, K. (eds.): *Government Law and Courts in the Soviet Union and Eastern Europe.* Vol., II. part V., Sovietization of Civil Law, Czechoslovakia, pp. 1238–1276.

discriminated against and confronted with provisions on individual property based on one's labour, such as objects of household, small family houses and savings accumulated from wages.

One of the prominent Czech lawyers who took part in the codification process was Viktor Knapp,[383] who later became a leading Czech legal theoretician; he explained the purpose of the adoption of the new Civil Code as follows: "to liquidate the remnants of bourgeois property relations, as well as bourgeois thinking in our society... to strengthen and protect socialist ownership and to observe the rules of the socialist community life..."[384]

The purpose of the Code and the new concept of private law were expressly stated in the first two parts: introductory provisions remarking on the building of socialism and people's democracy, and general provisions common to civil law as a whole. The concept of socialist ownership, together with other aspects of property law and mortgages, were contained in Part Three.

Part Four, dealing with obligations (arising both from contracts and from torts), underwent equally important changes. The Commercial Code had no place in the communist economic system and was abolished. Obligations could be formed not only on the basis of an agreement between parties, but in the case of "needs of economic planning" also by decisions of the planning authorities. Obligations could be changed or terminated for the same reason. When the Draft of the Civil Code was presented to the National Assembly, the Government expressly stated that "the law of contracts shall serve primarily the uniform economic plan... and the economic plan was designed to direct all the economic activities and in particular trades, production and transport." The most important entities were national enterprises, which were governed by special laws; for example, industrial national enterprises were regulated by the Act on National Enterprises of 1950. They were entrusted with national (state) property only for operational administration and were subjected to the economic plan and directives of the planning authorities. The Government, in the form of Governmental decrees (for example, Decree No. 33 of 28th May 1955) set specific rules for so-called economic contracts of national enterprises dealing with the supply of goods, performance of work, or rendering of services. Although a new Act on Joint-stock Companies was enacted in 1949, in practice most private companies were put under national administration, were nationalized, or simply ceased to be operational (even though they were sometimes liquidated years later).

Disputes between national enterprises and between national enterprises and other legal entities within the socialist sector were dealt with in most

---

383 See also his memoires, where is trying to play down his original zeal to bring about radical changes into the Civil Code, Knapp, V.: *Proměny času: vzpomínky Nestora české právní vědy*. Prague: Prospektrum, 1998, pp. 121–122.

384 See especially Knapp, V.: *Vlastnictví v lidové demokracii: právní úprava vlastnictví v Československé republice*. Prague: Orbis, 1952, pp. 67 and following.

cases (in particular, concerning production, services and work) through a new type of state sponsored and supervised arbitration, yet again according to the Soviet model.[385] There was a special Act No. 99/1950 Sb., on Economic Contracts and Government Arbitration, amended by Governmental decrees in 1953 and 1954. There was a specialized arbitration agency for co-operatives.

The Civil Code was not a complete departure from the Austrian Civil Code. This was mainly true of certain passages dealing with easements (servitudes) or the law of inheritance in Part 5. This was partly because the Code was prepared by leading Czech and Slovak professors educated in the Austrian times or in the interwar period (especially by professor Jan Krčmář), and partly because of a lack of time. The plan had to be fulfilled in a maximum of two years and at any price, including compromise in parts of law not so ideologically exposed. It is interesting that despite changes in the Constitution and in labour law, including the duty to work and many administrative interventions in the area of labour law, the Labour Code was not ready until 1965, and the part on labour contracts from the Austrian Civil Code remained in force. However, the Government introduced a number of regulations governing labour relations, for example that on absenteeism and job-switching issued in 1953.[386]

New civil proceedings resembled changes in the judiciary and administration of justice from 1948–1950.[387] Prosecutors were given the right to intervene in civil proceedings whenever they deemed it necessary for the protection of the interests of the Government (the People's Democratic State) or the working people. Again the class meaning of this concept was evident and was misused in practice against the "members of the former exploiting classes"; it violated the constitutional principle of equality of people before the law. The Government Attorney (from 1952 "Prosecutor") could apply all legal remedies under the Code of Civil Procedure.[388]

On 6th October 1948 a new Act on the Protection of the People's Democratic Republic (No. 231/1948 Sb.) was enacted to fortify the new regime through the potential of criminal law. Although most of the crimes contained in the Act were already punishable under the laws from the interwar period, a more severe punishment was introduced for political, military and

---

385 Hazard, L. N. – Shapiro, I. – Maggs, P. B.: *The Soviet Legal system. Contemporary Documentation and Historical Commentary*, pp.272–273.
386 Gsovski, V. – Grzybowski, K. (eds.): *Government Law and Courts in the Soviet Union and Eastern Europe*. Vol. II, part VI., Worker and factory, Czechoslovakia, pp. 1497–1514.
387 Gsovski, V. – Grzybowski, K. (eds.): *Government Law and Courts in the Soviet Union and Eastern Europe*. Volume 1, pp 885–893. See also Hikl, M.: *The Civil Codes in Communist Czechoslovakia*, pp. 47–60.
388 Táborský, E.: *Communism in Czechoslovakia: 1948–1960*, pp. 287–288. In comparative perspective Gsovski, V. – Grzybowski, K. (eds.): *Government Law and Courts in the Soviet Union and Eastern Europe*. Vol. 1, pp. 892–893.

economic crimes, in particular for high treason, terrorism, conspiracy, spying, incitement against the Republic, or sabotage, and certain other crimes, like propagation of Nazi ideology and misuse of religious functions. Crimes were defined broadly and loosely to enable courts to take arbitrary decisions in the first instance of political trials.

The Act on the Protection of the People's Democratic Republic was accompanied by the Act on the State Court No. 232/1948 Sb. The State Court together with state prosecutors and state security formed the major institutional bases for political trials, described in more detail below.

The new Criminal Code and the Code on Criminal Procedure (Acts No. 86 and 87/1950 Sb.) were enacted in 1950 as part of the two-year legal plan.[389] Criminal law enabled harsh punishment of real or potential opponents of the communist regime and, sometimes, simply people of different religious beliefs or political views, and also those coming from a "wrong" class or being of a "wrong" social origin.[390] The aim was not only punish individuals but also to deter and discipline the rest of the society. Naturally, traditional roles attached to criminal law and criminal justice were performed as well. New objectives set for criminal law by the communist legal science were to correct the shortcomings of the building of socialism, the "organization of social relationships" and of educating the society.

The purpose of the Code was expressly stipulated by Section 1:

"Criminal law shall protect the people, the People's Democratic Republic, its construction of socialism, the interests of workers and of individuals and shall teach the observance of the rules of socialist community life." The means to attain this purpose was the threat of punishment, the imposition and execution of punishments and of so-called protective measures.

The class character of the administration of criminal justice was connected with the concept of "socialist legality". According the leading textbook on criminal substantive law from the 1950s, socialist legality meant "the precise application and observance of such laws as are in accordance with the will of the working class and of workers. Its aim shall be to crush the enemies of the people and to protect and strengthen the dictatorship of the working class in order to build socialism and later communism". The principles of judicial independence were interpreted with regard "to the present social relationships" and as a "political principle".

The class character was discriminatory; for example it was possible to apply a milder punishment when a crime was committed by an offender who

---

389 Gsovski, V. – Grzybowski, K. (eds.): *Government Law and Courts in the Soviet Union and Eastern Europe.* Vol., II. part IV., New Substantive Criminal Law, pp. 994–1022. For the English translation of Criminal Code see Bulletin de droit Tchécoslovaque, No. 3–4, 1952, Prague: Union des juristes de Tchécoslovaque, pp. 345 and following.

390 Gsovski, V. – Grzybowski, K. (eds.): *Government Law and Courts in the Soviet Union and Eastern Europe.* Vol. II, part IV, pp. 998 and following.

was a worker and was living an orderly life. On the other hand, a "wrong social background" or an unfriendly attitude towards the People's Democracy constituted an aggravating circumstance and was followed by a harsher punishment.

The Criminal Code was divided into general and special parts.[391] The general part dealt with the general principles of criminal liability and the foundations for sentencing. The division between crimes and misdemeanours was abolished. New Soviet principles were introduced. The Criminal Code was based on the theory of both formal and "material" criteria for criminal acts, the former being elements set by the law, the latter representing a certain degree of danger to the society. The Code expressly stated that "The crime shall only be conduct dangerous to the society for whose consequences specified by statute the offender shall be liable...". The degree of danger to the society was used as a vague distinction between criminal offences and administrative delicts. The Administrative Criminal Code (Act No. 88/1950 Sb.) was seen as complementary to the Criminal Code.

On the other hand, some features of Soviet law were not followed by the Czechoslovak legislators. They particularly opposed the theory of analogy (i.e. to apply the criminal code to acts which do not exactly match the elements of an offence set by statute by analogy to the nearest applicable offence); the legislators bravely stated that such a theory is not suitable for Czechoslovakia because it was applied by the Nazi courts during the German occupation. The Czechoslovak Criminal Code prohibited the retrospective application of criminal law to the defendant's disadvantage.

There was an intended harshness to criminal law; for example, the death penalty could be imposed for 9 political offences, 3 common offences and 15 military offences. The sentence of imprisonment was either for life or for a maximum of 25 years, and correctional labour without imprisonment could be imposed. There were additional penalties, like deprivation of citizenship, deprivation of civic rights or military ranks, confiscation of property, fines, and prohibition of performing certain activities, and prohibition from staying in a certain town or region.

The special part of the Code reflected the higher significance attached to the protection of the state, economic and social system more than to the protection of the interests of individual citizens. The crimes against the state (taken virtually unchanged from the Act on the Protection of the People's Democratic Republic) and protection of socialist forms of ownership and economic planning came in the first two chapters.

---

[391] In more details see Hikl, M.: *The Penal Codes in Communist Czechoslovakia*. Toronto: The Czechoslovak Foreign Institute in Exile, 1957.

In the second half of the 1950s there were some changes also to substantive criminal law concerned with the reinforcement of an individual approach to punishment with regard to the offender (see also Chapter 21) on the one hand and increased protection of socialist property on the other, embodied in such Acts as Act No 63/1956 Sb., which brought a more moderate approach towards imposition of penalties including the death penalty, and Act No. 24/1957 Sb. on Disciplinary Prosecution of Stealing and Damage to Property in Socialist Ownership.

Criminal law was used also for solutions of some social problems including the attempt to settle the Roma (Gypsy) population. Act No 74/1958 Sb. punished those who refused to settle and continued their "nomadic style of living", although they were offered new housing.

The Code of Criminal Procedure 1950 introduced important changes to the Austrian model.[392] Two main stages of proceedings – pre-trial proceedings, and trial before a court – were introduced.

The system of an independent investigative (examining) judge was abolished. Pre-trial proceedings were conducted by the police forces of the communist regime, the State and Public Security, and supervised by the office of the Prosecutor; as such they prevailed in practice over the main trial, and the results and evidence presented during the pre-trial stage influenced the majority of judicial decisions during the trial before a court. This was true not only in the case of political trials. The prosecutor personally supervised and directed the execution of custody and the sentence of imprisonment.

Courts usually did not take into account the evidence and defence strategy of the accused; such an approach was broadened by changes in the legal profession of attorneys. Although the Code of Criminal Procedure contained provisions for appeal and other types of remedial measures, in practice the right of the accused to any remedy was limited. A so-called limited revision principle applied in accord with the Soviet model.

In 1950 new Codes on Administrative Criminal Law and Procedure for Administrative Authorities (Acts No. 88 and 89/1950 Sb.) supplemented the Criminal Code and the Code of Criminal Procedure, as the administration of justice in criminal matters was carried out by two types of criminal (penal) authorities – by criminal courts and certain administrative authorities, especially national committees. National committees dealt with administrative transgressions; in practice they imposed quite severe penalties, including confinement in labour camps, confiscation of property, imposition of fines and public reprimand, prohibition of certain activities, or publication of the sentence. There was a specific class character to administrative criminal law,

---

392 *Ibidem.* See also Gsovski, V. – Grzybowski, K. (eds.): *Government Law and Courts in the Soviet Union and Eastern Europe*, vol. I. Judicial Procedure, Czechoslovakia, pp. 848–849.

since those offenders who showed a hostile attitude towards the People's Democratic Order could be awarded a double fine instead of a regular one. Act No. 102/1953 Sb. transferred the authority to impose the most severe penalties to criminal courts and milder punishments were introduced.

/21/
Political trials and other forms of persecution

The developments of the two-year legal plan formed a required legal frame-work not only for changes in the concept of criminal law but also for its implementation in practice in compliance with the political goals of the Com-munist Party. The real character of the new communist regime was evident very soon, particularly in the conducting of political trials.[393] The political trials began with the renewal of the legal effect of the Retributory Decrees just one month after the February coup d'état. As a result, it was possible to commence new proceedings or to reopen proceedings which had already been terminated; thus the first wave of political persecution was built upon false accusations of collaboration with the Nazis during the occupation. In 1948 the first round of imprisonment of non-Communist politicians or army officers followed; however, their sentences were based on pre-February legis-lation and were not so draconic.

---

393 For this phenomena see Pelikán, J.: (ed.): *The Czechoslovak Political Trials 1950–1954.* The Sup-pressed Report of the Dubček Government 's Commission of Enquiry 1968, Stanford 1971, especially pp. 69–147 and Cotic, M: *The Prague Trial, The First Anti-Zionist Show Trial in the Communist Bloc.* New York: Herzel Press, 1987, introduction by K. Kaplan, pp. 9 and following.

The main bulk of political trials took place between 1949 and 1955. It was a systematic, mass and planned activity of the communist regime aimed at the liquidation, intimidation and persecution of all strata of any potential ideological, political or social opponents to the People's Democracy. The number of accused and sentenced gradually rose from 1949 until 1952.

Laws and justice played their role as tools of the communist political strategy.[394] The atmosphere of fear was to intimidate the majority of the society; officially the regime claimed to use criminal persecution also for the "education" of the society, so that it could acquire a "positive approach" towards the People's Democracy. The most important role in the political trials was vested in the police structures, especially the State Security. Theoretically, the State Security was under the control of the leaders of the Communist Party; however, the most important say in the preparation of political trials at the central level was in the hands of the Soviet security forces.[395]

The political trials are regarded as one of the main features of the period of Stalinism. In the USSR the method of publicly exhibited show trials was used as early as in the 1930s, and usually the trials had ideological labels used to a certain extent in the states of the Soviet Bloc after 1948. In Czechoslovakia the most important political trials were connected with the interests of Soviet foreign policy; thus cases of high treason in particular were alleged to have been committed in the interest of the imperialistic Great Powers, Zionism, Holy See, etc.[396]

The State Security was a combination of police and investigative roles. It used provocations, agents-provocateurs and particularly cruel and illegal methods of interrogation, including beating, torturing or even using drugs and psychical intimidation. The role of the State Security was defined in the new Act on National Security, No. 286/1948 Sb. of 21st December 1948; and the State Security was seen as part of the new Czechoslovak police forces, called the National Security.

The political trials misused the principle of publicity of proceedings. In accordance with a special decree of the chief of the State Security from 1951, the secret police selected certain cases in advance to be treated publicly for propaganda aims. The trials were publicized in the media, including radio and film, and sometimes even excursions were organized for the public to see the cases of traitors and enemies of the People's Democracy. On the other hand, in case of the trials of army officers the public was excluded.

In the years 1949–1953 political trials were not only hand-picked by the State Security, but they were debated in advance in political terms with

---

394 Kühn, Z.: *The Judiciary in Central and Eastern Europe, Mechanical Jurisprudence in Transformation?*, pp. 26–28.
395 Cotic, M: *The Prague Trial*, pp. 20–21.
396 In more details see works by K. Kaplan. In English especially Kaplan, K.: *Report on the Murder of the General Secretary*, pp. 14 and following.

representatives of the Communist Party and state officials. In the most important cases the judgments were resolved by the leaders of the Communist Party, and the cases prepared by representatives of the Ministry of Justice working with selected judges and prosecutors. The same manner of organization applied to political trials on the regional and local levels, where special committees of "five" or "three" representatives of the State Security, Communist Party, respective national committees and the state prosecutor discussed the cases beforehand. After the political decision had been issued, the cases were placed under the special supervision of regional prosecutors. There were special instructions and training for the judiciary to "understand properly the main political lines of the trials".

There were certain types of political trials based according to groups of persons selected for the trial. A special type of trial was connected with some representatives of the Communist Party and was built mostly upon their alleged failures and misconceptions.

Special trials were conducted against the members of former non-communist political parties, army officers, the church, Catholics, teachers, members of the Youth Organizations, as well against those who opposed the collectivization in the countryside and villages or opposed nationalization.

At first the former political opponents were put before the State Court. The communist regime tried to secure its picture of post-war development and the legitimacy of the take-over in February 1948. The most important case of that time was the trial of "Milada Horáková and her anti-state espionage centre", in which 13 former representatives of the National Socialist and Social Democratic parties were, without any relevant evidence, accused of high treason, espionage and other subversive activities. The case was a typical ideological show trial, prepared in advance; in June 1950 Milada Horáková and three others were sentenced to death and executed despite protests from the democratic world, including a personal letter of Clementine Churchill.[397] After this case, some thirty five "follow-up cases" were prepared and orchestrated by the State Security, and 639 people sentenced, usually to long terms of imprisonment.[398]

Important political trials were set up for Czechoslovak army officers; most of these were those who had fought for Czechoslovak liberation in the West or opposed the communist-drafted legends related to WWII and cooperation with the USSR. In 1949 General Heliodor Píka was sentenced to death and executed. The hero of the Prague Uprising in 1945, General Karel Kutlvašr, was accused of high treason, but, because of a lack of evidence, sentenced to "only" 10 years of imprisonment. A sentence of imprisonment was imposed on

[397] For this initiative supported by Czechs in Exile see Jaroslav Stránský Collection, Hoover Institution Archives, box No. 8.
[398] Cotic, M: *The Prague Trial*, pp. 72–73.

Air Marshall Karel Janoušek and, together with him, on most of the Czechoslovak airmen having served in the Royal Air Force during WWII.[399]

Persecutions, including political trials, were designed with respect to bishops and priests, particularly of the Catholic Church; but other churches were also exposed to communist threats. This type of political trial was closely connected with the communist policy in religious matters.[400] In the beginning the new People's Democratic regime tried to avoid open confrontation with the Catholic Church. However, in 1949 mutual relations deteriorated, and the Communists launched an anti-Church campaign, seized all Church property (not only of the Catholic Church but of all Churches and religious communities), and in October 1949 enacted so called "Church laws" (Acts No 217 and 218 /1949 Sb. and governmental ordinances for individual Churches), which from 1949 put Churches under state supervision (under so called State Board for Church Questions) including financial and property questions.[401] Church representatives and priests were able to continue their work only under special "state consent" accompanied with "pledge of alliance to the regime of people's democracy". Failure to obtain it resulted also in administrative or criminal prosecution.

The Communist regime also prepared a series of trials of clergy. The Archbishops of Prague and Olomouc, Josef Beran and Josef Karel Matocha respectively, as well as all other bishops were interned. Two political trials, one in the Czech lands and the other in Slovakia, with Catholic clergy, including some bishops, followed before the State Court in 1950 and 1951.[402] The allegations included cooperation with the Holy See against the interests of the Soviet Bloc, collaboration with Germans during WWII, and, especially, a hostile attitude towards the People's Democracy. In April 1950 the so-called "Action Monasteries" resulted in the closing down of convents and religious communities, and 2,376 monks and nuns were interned. It was clear that the Communists regarded the Catholic Church (and religion as such) as its chief ideological opponent.

There were also "minor" or "follow up" trials with priests, students of theology or Catholic intellectuals. It is estimated that the State Court had dealt with the cases of at least 280 priests by the end of 1952.

399 For the background see Brown, A.: *Airmen in Exile: The Allied Air Forces in the Second World War*. Sutton Pub Limited, 2000.
400 From wider historical context see especially Bušek, V.: *State and Church*: In: Bušek, V – Spulber, N. (eds.): *Czechoslovakia. East-Central Europe under the Communists*. Mid-European Studies Center of the Free Europe Committee. New York: F. A. Praeger, 1957, pp. 130 and following, especially pp. 148–153. See also Böhmer, A. – Kočvara, S. – Nosek, J.: *Church and State in Czechoslovakia*. In: Gsovski, V. (ed.): *Church and State behind the Iron Curtain*. New York: F. A. Praeger, 1955, pp. 37 and following.
401 English translation of Czechoslovak laws on Church affaires from 14th October 1949. *Ibidem*, pp. 40–45
402 *Ibidem*, pp. 37–40.

It should be noted that there were purges within the ranks of the Communist Party. These formed part of the wider course of action pursued by the Soviets in all other people's democratic regimes, including the trials of Laslo Rajk in Hungary and Wladyslaw Gomulka in Poland.[403] The purges came late to Czechoslovakia, but they were executed fiercely. Soviet advisers, two of them personally connected with the purges in Hungary, were sent to Prague to help the Czechoslovak State Security prepare trials.[404]

In the spring of 1950, the Slovak communists Gustav Husák and Clementis were accused of "bourgeois nationalism" and, in the case of Clementis, also of disloyalty to the USSR, as he had criticized the Hitler-Stalin Pact of 1939.[405] Another party conspiracy group was uncovered in Brno, where Regional Party Leader Otto Sling was arrested in October 1950.[406] Since the interrogators and their Soviet advisers became worried that they were not able to construct a sufficiently strong case, they looked for someone from the very top of the Communist leadership to please Stalin's paranoia. In the end Rudolf Slánský, Secretary General of the Communist Party, was chosen as a suitable candidate for this "monster trial."[407] He was arrested on 24th November 1951, and the preparation for the trial took almost a year. Proceedings were carefully planned in advance, and the accused had to plead guilty and to even rehearse a written script of their answers before the court. A group of the alleged "espionage, anti-state centre" headed by Slánský was formed by the Secret Police and consisted of fourteen high rank communists, eleven of them of Jewish origin.[408] This again served the Soviet foreign policy well, because members of the conspiracy centre were accused of Zionism, Trotskyism, cooperation with imperialistic powers, and of causing damage to the national economy (in order to find someone responsible for the economic failures of the first five-year economic plan).[409] The trial opened in November 1952. It was broadcasted live by Czechoslovak radio. The result and the main scenario of the process were resolved in advance by the Central Committee of the Communist Party and the investigators used brutal interrogation methods. The process

403 Kaplan, K.: *Report on the Murder of the General Secretary*, pp. 7–25, and Cotic, M: *The Prague Trial*, pp. 9–21.
404 Pelikán, J. (ed.): *The Czechoslovak Political Trials 1950-1954*, p. 130. K. Kaplan also claims that purges were personally influenced by Stalin, Cotic, M: *The Prague Trial*, pp. 27–37.
405 Pelikán, J.:(ed.): *The Czechoslovak Political Trials 1950-1954*, pp. 87–89.
406 Cotic, M: *The Prague Trial*, pp. 22–23.
407 Táborský, E.: *Communism in Czechoslovakia: 1948-1960*, pp. 95–96.
408 Pelikán, J. (ed.): *The Czechoslovak Political Trials 1950-1954*, pp. 48–50. For personal experience see Kovaly, H. *Under a Cruel Star: A Life in Prague 1941-1968*. Cambridge Mas: Plunkett Lake Press, 1986, pp. 140–143.
409 Pelikán, J. (ed.): *The Czechoslovak Political Trials 1950-1954*, pp. 179 and following. See also Loebl, E.: *Sentenced and Tried, The Stalinist Purges in Czechoslovakia*. London: Elek Books, 1969, pp. 78–80, where Loebl claims that he was accused also because he negotiated the compensation for foreign investors (especially Unilever) for nationalized property.

was a plain "show trial" rehearsed in advance. As a result, eleven death penalties and three lifelong imprisonments were adjudicated.[410]

The total number of victims of the communist repression has been estimated at 250,000 to 280,000. Between October 1948 and the end of 1952, 233 death penalties were passed and 178 persons executed, 90 percent of them for political offences.[411] Death penalties in 22 politically motivated cases were executed between 1954 and 1956, during which time the cases were reviewed by the Political Secretariat of the Central Committee of the Communist Party. It is estimated that at the end of 1949 more than 6,700 people were in prison for political offences under the Act on the Protection of the Republic; in December 1950 the number was increased to almost 15,000. The State Police arrested about 16,000 people between 1951 and 1952.[412]

There were other forms of persecution, including administrative, property, or economic consequences, or persecution through discrimination in labour law and social security. After February 1948 persecution was aimed at university students and their non-Communist teachers. Most of them were expelled from universities. There was a possibility that some politically motivated punishments took the form of sentences for economic crimes, such as in some cases of persecution of the Catholic clergy or the former owners of nationalized enterprises; this feature returned, although in a different role, in the 1970s and 1980s.

A typical form of persecution in the early 1950s was connected with the phenomena of forced labour camps.[413] The Act on Forced Labour Camps (No. 247/1948 Sb.) was enacted on 25th October 1948.[414] It established special boards (commissions) within regional national committees consisting of three members appointed by the Ministry of the Interior. The boards were entrusted with the authority to confine to forced labour camps "persons who were not younger than 18 and not older than 60 years and who were physically and mentally capable of working, but who have evaded work or endangered the establishment of the people's democratic order or economic life..." The Act on Forced Labour Camps represented, on the one hand, a specific result of the duty to work set by the Constitution and, on the other, an effective tool of persecution. Its aim was to re-socialize persons considered detrimental to the "new society", including even persons who did not commit any crime.

---

410 Kaplan, K.: *Report on the Murder of the General Secretary*, pp. 227–236 and Loebl, E.: *Sentenced and Tried*, documents on the trial, pp. 82–242.
411 Pelikán, J. (ed.): *The Czechoslovak Political Trials 1950–1954*, p. 36.
412 *Ibidem.*
413 Forced labour was a typical feature of Stalinist period. International Labour Organization in 1952 set an Ad hoc Committee on forced labour. International League for the Rights of Man prepared a comparative report published in 1955 under the title *Forced labour in People's Democracies* by editor Richard L. Carlton. New York: F. A. Praeger, 1955.
414 *Ibidem*, part devoted to Czechoslovakia, pp. 111–140.

The forced labour camps had a certain tradition in Austro-Hungary, within the interwar period and during retribution, when institutions forcing certain categories of people to work for a set term were combined with duties imposed upon them after they were released from jail. However, after 1948 forced labour camps reached a different stage and extent.

The boards of regional national committees were authorized to send persons to a forced labour camp for a period from three months to two years. The same boards could decide on some other restrictions. The boards had the power to prohibit such persons from staying in a particular place or order them to stay in a particular place, to order them to vacate their flats, deprive them of their business license, or to introduce national administration or confiscation of their property.

Persons were sent to labour camps even without having committed a particular offence. The Act was very elastic, and a decision could be, for example, taken only for "intentionally evading work, a negative attitude towards constructive work or building socialism". It applied to offenders after they had served a term in prison, and when they appeared to the regime to remain "hostile towards the State" further means applied. The whole concept was heavily based on the new ideology, and the Act was viewed as a means of "effective struggle against the remnants of the capitalist society endeavouring to restore capitalism, or at least to try to slow down or render more difficult our way to socialism."

The camps were established by the Ministry of the Interior. By the end of 1949 there were fifteen camps, and more were established between 1950 and 1951.[415] A special labour camp was established for military personnel; forced labour continued to be used as a part of imprisonment, especially in cases of political offences. Harsh conditions existed in camps built near heavy industrial centres. The Ministry prepared detailed instructions for regional national committees to implement the law. Upon proposals from the police, organizations of the National Front and individual "trustworthy" citizens, the security officers of the respective national committee prepared a list of "candidates" for labour camps and submitted it to the board. Any potential appeal against a decision of the board did not have a suspensory effect.

In 1950 the forced labour camps were incorporated into the new Administrative Criminal Procedure Code. According to this code, camps were intended for the "real class enemies of the working people", and punishment in the form of forced labour was expanded to cover misdemeanours. Some of the forced labour camps were situated also near uranium mines. On 22nd December 1953 (with effect from January 1954) most of the provisions for labour camps as well as the provisions of the Administrative Criminal Code on this type of

415 For the map and list of the camps *Ibidem*, pp. 132–140.

punishment were repealed by Act No.102/1953 Sb. Most new provisions provided for correctional labour without confinement in the camps combined with fines.[416]

After their shocking experience with political trials and after the end of the period of Stalinism, the Czechoslovak Communists came up with proposals to change the penal proceeding and some aspects of substantive criminal law in 1956 and not to repeat such open misuse of police powers. The institution of investigators attached either to the office of prosecutor (state prosecutor) or the Ministry of the Interior was introduced; however, this fell short of the previous guarantees of an investigating judge. These procedural innovations were again mainly copied from the Soviet criminal procedure laws.

An extraordinary remedy under both criminal and civil proceedings open to the Prosecutor General was introduced. He could lodge an appeal with the Supreme Court on the final decision of any court not subject to regular appeal in order to correct a violation of law, or against the decision of a prosecutor. In 1956 conditions for this extraordinary remedy were set in more detail; and the reason for this remedy was given that the decision at issue "violated law", was issued "on the basis of an improper procedure", or, in criminal law, when the penalty imposed was in "obvious disproportion to the degree of the dangerousness of the act to the society". However, such an extraordinary remedy was used also to the defendant's disadvantage; as a legal institution it was far from being supportive of the stability and predictability of the legal order.

After 1956 the Communist Party was forced to review some of the injustices committed during political trials;[417] however, in the beginning, rehabilitation was opened mainly for "purged" members of the Communist Party. The majority of political prisoners could apply for parole, and, eventually, amnesty was promulgated in 1960. A more thorough rehabilitation and condemnation of the political trials was demanded by Czechoslovak society especially in the second half of the 1960s as part of the emerging Prague Spring of 1968.[418]

---

416 *Ibidem*, pp. 118–119.
417 It was a part of wider political changes within the Soviet block reflected by the Czechoslovak communists. See interesting analyses in Kusin, V. V.: *The Intellectual origins of the Prague Spring. The Development of reformist ideas in Czechoslovakia 1956–1967.* Cambridge University Press, 1971, especially pp. 19–22 and 28–30.
418 Pelikán, J. (ed.): *The Czechoslovak Political Trials 1950–1954*, pp. 148 and following.

/22/
Changes in land law – forced collectivization

Immediately after the 1948 February coup the National Assembly enacted a series of Agricultural Acts, including the Act on the Second Land Reform No. 46/1948 Sb. The Constitution promised to leave land to those who work on it under the condition that the land did not exceed 50 hectares.[419]

In the autumn of 1948 the Communist Party leadership re-thought its original concept of agricultural policy and launched a strategy of socialization of villages to be built upon people's cooperative farms and large scale agricultural production based on the Soviet model.[420]

Beginning in 1949 Uniform Agricultural Cooperatives, as a new legal entity, were promoted in conjunction with the state owned farms and special tractor and farm machinery stations (abolished in 1960), following again the Soviet example. The legal basis for cooperatives was enacted in February 1949. Cooperatives had to adopt their statutes in accordance with model bylaws

---

419 See official governmental publication Koťátko, J.: *Czechoslovak Land Reform*. Prague: Orbis, 1948, which included also previous legislation from 1947.
420 Gsovski, V. – Grzybowski, K. (eds.): *Government Law and Courts in the Soviet Union and Eastern Europe*. Vol. II, part VII, Law and Peasant, Czechoslovakia, pp. 1757–1785.

adopted by the Central Council of Cooperatives and approved by the Ministry of Agriculture.

In the beginning, the Communist Party emphasized the voluntary character of cooperative membership, although joining cooperatives seemed to be more advantageous from an economic perspective. Simultaneously, stricter and stricter demands were imposed on peasants resisting cooperative membership: they had to fulfil compulsory delivery quotas of agricultural products (originally introduced during the war years) to the state agencies.[421]

It was evident quite soon that educational, propaganda and economic methods alone were not working, and various forms of persuasion including coercion were applied, especially with respect to larger and medium sized farmers. The Ministry of Agriculture and national committees became responsible for speeding up collectivization in their respective regions.

From 1950 a new political line spoke about larger farmers (sometimes having only 20 hectares) in terms of being class enemies of the People's Democratic order, and the Soviet expression "kulak" was used to identify class enemies in the countryside. In February 1951 an even harder line was introduced, and those who refused to join cooperatives were subject to larger obligatory quotas of production to be delivered to the state; in most cases administrative and penal punishments and persecution of various kinds were imposed.

Deportations, fines and criminal prosecution were applied if contractual duties to deliver higher and higher quotas of agricultural products were not fulfilled. Repeated failure was often followed by political trials, as the kulaks were sometimes accused of sabotage or even high treason. They were usually sentenced to a long term in prison, including confiscation of their property and a prohibition from staying (together with all their family) in the region where their farms were located.

This "action K" (Action Kulak), based on the instructions issued by the Ministry of the Interior, Ministry of National Security and the Ministry of Justice, was directed against wealthy farmers as class enemies, deprived them of various human and civic rights, subjected their property to confiscation, forced them to leave their regions, and their children were not allowed to study at secondary schools and universities.

From 1953 the Ministry of Agriculture tried to solve many economic problems of the whole system of cooperatives, especially to improve their management, because many of them were economically ineffective and were close to bankruptcy. The Ministry also introduced a new legal form of Standardized Charters for the cooperatives.[422] It was not only necessary to punish

421 Bušek, V. – Spulber. N. (eds.): Czechoslovakia, pp. 253–254.
422 For its text in English see Kočvara, Š.: The Sovietization of Czechoslovak farming. Standard Charter of the Unified Agricultural Cooperative in Czechoslovakia of February 17, 1953, Mid European Law Project, Library of Congress, Washington, 1954, part B.

those opposing cooperatives but also to assist the cooperatives to improve their economic outcomes. As a result of changes forty percent of arable land was, in 1953, controlled by cooperatives, in addition to fourteen percent of land owned by state farms. In 1956 and 1957 a new wave of collectivization was launched, and the process was virtually completed by 1958. The number of cooperative farms found its peak in 1960, where the majority of land (almost ninety percent) was part of the "socialist sector". The importance of cooperatives in the communist ideology and the Soviet model gave rise to discussions within academia in the 1950s resulting in the establishment of a new branch of law called agricultural cooperative law. Cooperatives formed the basis of Czechoslovak agriculture, and the process of concentration of agricultural production in even bigger units began in the early 1960s.

/23/
<u>Social security and labour law</u>

Fundamental changes were brought to the system of social security and labour law. During the period between 1945 and 1948 the pre-war system, with some changes in unemployment security, continued. It was still a Bismarckian system of social security, adapted to the Austrian and later Czechoslovak environments. Immediately after February 1948 steps were taken to introduce a universal welfare state protecting all citizens, and not only those who were insured; this was inspired by the programme of the British reformer William Beveridge and Acts on National Insurance and on National Assistance proposed by Attlee's Labour Government. It was called a national insurance scheme and was accepted by the Communists as their own programme.[423] It was embodied in Act No. 99/ 1948 Sb. However, after 1951 the process of reforming the national insurance in order to establish the Soviet scheme of social security was launched.[424] The reform was completed

---

423 In more details see Hrachová, S.: *Social Security and National Insurance Act in Postwar Czechoslovakia (1945–1948)*. In: Prague Economic and Social History Papers. Prague: fakulty of Arts, Charles University, vol. 13/ 2011, pp. 30–44.
424 See for example *80 Years of Social Insurance*, Czech Social Security Administration 2004, p. 25 and in more details De Denken, J.-J.: *Social Policy in Postwar Czechoslovakia. The Development*

by 1956. It represented a gradual disintegration of insurance principles, and the replacement of these with a state-paternalistic model in accordance with the Soviet pattern. For example Act No. 102/ 1951 Sb. stipulated that sickness insurance was newly administered by the Revolutionary Trade Unions together with employers.

The social protection of the population was financed thoroughly from the state budget. The decline of living standards, caused both by huge investments into heavy industry and by the influence of the Monetary Reform implemented in 1953, accelerated the efforts to improve the quality of life of the population by means of growing consumption. In the years following a repeated drop in prices and a partial improvement in supplies could be traced. In 1956 new laws were passed for retirement pensions and health insurance. These represented the final stage in adopting the Soviet model of social security that had been initiated in the beginning of the 1950s.

Some branches of social law (especially health care) were based on high and effective standards; other policies, like housing, were less successful. The system of nationalized, centrally planned economy was incapable of satisfying the increasing demands of citizens in social care; this trend worsened even more during the later decades of the communist dictatorship. Most of the provisions in both the Constitution and social security laws therefore remained mere proclamations.

An interesting development was seen in labour law. Although the Constitution of May 1948 proclaimed new provisions for employment, it should be noted that labour law as such remained uncodified throughout the whole period of the 1950s, even though there were several attempts to pass a brand new Labour Code in compliance with the socialist ideology. Instead, the provisions for labour contracts of the Austrian Civil Code still remained in force. Nevertheless elements of private law in labour contracts were diminished. Labour law dealt mainly with the practical application of the duty to work connected with the implementation of new goals set by Five-Year Plans. New provisions of Czechoslovak labour law therefore dealt with the distribution of the work force and penalties. For example, the 1953 Governmental Decree on Absenteeism and Job-hopping tried to solve the shortage of workers through repressive measures.[425] There were attempts to send administrative employees to help industry as manual workers and to implement a strict system of placing medical doctors, technicians and teachers immediately after their graduation to satisfy the needs of individual regions. The shortage of workers

---

of *Old-Age Pensions and Housing Policies During the Period 1945–1989*, European University Institute working papers in political and social sciences, Florence, 1994, pp. 73 and following.

425 See English summary in Státník, D.: *Sankční pracovní právo v padesátých letech: vládní nařízení o opatřeních proti fluktuaci a absenci č. 52/1953 Sb.*. Prague: Ústav pro soudobé dějiny, 1994, pp. 174–176.

in certain branches of industry and agriculture led to launching a system of compulsory as well as voluntary work by students during their studies at both secondary schools and universities.

Labour law dealt with the increased role of trade unions especially in securing the improvement of working conditions or settlement of disputes arising from labour contracts. New provisions concerning safety and health at work were adopted, and the regime tried to improve the social conditions of workers, including a paid leave or holidays, organized by the trade union organizations. The best workers were publicly awarded special honours; a competition for the best results at work, in accordance with the Soviet style "Stachanov movement" (named after Aleksey Grigorevich *Stachanov*, a coal miner in Soviet Donetsk Basin in the 1930s),[426] was promoted.

426 See instructive propaganda brochure by Stakhanov himself designed by the USSR Government for distribution at the 1939 New York World's Fair: *The Stakhanov Movement Explained by Its Initiator Alexei Stakhanov.* Moscow, 1939.

/24/
The Socialist Constitution of 1960

The Constitution of the Czechoslovak Socialist Republic was enacted by the National Assembly as Constitutional Act No. 100/1960 Sb. on 11th July 1960.[427] The National Assembly met in the Vladislav Hall of the historic Prague Castle and the document was approved ceremoniously and unanimously. It was prepared by the Communist Party bodies, which decided that the draft of the Constitution would be discussed within the National Front and with the people; nevertheless the discussion was a mere formality.

The Constitution consisted of an initial Declaration and nine Chapters. The Constitution was heavily influenced by ideology, and the communist regime openly described its foundation. It was a constitution of the socialist state in accordance with the Soviet pattern of 1936.[428]

---

427 For English translation se Bulletin of Czechoslovak law,, No. 1–2, Union of Lawyers of the Czechoslovak Socialist Republic, Prague, 1960, pp. 19 and following with commentaries and speeches by A. Novotný and Deputy Secretary of the Central Committee of the Communist Party J. Hendrych and *Constitution of the Czechoslovak Socialist Republic*. Prague: Orbis, 1960.
428 See commentary in Bulletin of Czechoslovak law, No. 1–2, 1960, pp. 28–32. See also Skilling, H, G.: *The Czechoslovak Constitution of 1960 and the Transition to Communism*. The Journal of Politics. New York, XXIV, No. 1 (February, 1962), especially pp. 142–146.

The semi-democratic facade of the 1948 Constitution was abandoned.[429] This was clearly visible in the introductory Declaration. The Declaration was made in the name of the working people of Czechoslovakia and declared that "Socialism has triumphed in this country under the leadership of the Communist Party of Czechoslovakia". Its aim was to construct even a more advanced socialist society and to lay down the foundations and "to gather strength" for Communism. The Declaration mentioned the friendly alliance and union with the Soviet Union and other countries of its block.[430]

The Declaration provided an ideological view of the development after 1945 and 1948; the socialist stage of social development was depicted as a possibility to create a harmonic relationship between Czechs and Slovaks.

Chapter One dealt with the definition of the socialist social order. The socialist state was, according to its Article 1, "a state of workers, farmers and working intelligentsia headed by the working class"; the Communist Party was the leader of the working class. The Constitution was officially based on the principle that the power belonged to the working people, who exercised it through constitutional bodies. However, the Constitution tried to establish the socialist principle of more activeness, initiative and direct participation of the working people and their organizations in the exercise of power within the state together with its representative bodies. The Constitution stated that the transfer of part of the responsibilities of the state to the Revolutionary Trade Unions and other socialist organizations of the National Front was possible.

In other respects the Constitution was centralistic, with most power vested in the centre of the state, with the exception of a certain degree of autonomy for Slovak bodies.

The most important ideological and political indoctrination in the Constitution was represented in Article 4, which stipulated the leadership role of and guiding force of the Communist Party within the Czechoslovak state and society. The Communist Party was depicted as a "combative association of the most active and most politically conscious citizens from the rank of workers, farmers and working intelligentsia". The system of the National Front headed by the Communist Party was for the first time officially approved at the constitutional level.

The socialist system was also defined from the economic point of view. It was based on the exclusion of exploitation of workers, re-emphasized successful changes in ownership structures, including nationalization and collectivization; these along with central planning and labour for the benefit

---

429 Táborský, E.: *Communism in Czechoslovakia: 1948–1960*, pp. 180–182.
430 It should be noted that Czechoslovakia was from 1955 loyal member of the Warsaw Pact. Skilling, H. G.: *The Governments of Communist East Europe*, pp. 218–219 and Johnson, R. A.: *The Warsaw Pact: Soviet Military Policy in Eastern Europe*. In: Terry, S. M. (ed.) *Soviet Policy in Eastern Europe*. New Haven: Yale University Press, 1984, pp. 255–284.

of the society were stipulated as the main features of the socialist economic system.

The 1960 Constitution enacted a new definition of socialist ownership,[431] having two basic forms: (a) state ownership (called national property) and (b) the ownership of people's cooperatives (especially uniform agricultural cooperatives). National enterprises were established for the administration of national property. Private ownership was limited only to small businesses based upon the labour of the owner, and exploitation of another's labour was prohibited. The Constitution, on the other hand, promoted and legally protected citizens' personal ownership of consumer goods, especially articles for domestic and personal use, family houses, and savings generated by their labour. It guaranteed inheritance only of this kind of property.

The Constitution determined basic conditions for long-term economic planning and considered the economy as the foundation to its ideological, political and social plans, including a predicted rise of the social standard of living and a gradual reduction of working hours. It should be emphasized that, from a constitutional perspective, the 1960 Constitution enabled Czechoslovakia to take part in the Council of Mutual Economic Assistance (CMEA), established in 1949; as a result, it stipulated the principle of the international socialist division of labour.[432]

Another example of the ideological indoctrination of the Czechoslovak Constitution of 1960 was Article 16, regulating cultural, educational and scientific policies. The entire cultural policy and all forms of education were directed in "the spirit of scientific world opinion – Marxism-Leninism" and closely "linked to the life and work of the people". The Communist Party and the whole regime openly declared that they wished to achieve the goal that the "minds" of the Czechoslovak people "be liberated from surviving influences of a society based on exploitation".

The Constitution contained another key mantra of socialist law, so-called socialist legality. It was described as a duty of citizens, state and socialist organizations to direct all their activities in accordance with the legal order of the socialist state; particularly, the people's organizations of the National Front were obliged to guide the citizens to uphold the law, to maintain the work discipline and the principles of socialist conduct. The respective chapters of the Constitution show that especially this provision influenced new codifications of criminal and civil law and brought, to a certain extent, an idealistic approach towards the functioning of certain parts of socialist legislation.

---

431 See again a chief Czech expert in this question Knapp, V.: *Questions of Ownership in the New Constitution of the Czechoslovak Socialist Republic.* In: Bulletin of Czechoslovak law, No. 1–2, 1960, pp. 46–50.
432 For the establishment of CMEA and its first period see Grzybowski, K.: *The Socialist Commonwealth of Nations: Organizations and Institutions.* Yale University Press, 1964, pp. 64–75. See also Skilling, H. G.: *The Governments of Communist East Europe*, pp. 218–226.

Chapter Two dealt with the rights and duties of citizens.[433] The socialist character of the state was expressed by a new view of the rights and freedoms of citizens, which were seen in connection with the development of the whole society. The individualistic and liberal concept of civic rights and freedoms was superseded in favour of a collectivistic one.[434] Article 19 expressly stated that "in a society of working people the individual can fully develop his capabilities and assert his true interests only through his active participation in the development of the society as a whole and particularly by undertaking an appropriate share of social work". Therefore work in the interest of the community was proclaimed as a primary duty and the right to work a primary right of every citizens.

The Constitution formally guaranteed the equality of all citizens without regard to nationality and race, but no special protection of minorities was enacted. The socialist character of the Constitution was strengthened by putting the social rights first, including the right to work, to remuneration for work according to its quantity, quality and social importance, to the protection of health and free medical care, as well as to leisure time after work. Social rights included material welfare during old age and during incapacity to work, together with free education. The Constitution pointed out that socialist countries did not experience economic crises and unemployment. Maternity, marriage and family were protected by the state. Article 27 expressly stated that the equal status of women within a family, at work and in public life should be secured by special adjustment of working conditions and special health care during maternity and pregnancy.

Yet again, the main problem of the Constitution subsisted in the contrast between its proclamations and the actual implementation of civic rights in practice. Freedom of speech and press were limited not only by practice and laws enacted for its implementation (for example laws on Czechoslovak Radio and Television adopted in 1964), but also by a new provision in the Constitution, that such civic rights should be consistent with the interests of the working people. In 1966 a new Act on Periodical Press and other mass-media No 81/1966 Sb. was enacted. This Act declared the educative role of the media in the socialist manner and in accordance with the "leading role" of the Communist Party stipulated in Article 4 of the Constitution. In order to protect the interests of the socialist society, a Central Publishing Authority was established, which was entrusted with the right of preliminary censorship. Documents to be published in newspapers were submitted to the Authority. According to a special Governmental Order No. 119/1966 Sb., on the Charter of the Central Publishing Authority, this authority could decide whether a

---

433 From the socialist point of view see Moural, J.: *Rights and Duties as Stated in the New Constitution of the Czechoslovak Socialist Republic.* In: Bulletin of Czechoslovak law, No. 1–2, 1960, pp. 53 and following.
434 Táborský, E.: *Communism in Czechoslovakia: 1948–1960*, pp. 181–182.

particular piece of information would or would not be published; reasons for refusal were that the respective document was "contrary to the political and ideological line" of the Government and the Communist Party or "detrimental to the interests of the society", i.e. against the socialist order.

Similarly, the socialist character of the state and the system of the National Front limited the freedom of assembly, to hold public marches and demonstrations. The Constitution promised other individual freedoms, like inviolability of the person, inviolability of home, and the privacy of mails. In an attempt to promote more activity within the society the Constitution stated that citizens and organizations had the right to submit their proposals, suggestions and complaints to representative bodies and to other bodies, and that it was the duty of state bodies to take responsible and prompt action in response of those initiatives.

The freedom of confession was accompanied by an express freedom to be without any religious beliefs. The exercise of one's religious belief should not contravene the law; religious faith or conviction could not constitute grounds for refusal to fulfil civic duties laid down by the law. The limits on religious freedoms became visible in the period after 1960 and especially 1968 in several cases of criminal prosecution related to witnesses refusing compulsory military service (conscientious objection).

Article 33 enacted a special provision for granting asylum to citizens of a foreign state "persecuted for defending the interests of working people, for participating in the national liberation movement or for activities defending peace". This enabled socialist Czechoslovakia to serve the interests of Soviet foreign policy.

The 1960 Constitution governed the duties of citizens. There were duties to defend the country and its socialist order, to endorse the Constitution and other laws, to pay attention to the interest of the socialist state and society, to protect and strengthen national property and to fulfil public functions "entrusted to them by the working people" conscientiously and honestly.

Chapters Three, Four, Five and Six regulated Constitutional bodies.[435] The Constitution deserted the theory of the division of powers; on the contrary, it applied the Soviet principle of one uniform centre of powers in the socialist state. The Constitution was centralized, and the Slovak national bodies were again restricted in their powers.[436] The real centre of power was not vested in the constitutional bodies stipulated by the Constitution, but in the Central Committee of the Communist Party.

435 See Levit, P.: *The Supreme Organs of the State in the New Constitution.* In: Bulletin of Czechoslovak law, No. 1–2, pp. 65–78.
436 Matoušek, S: *The Slovak National Council, Ibidem,* pp. 93 and following.

Chapter Seven focused on national committees as forming the basis for state power and administration at local, district and regional levels.[437] National committees were elected for a period of five years. However, the system of elections to them as resembling elections to Parliament (although they were modified by the so called imperative mandate of a deputy) [438] was becoming a farce. Although the Constitution provided for active participation of local citizens in the activities of national committee, they were mainly bodies of state direction and administration as regards general internal administration and various other administrative matters.[439] The Constitution expressly stipulated the manner for planning of the development of their respective territories and the importance of economic, cultural and social development of the communities. On the other hand, the interests of the whole society stood, according to the Constitution, above local or partial interests.

Competences of national committees were reflected in their binding orders. A national committees, headed by a chairman, established their executive council, commissions and other bodies. National committees at a superior level directed, guided and supervised the activities of national committees at a lower level; the whole system was supervised by the Government and individual ministries. The Government or national committees at a superior level could even annul a decision of the respective national committee at a lower level if it was in contradiction not only with the law or governmental directives but also with directives of the superior national committee. This helped the centralization of the whole country and of the system as implemented by three special laws in 1954 (Acts No. 12–14/1954 Sb.) which laid down its foundations and which, with certain reforms in 1967 and 1968 and again in the late 1980s, survived until the end of the communist regime in 1989.

Chapter Eight dealt with the judiciary and the Office of the Prosecutor. They were both entrusted with the protection of the socialist state, its social order and the rights of citizens and of organizations of the working people. The ideological indoctrination was apparent in the duty of courts and prosecutors to educate the citizens to be loyal to their country and Socialism, to abide by the laws and rules of socialist conduct, and to honourably fulfil their duties towards the state and the society.

The Constitution set elective and independent courts. The feature of electing judges helped to strengthen the loyalty of professional judges, since they

---

437 Jičínský, Z: *National committees in the New Constitution of the Czechoslovak Socialist Republic.* Ibidem, pp. 79–92.

438 In theory it meant that the deputies should be in permanent contact with their voters and that voters could recall the deputy on any time Krejčí, O.: *History of Elections in Bohemia and Moravia*, p. 220.

439 See also Kočvara, Š.: *Czechoslovakia: Local Councils (People's Committees) at the Village Level (outline of Principal Laws)*. Washington: Library of Congress, 1956.

were elected for a term of ten years by national committees, and the judges of the Supreme Court elected by the National Assembly.[440]

Judicial independence meant that judges were bound by the legal order of the socialist state and that they were expected to interpret laws in the spirit of socialist legality. Professional judges usually sat as single judges or as person in charge of panels consisting of professional and lay judges. The Constitution set basic principles for court proceedings, which were later used for the new codification of civil and criminal procedure. This part of the Constitution was implemented by special Act No. 62/1961 Sb., on the Organization of Courts, which was replaced in 1964 by Act No. 36/1964 Sb., on the Organization of Courts and Election of Judges.

The Office of the Prosecutor was entrusted with supervision over the precise fulfilment and observance of the laws and other legal regulations by ministries and other bodies of state administration, national committees, courts, national enterprises and other economic entities and by individual citizens. The system of Offices of Prosecutor was headed by the Prosecutor General, appointed and recalled by the President of the Republic. In addition, there were special military prosecutors. Initiatives for the working people and their organizations and cooperation with these were proposed as a new feature of socialist prosecutors. In practice, they remained loyal and frightful watchdogs of the communist regime.

Chapter Nine, general and final provisions changed the state emblem of the Czechoslovak Socialist Republic to a new one consisting of a red escutcheon in the form of a Hussite shield with a five-pointed star in the upper part, with a white, two tailed lion bearing a red shield on its chest showing a blue outline of the Slovak Kriváň mountain and a golden fire of freedom. It was a classic example of the misuse of Czech and Slovak national history for the communists' sake.[441]

440 Kühn, Z.: *The Judiciary in Central and Eastern Europe. Mechanical Jurisprudence in Transformation?*, pp. 60–62.
441 Sedláček, P.: *Symbols of the Czech Republic, Prague*: Office of the Czech Government, 2007, pp. 15 and 21. See also History of the Czech national emblem, Government of the Czech Republic. *www.vlada.cz/en/.../1---the-oldest-history-19169*.

/25/

Recodification of criminal law in the 1960s

During the 1960s the communist system gradually took on a more liberal facade but this was still heavily based on ideology. After the 1960 Socialist Constitution had been enacted the leadership of the Communist Party proclaimed its main political goal in the field of law, namely that new codes would be enacted in order to reflect the socialist character of society.

The meeting of the Central Committee of the Communist Party in December 1960 highlighted the necessity to change criminal law. A new proposal of the Criminal Code was ready relatively quickly by the summer of 1961.[442] Even though there was continuity with the principles of criminal law laid down in 1950, the open form of the dictatorship of proletariat was replaced by a "milder" form of repression, as well as by an "educational" concept of criminal law related to the socialist period, particularly where "education" aimed at the fulfilment of civic duties was concerned. The Criminal Code ceased to be seen primarily as a tool used to suppress political opponents of the regime, and general criminological aspects were highlighted. A declining number of crim-

---

442 See leading Czech specialist in criminal law Solnař, V.: *The Conditions of Criminal liability under the new Czechoslovak Penal Code of 1961*. Bulletin of Czechoslovak Law. Prague: Union of Czechoslovak Lawyers, 1961, No. 2–4, pp. 1–9.

inal offences committed, if compared with the interwar period and even with the 1950s, was used by the communist regime as an example of the success of the socialist society. The codification was again influenced by the Soviet experience – this time from its "socialist period".

The Czechoslovak Criminal Code of 1961 (Act No. 140/1961 Sb.) was divided into three main parts: Part One, the General Part, dealt with definitions and general terminology concerning the crime and punishment. Part Two, the Special Part, classified individual groups of crimes and punishments set for them. Part Three contained transitional and final provisions.

The purpose of the Criminal Code and of the whole of socialist criminal law was to protect the interests of the state, the social and economic foundations of the Czechoslovak Socialist Republic, socialist ownership, and the rights and legitimate interests of individuals. It was expressly stated that criminal law was not only intended for the punishment of offenders but had also an educational objective in accordance with "the rules of socialist cohabitation between citizens".

A crime (referred to as a "criminal act") was defined as an act which was dangerous to the society and its elements were laid down in the Code. It was a combination of formal and dangerousness criteria.[443] The commission of a crime required an intent and the culpability of the offender to be proven, unless it was expressly stipulated that an act committed by negligence was considered a crime.

However, an act representing only a negligible danger to the society did not constitute a crime. Conduct determined as "less dangerous to the society" was dealt with in the Administrative Transgression Act and other laws authorizing national committees or special People's Courts to impose punishment upon the transgressor. Criminal liability was applicable to an offender who was at least 15 years of age and of sound mind. Offenders between 15 and 18 were referred to as "juveniles" and were subject to more tolerant conditions for determining their criminal liability and for sentencing.

The degree of danger to the society (i.e. "material elements" of a crime) corresponded to the importance of protected interests affected by a criminal act, the manner in which the act was committed and its consequences, the circumstances under which the act was committed, the personality of the offender, the degree of his or her culpability and/or motives behind the act. The debates on the proposal of the Code in the National Assembly resulted in the inclusion of an interpretive possibility for judges to consider the danger caused to the society according to the existing situation within the society and the degree of the development of social relations. This flexible clause enabled the communist regime to use the same code in a quite liberal way in the 1960s, as well as for severe persecution after the reform movement of the

---

443 *Ibidem.*

Prague Spring was crushed and the period of so-called normalization in the 1970s and 1980s followed.[444]

The types of punishment which could be imposed under the new Czechoslovak Criminal Code were the death penalty, imprisonment, deprivation of honorary titles and awards, deprivation of military rank, prohibition from undertaking a certain activity (including the prohibition against drinking alcohol, or deprivation of one's driving licence), fines, forfeiture of property, forfeiture of a particular item of property, expulsion and prohibition from staying at a particular place.

The Code provided for a suspended or unsuspended term of imprisonment to be imposed. An example of the "educative" aim of the Code was the possibility to not impose a penalty if a particular court hearing appeared to be sufficient for the correction of an offender. A term of imprisonment could be converted into instalment payments of a fine to be deducted from the offender's wage. A suspended term of imprisonment was usually connected with a guarantee pledged to the court by a socialist organization, like a trade union or youth organization.

The death penalty was reserved for crimes showing an "extremely high danger to the society", including high treason, terror, sabotage, espionage and murder. As an exceptional punishment a term of imprisonment for 15 to 25 years or a life sentence could be imposed. The experience of political trials from the 1950s led to a more cautious attitude towards the death penalty.

Part Two, the Special Part, contained provisions for individual crimes and their respective punishments and was subdivided into twelve chapters. The chapters again reflected the higher significance attached to the protection of the state, economic and social system more than to the protection of the interests of individual citizens.

Chapter One provided for crimes against the Republic and was subdivided into three subchapters. The most serious crimes were high treason, along with subversion of the Republic, terror, and sabotage committed in connection "with a foreign power".

In practice the communist regime often used a new crime of destabilizing the Republic to punish its remaining political opponents. This crime was especially important in the prosecution of the dissident movement in the 1970s and 1980s, as its elements were set in a very flexible manner. It was required to prove an offender's hostile attitude towards the socialist system and his or her intention to destabilize the social and state arrangements of socialist Czechoslovakia. It was usually connected with the crime of public incitement and public campaigning against the Republic and its representatives. It should be noted that, because of the leading role of the Communist Party, stipulated

444 See for example Riese, H. P.: *Since the Prague Spring: The Continuing Struggle for Human Rights in Czechoslovakia*, Random House, 1979, pp. 41–53.

in the 1960 Constitution, the Chairman of the Communist Party was regarded, for the purposes of prosecution, as an official representative of the Republic. The Chapter also dealt with the protection of interests of the Soviet Union and the states of the Soviet Bloc. An escape of citizens into exile was considered a specific crime against the Republic.

Chapter Two classified economic crimes. It concentrated on the protection of economic interests of the socialist sector of the economy, including central planning, socialist property, work discipline, and monetary and financial issues. For example, crimes of stealing items of socialist property were punished more severely than thefts aimed against the property of an individual. Crimes in this chapter enabled the communist regime to punish the most provoking examples of the "grey economy" or sometimes to punish political and ideological opponents of socialism to "mask" real reasons for their respective persecution.

Crimes against the public order were seen as crimes which could endanger the bodies of the socialist state, especially in the form of attacks against the representatives of the state and socialist organizations. On the other hand, this chapter of the Criminal Code made the prosecution of corruption and bribery possible. It demonstrated that corruption had become a significant feature of "real socialism" despite the optimistic forecasts.

Crimes against public order were closely linked with that group of crimes causing a general danger. Subchapter Five dealt with crimes infringing civic coexistence, and its enactment was based on the communist ideology. The aim of the Code in this respect was to fight alcoholism, public disturbances and other forms of a "parasite" lifestyle not fitting into the socialist society. In practice it was often used as a basis for persecution of those strata of the society which were unwilling to accept the new, socialist way of living. Subchapter Six, with a similar aim, contained special provisions concerning crimes against family and young people, which was an attempt to enforce the fulfilment of the duties of parents and of raising youth through criminal law.

Crimes against life and health were contained in Chapter Seven of Part Two of the Code which was intended for the protection of individual interests. The most important crimes were murder and attacks against the physical integrity of an individual. Crimes against freedom and human dignity, as well as criminal assaults and rape, were intended to protect individual rights and freedoms proclaimed by the Constitution.

Crimes against property covered illegal acts against the property of an individual, in particular robbery and theft. As suggested earlier, individual property was protected less strictly than the property of the socialist state and cooperatives.

Crimes against humanity implemented the international convention on genocide, whereas the last two chapters entitled "crimes against conscription and military crimes" were connected with the duty to serve in the army and with the special position of the criminal liability of army personnel. The link between criminal law and the Czechoslovak army represented another example of a repressive tool used by the communist regime against potential opposition from the young generation. Crimes against conscription were misused against religious movements refusing compulsory military service and against conscientious objectors.

In 1961 a new Criminal Procedure Code (Act No. 141/1961 Sb.) was enacted [445] to implement the above mentioned "new spirit" of substantive law; and that is why both codes were based on similar and complementary principles.[446] The new procedural code, to a certain extent, modified the original strict implementation of Soviet principles. The modified principles were seen as a safeguard to not repeat the worst unlawfulness of the first half of the 1950s and to implement a new educative role into the socialist stage of social development. They were, for example, intended to expand the role of employees and social organizations in criminal proceedings.

The main purpose of the new Code was to regulate procedures used by those "bodies acting in criminal proceedings", i.e. the investigative, prosecuting and adjudicating bodies (the police, prosecutors and courts), to ensure that offences were properly investigated and their perpetrators justly punished under the law. Criminal procedure was also intended to strengthen "socialist legality", to prevent and suppress criminal activities, to educate citizens to consistently abide by the law and the rules of the socialist civil coexistence and to honestly fulfil the duties they owed to the state and the socialist society.[447]

The Code stipulated basic principles of criminal procedure. It stated that no one would be prosecuted as the accused on other than legal grounds and in any other manner than that provided for under the Code, and that every person charged with an offence would be presumed innocent until proven guilty by a final judgment of conviction delivered by a court. Prosecutors had the duty to prosecute all criminal offences of which they became aware. Criminal proceedings before courts commenced only upon an indictment filed by the prosecutor. Other basic principles of criminal procedure were to carefully consider all facts of the case, to search for the objective truth, to hold public and oral proceedings. All investigative, prosecuting and adjudicating bodies had to co-operate with socialist organizations and associations of the National Front and should produce an educational impact thereon.

---

445 For its text in English see *Czechoslovakian Law on Criminal Judicial Procedure*, United States. Joint Publications Research Service, volume 13, Collection of laws of the Czechoslovakian Socialist Republic, 1962. See also alternative version in Bulletin of Czechoslovak law, No 3–4, 1962, pp. 50 and following.
446 See Přichystal, V.: *New Provisions Governing the Penal Procedure in the Czechoslovak Socialist Republic.* In: Bulletin of Czechoslovak law, No 3–4, 1962, pp. 145 and following.
447 *Ibidem.*

The decision in criminal proceedings was taken either by a panel of judges or by a single judge. Decisions made in pre-trial proceedings by a first-instance court were made by a single judge; more serious crimes and appeals were always heard by a panel.

The communist criminal law of the 1960s took on a more liberal suit of clothes and reduced the class approach. However, persecution of political and ideological opponents, as well as of young people from nonconformist strata of society, continued, and the regime applied harsher punishments, for example, for illegally leaving the country (emigration) or for economic crimes. In 1965 a new law (Act. No. 58/1965 Sb.) on a more strict punishment for social parasitism and evading work was adopted; the regime admitted that its propaganda on a new socialist epoch in the development of the Czechoslovak society was too optimistic.[448]

---

448 See for example Nezkusil, J.: *Amendment of the Czechoslovak Penal Code.* Bulletin of Czechoslovak law 1965, volumes 6–7, pp. 257 and following.

/26/
New civil law of the 1960s

The socialist character of the new social order adopted by the Constitution of 1960 had an impact upon the preparation of a new Civil Code. The proposal to amend the Civil Code of 1950 was quickly abandoned with an explanation from the Communist Party leadership that a new socialist era needed a brand new socialist Civil Code and that the 1950 Code represented a hold back. The draft was ready by 1964 and was so radical that it represented a unique example of socialist law not only in Czechoslovakia but also in comparison with other countries of the Soviet Bloc.[449]

The civil law tradition was ignored to an even greater extent if one compares it with the Civil Code of 1950.[450] It was stressed also in the initial Preamble, which closely connected the Civil Code with Socialist Constitution, Economic planning and socialist society.[451] Traditional institutions and

449 For its characteristics see Elišer, D. – Frinta, O. – Pauknerová, M.: *Recodification of Private Law in the Czech Republic*. In: Rivera, J. C. (ed.): *The Scope and Structure of Civil Codes*. Dordrecht: Springer, 2013, pp. 113–114 and 118–120.

450 See also Pauknerová, M: *Codification of Czech Private Law in the Middle and on the Outskirts of Europe*. In: *Liber Amicorum Valentinas Mikelenas*. Vilnius: Justitia, 2008, pp. 239–245.

451 *Commentary on the Czechoslovak Civil Code* by Th. J. Vondracek, Dordrecht: Martinus Nijhoff Publishers, 1988, pp. 1–2.

terms such as possession, servitudes (easements), tenancy or neighbours' rights were either transformed or disappeared entirely. Other terms like "natural persons" and legal entities were replaced with "participants in the civil relationship" and socialist organizations respectively, "proper morals" were transferred into "the rules of socialist common life". Contracts were transformed into mere "services".[452]

Moreover these changes in terminology were not the only effect of the socialist mode of codification. The Civil Code was not anticipated as a general code of civil law. On the contrary, the whole codification process of the 1960s led, in accordance with Soviet legal theory, to the disintegration of civil law into several legal branches, represented by their special acts and codes, i.e., the Family law Act, the Economic Code, the Labour Code and the International Trade Code.[453]

The Civil Code (Act No. 40/1964 Sb.) was devised mainly as a code governing proprietary and consumer relations; other aspects of private life were underrepresented in the Code. Moreover, the Civil Code implemented a large number of mandatory provisions with a limited possibility for citizens to use the autonomy of their will in individual circumstances. It was a very good example of state intervention into the private sphere of citizens as a result of the abolition of dividing legal branches into private and public law under the socialist doctrine. The third important aspect was that the Civil Code was drafted with a codification optimism towards the new socialist era based upon belief in the "higher" moral rules of socialist common life leading to the next communist phase.[454] This aim together with an attempt to "eradicate the remnants of the past in the consciousness of men" soon proved to be rather illusionary.[455]

The Civil Code of 1964 was divided into a Preamble and eight Parts. The short Preamble stressed the main ideological reasons for the enactment of the Civil Code and repeated the connection between the new socialist Constitution of 1960 and the Civil Code. It confirmed the economic foundations of the central planned economy and socialist ownership to be the keystones for civil law, which was to serve primarily for the fulfilment and satisfaction of citizens' material or cultural needs. However, the rights of citizens had to be interpreted in accordance with the interests of the whole society and the protection of rights was based on the vague term of "socialist legality".

452 Elišer, D. – Frinta, O. – Pauknerová, M.: *Recodification of Private Law in the Czech Republic*, pp. 118–119.
453 *Ibidem*.
454 See also interesting study by Ulč, O.: Class Struggle and Civil Law: The Case of Czechoslovakia. In: Rechcígl, M. (ed.): *Czechoslovakia Past and Present: Political, international, social, and economic aspects*. Volume I, Published under the auspices of the Czechoslovak Society of Arts and Sciences in America, by Mouton, 1968, pp. 537–555.
455 See again the Preamble of the Code Commentary on the Czechoslovak Civil Code by Th. J. Vondracek, pp. 1–2.

The introductory part, General Provisions, provided the definition of "civil law relationship" and its parties. It included every relationship, which was of a proprietary nature, i.e. "property relationships between citizens and socialist organizations, property relationships between these persons and the state, as well as relationships arising from the protection of personal rights, unless these relationships were regulated by other acts".[456] There were provisions concerning legal capacity and competence to perform legal acts. Explanatory definitions of some general concepts, like household, close persons, computation of time, or division of things, were included, with significance for the whole legal system. Part One also covered general provisions regarding contracts concluded between citizens.

Part Two dealt with socialist ownership and personal ownership.[457] The Code applied the theoretical division of types of ownership according to socialist legal theory. Three kinds of ownership were distinguished, and a strict hierarchy among the different forms of ownerships applied. Only state socialist ownership (state and cooperative) was the most promoted and protected under socialist civil law. Ownership of individuals was divided into personal ownership (intended for the personal use of citizens) and private ownership, which was treated as a relic of the capitalist era and was limited and restricted. The Civil Code set the definition of personal ownership by enumerating things which could be considered as part of the personal property of citizens, such as income and savings generated from one's work and the social security system, things of domestic or personal use, family houses and recreation cottages. There were detailed provisions for co-ownership and the community property of spouses. In the latter case it was important to set rules not only for its creation, but especially for its distribution in the case of divorce.

The Code departed from the traditional definition of an owner, who was entitled, within statutory limits, "to possess, use, enjoy its fruits and benefits and to handle the object of his ownership", but was not recognized as a master allowed to exercise his dominion over his property; and there were serious restrictions to his rights, sometimes applied even without any statutory basis.

Part Three dealt with the personal use of apartments, other premises and land.[458] This so-called personal usage was projected in accordance with socialist legal theory as a specific institution of new "socialist law" to bypass traditional concepts of ownership or to act as a substitute for private ownership of land. Socialist organisations (particularly state organizations and cooperatives) used this concept to build new housing estates and left apartments to citizens' personal use in return for payment, without fixing the

---

456 *Ibidem*, pp. 11–132.
457 *Ibidem*, pp. 135–168.
458 *Ibidem*, pp. 169–216.

period of use. The right to personal use of land served citizens as title to build family houses, recreation cottages or garages, or just to have a garden on the land. This right was not limited in time and was transferable to heirs.

Part Four was entitled "Services" and replaced the traditional concept of contract in relationship to the socialist organizations.[459] Services were provided by socialist organisations to citizens and could have a form of real or material performance. According to the Code the main aim was to satisfy citizens' material and cultural needs. Services were provided in return for payment, or for free if the law provided so. This part of the Civil Code stipulated the duties of socialist organisations to be followed in the course of supplying special types of services. Particular provisions regulated the buying of goods in shops.

The fundamental problem of this approach was that it was so closely connected with central planning, which in the case of the production of goods never met demand and could not satisfy the "material and cultural needs" of citizens. The nearly absolute nationalization of medium and small businesses proved to be rather problematic. The "supply" was either lower than the demand or inadequate. People then started to help each other. Subsequently illegal businesses and crafts in the "grey economy" flourished, and, to a certain extent, the communist regime tolerated them. Another problem was the deterioration of the quality of products and a low level of protection of consumers.

Part Five dealt mainly with "civic assistance" among citizens, when one citizen executed some work for another citizen (especially in a neighbourhood) upon the latter's demand, or provided him with a loan, or helped him with some work.[460] Rights and obligations resulting from this civic assistance had to be in accordance with the rules of socialist community life, i.e. they were not intended to replace private initiatives in the business sphere, and, primarily, they should not be intended to generate profit. This section of civil law was under the heavy influence of the socialist ideology and proved to be inadequate to stop the expansion of the grey economy.

Part Six regulated liability for damage and for unlawful benefit from use of property.[461] Liability for damage arose to a party who breached the primary legal obligation, resulting from the law or a contract. Everybody was deemed liable for damage caused by his or her fault and unlawful conduct. This part was based on a general liability clause, and different individual cases of liability for damage were set down in special provisions. The Civil Code attached great importance to the general duty of prevention.[462]

459 *Ibidem*, pp. 218 and following.
460 *Ibidem*, especially pp. 341–363.
461 *Ibidem*, pp. 369–403.
462 *Ibidem*, pp. 370–375.

Part Seven governed the law of succession concerning personal property.[463] The Civil Code distinguished succession based on a last will and on intestate succession. A combination of both titles was possible. However, the socialist legal theory supported the idea that there was no real interest of the socialist society in allowing the testator to dispose of his belongings after death freely. Succession law therefore failed, to a certain extent, to respect the last will, and the whole law of inheritance was simplified.[464] The last Part of the Code covered final, transitional and repealing provisions, in particular with regard to the Civil Code of 1950.[465]

Already in December 1963 the changes in civil law began with the new Code on Civil Procedure (Act No. 99/1963 Sb.).[466] It strengthened the socialist idealism, typical for the beginning of the 1960s. The new civil procedure rules aimed at the reaching of objective truth notwithstanding the claims of the parties to the trial. The judges were for example free to decide what evidence could be admitted. The trials were also made less speedy, because the idea of concentration of procedure was abandoned and the priority of out-of-court settlement of disputes (in accordance with the socialist morality) was fostered. The Code also promoted the idea of making proceedings understandable to laymen – there was for example the strict obligation of judges to instruct the ignorant citizen about his right and duties.[467]

The first departure of family law from the Civil Code happened in 1949, and the trend was confirmed by the new Family Act of 1963 (Act No. 94/1963 Sb.).[468] Initially, the latter was proposed to only amend the Family Act of 1949, but the nature of changes in the 1960s led to the enactment of new legislation. The Family Act came into force on 1st April 1964, i.e. on the same day as the Civil Code. The Family Act governed mutual relationships between spouses, between parents and children, and relationships arising from foster care. It even strengthened basic considerations of socialist family law, including an obligatory civil marriage, equality of spouses, and various interferences of public authorities into the private sphere of families. The state intervened through national committees particularly where education and the upbringing of children were concerned; general parental responsibility was adopted.

---

463 *Ibidem*, pp. 411–436.
464 For the influence of Soviet legal theory see Hazard, L. N. – Shapiro, I. – Maggs, P. B.: *The Soviet Legal system. Contemporary Documentation and Historical Commentary*, pp. 401–407.
465 *Commentary on the Czechoslovak Civil Code* by Th. J. Vondracek, pp. 437–462.
466 For its text in English see *The Code of civil procedure* of 4th December 1963. Bulletin of Czechoslovak law 1965, volumes 6–7, pp. 152 and following. For its interpretation from the socialist legal theory point of view see Češka, Z.: *The New Czechoslovak Rules of Civil Procedure. Ibidem*, pp. 149–152.
467 Kühn, Z.: *The Judiciary in Central and Eastern Europe. Mechanical Jurisprudence in Transformation?*, pp. 41–43.
468 Elišer, D. – Frinta, O. – Pauknerová, M.: *Recodification of Private Law in the Czech Republic*, pp. 125–126.

New provisions concerning the determination of parenthood, adoption, tutorship and curatorship were enacted in the 1963 Family Act.

However, provisions concerning the community property of spouses were transferred to the Civil Code, and its concept was based on property being undivided into individual shares. Such an approach resulted from an idea that all relationships regarding property matters should be regulated by the Civil Code. The Family Act stipulated that the provisions of the Civil Code would apply unless something else was stipulated by the Family Act. The idea of isolating family law as a separate branch of law was, to a certain extent, overcome and the supportive role of civil law was admitted.

In 1965 the Labour Code was finally enacted (Act No.65/1965 Sb.); it came into effect on 1st January 1966.[469] On this date the provisions of the Austrian Civil Code of 1811 on employment contracts, however in an amended form, ceased to be part of the Czechoslovak law. The Labour Code implemented several principles of the Czechoslovak Socialist Constitution of 1960, especially the right to work.

The relationship between the Labour Code and the Civil Code was not settled by legislation; in practice both codes were treated as separate branches of law. This was for ideological reasons, because work was not seen as a part of proprietary relations. The Labour Code was proposed in order to constitute a complex and cogent branch of law. The Code was applicable to all legal relationships arising from work. It dealt with the position of trade union organizations and strengthened their status as the sole representation of employees within factories or socialist organizations through collective agreements of a socialist type.[470] The whole Code was based on the principle of a uniform approach towards labour relations and aimed at the dissolution of former differences between various types of work and occupations. These differences applied mainly to public services, police, army and justice and cooperative farms.

Parties to a labour contract were not allowed to agree on something that the Code did not explicitly address, and contractual freedom was limited to certain minor points. The Labour Code was divided into six parts. Part One were general provisions and an explanation of basic terminology applicable to labour law. Part Two governed labour relationship; Part Three dealt with apprenticeship; Part Four regulated labour contracts made outside regular labour relationships; Part Five contained common provisions; and Part Six were final provisions.

The Labour Code enacted a maximum of 46 work hours per week, with a prospect of fulfilling the Constitutional promise to shorten the length in the

469 Bulletin of Czechoslovak Law, vol. 6–7, pp. 67 and following.
470 See Mařík, V. – Urbanec, A.: *The Czechoslovak trade unions and labour legislation.* Prague: Práce, 1967, pp. 70–72.

future. At the same time socialist labour law predicted an increase in the living standard through increased effectiveness of work. This was connected with other social benefits for employees, including a guaranteed paid leave. Key institutions of the socialist labour law were labour discipline and liability. The Labour Code enacted more detailed provisions regarding safety and health at work.[471]

Economic relationships (especially those connected with national economy and planning) were removed from the Civil Code and incorporated into a special Economic Code No. 109/1964 Sb., which came into effect on 1st July 1964. It was the result of a long theoretical discussion on the concept of socialist law regulating economic relations between socialist organisations (i.e. state enterprises and other legal entities) in the environment of the planned economy.[472] The Economic Code was not a simple replacement for business law (the Business Code was abolished in 1950) and tried to apply some reformative reforming concepts which originated within Czechoslovak society in the 1960s.[473]

According to the Economic Code, the national economy of the Czechoslovak socialist Republic was governed by the principle of democratic centralism and was under the guidance of the Communist Party. Central planning was proclaimed as a basic principle for organization of economic relationships. Socialist organizations were obliged to take care of socialist ownership, to fulfil the tasks of the state plans and to cooperate with other socialist organizations.

The Economic Code dealt with the relationships between socialist enterprises, along both horizontal and vertical lines. The Economic Code consisted of a Preamble, ten fundamental Articles and twelve parts divided into 400 sections.

The content of the Economic Code focused on the direction of the national economy through central planning, financing and other forms of administrative management of national enterprises. The Code confirmed the key role of five years economic plans.

The Economic Code acknowledged the socialist theory of types of ownership and concentrated on socialist ownership. The Code provided for the types of socialist organizations. There were five basic types: state owned economic organizations (mainly national enterprises), organizations directly financed from the state budget (especially bodies of state administration or organizations set for administration of health care and culture), organizations

---

471 *Ibidem*, pp. 75–76.
472 See especially Hazard, L. N. – Shapiro, I. – Maggs, P. B.: *The Soviet Legal system, Contemporary Documentation and Historical Commentary*, pp. 286–289.
473 Stuna, S.: *The development of Economic Legislation in the Czechoslovak Socialist Republic and the Subject of the Economic Code*. In: Bulletin of Czechoslovak law 1965, volumes 6–7, pp. 1–9. Text of the Code in English. *Ibidem*, pp. 39 and following.

subsidized from the state budget, cooperatives, and socialist social organizations in a political and cultural area.

Another part of the Code contained special provisions for "economic obligations" concluded between the socialist organizations. The Economic Code tried to solve the basic problem of the whole socialist economy, i.e. to find a balance between the central economic planning and the initiative and individual decision-making of national enterprises and other organizations at the basic level of the national economy.

Individual ministries usually set standard rules for the supply of individual categories of goods and services. The realization of the plan was connected with a special type of economic contract concluded between national enterprises and socialist organizations establishing the relations of "supply and delivery". The Code set obligatory conditions for the contracts, and there was only a limited scope for enterprises to negotiate supplementary terms. In the event of the fulfilment of the economic plan there was an obligation to conclude a contract with another socialist organization.

The special character of economic relations within the central planned economy was connected with the establishment of state arbitration in accordance with the Soviet pattern. Arbitration was introduced in 1950 together with special provisions for contracts concluded between national enterprises. Arbitration not only resolved disputes arising from economic relations but also ensured there was discipline within the planned economy.[474]

There was a clear separation of economic relations within the national economy and those related to foreign trade. Special provisions applied in respect to the Council for Mutual Economic Assistance, which was established in 1949 to coordinate economic relations within the Soviet Bloc. In 1963 the International Trade Code (No. 101/1963 Sb.) was enacted to focus on international trade relations.[475]

---

[474] Hazard, L. N. – Shapiro, I. – Maggs, P. B.: *The Soviet Legal system. Contemporary Documentation and Historical Commentary*, pp. 230 and following.

[475] In more details Kalensky, P. – Kopač, L.: The new Czechoslovak code of international trade. In: *Bulletin of Czechoslovak Law*, 1964, Nos. 3–4, pp. 143 and following.

/27/
<u>Prague Spring</u>

In the second half of the 1960s a new wave of liberal changes started within the Communist Party and Czechoslovak society. The changes were initiated in response to a call for economic and subsequent political reforms.[476] The Communist Party allowed for liberalization in areas of culture, particularly in film and literature.[477]

In 1965 the Communist Party approved changes in the economic model. The economic programme proposed by the Czech economist Otto Šik called for both intensive and extensive economic development, emphasizing technological improvements. Under the programme, central planning was to be limited to covering overall production and investments on the one hand, and basic prices and wage guidelines on the other. Management and councils of workers were to be attracted to take a more active part in decision-making within national enterprises. The plan tried to combine central planning with certain free market features.

---

476 For connection between economic, socio-cultural and political reform see for example Golan, G.: *The Czechoslovak Reform Movement.* Cambridge University Press, 1973, especially pp. 50 and following.
477 *Ibidem*, pp. 94 and following.

The movement to reform the socialist system in Czechoslovakia acquired a new dynamism in the beginning of 1968, usually referred to as Prague Spring. A progressive Slovak communist, Alexander Dubček, was elected the new leader of the Czechoslovak Communist Party. The first proposals to reform the political and economic system were presented in March. One month later, a so-called Action Programme of the Communist Party was adopted. The programme proposed a new model of socialism combining democracy and socialist ideas adjusted to the Czechoslovak environment.[478]

Changes in the Constitution, including real guarantees of civic rights and principles of federation of the Czechoslovak state, were proposed along with forming a state administration independent of the direct political will of the Communist Party.[479] Some civic rights proclaimed by the 1960 Constitution regained real content; as a result, many Czechs and Slovaks got their passports and were allowed to travel for the first time in their lives. Several partial reforms touching the Constitution and law followed, like the abolishment of preliminary censorship and of the Central Publishing Authority in June 1968, proposals to strengthen the role of the Government and Parliament, and a new wave of rehabilitation of victims of the political trials of the 1950s. After the report of a special commission set in April 1968 proved necessity of rehabilitating more than just members of the Communist Party, special Act No. 82/1968 Sb., on Judicial Rehabilitation, was enacted. The Act made it possible to not only repeal judgments, but also to ask for compensation or rehabilitation of civic rights. By 1969 more than 1200 cases were resolved in favour of the victims.

The movement of reforming communism gained popular support. New political organizations were established, demanding at least "socialism with a human face" and the possibility to form political opposition to the Communist Party and the National Front organizations. Changes were proposed to the rigid central planning system and foreign policy.

The Prague Spring was perceived by the communist hardliners in the Soviet Union and within the Soviet Block (especially in German Democratic Republic) as a clear danger.[480] They feared for the integrity of the Soviet empire and especially condemned and refused any democratic reforms. In the end the leader of the Soviet Union, Leonid Brežněv, ordered a military intervention. In August 1968 Czechoslovakia was occupied by the armies of the Warsaw Pact, and the Czechoslovak reform communist leaders finally capitulated during negotiations in Moscow, where they signed the so called

478 For extracts in English see Navrátil, J. (ed.): *The Prague Spring 1968: A National Security Archive Documents Reader*. Central European University Press, 1998, doc. No. 19, pp. 92–95. See also Zeman, Z. A. B.: *Prague Spring: A Report on Czechoslovakia 1968*. London: Penguin Books, 1969, pp. 115–127.

479 Golan, G.: *Reform Rule in Czechoslovakia: The Dubček Era, 1968–1969*. Cambridge University Press, 1973, pp. 147 and following.

480 Skilling, G. H.: *Czechoslovakia's Interrupted Revolution*. Princeton, 1976, pp. 675–680.

Moscow Protocol.[481] On 16th October 1968 the shameful Agreement on Temporary Presence of Soviet Forces on Czechoslovak Territory was concluded and hurriedly rushed through Czechoslovak parliament. Four deputies who voted against the Agreement were soon stripped of their mandates.[482] Within a year domestic collaborators with the Soviets and the conservative wing within the Communist Party finally prevailed. Gustáv Husák was elected the new leader of the Czechoslovak communists, and a period of stagnation, called "normalization", began.[483] Reform communists were expelled from the Party, and emigration grew in numbers after 1968. After the popular protests in 1969 were crushed and their organizers punished, the rest of the population gradually sank into apathy.

Some reforms of the Prague Spring were reversed almost immediately after the Soviet invasion; for example, as early as on 13th September 1968 Act No. 127/1968 Sb. on certain temporary measures in the area of press and other mass-media re-installed the previous censorship and established the Press and Information Bureau. The same day Act No. 126/1968 Sb. was passed to curtail the freedom of assembly, and the national committees were entrusted with authority to forbid public meetings if they were contrary to the international interests of the Czechoslovak state or were aimed against the socialist order. The same fate was designed for other political and economic reforms. Rehabilitation of victims of political trials was stopped, and some resolved cases even reversed.

In May 1970 Czechoslovakia and the Soviet Union signed the Treaty on Friendship, Cooperation and Mutual Assistance. It strengthened the principle of a limited sovereignty for Czechoslovakia within the Soviet Bloc, and the Soviet troops remained stationed in Czechoslovakia until 1991.

The promises of the Prague Spring were fulfilled only in the introduction of a Czechoslovak federation. The question of federalization was an important part of political discussions during the liberalization of the communist regime in the second half of the 1960s; it became an important point in the political agenda mainly after Slovak Communists, punished for their national policies in the political ("bourgeois nationalist") trials of the 1950s were rehabilitated.[484] However the real importance of federalization and of its content was clearly viewed differently by Czech political elites and this fact created yet another problem for future Czech-Slovak relations within a common state.[485]

---

481 For English text of Moscow Protocol of August 26, 1968 see Navrátil, J. (ed.): *The Prague Spring 1968: A National Security Archive Documents Reader*, doc. No. 119, pp. 477–481.
482 *Ibidem*, doc. No. 133, pp. 533–537.
483 Golan, G.: *Reform Rule in Czechoslovakia: The Dubček Era, 1968–1969*, pp. 264–268.
484 In more details Sikora, S.: *Slovakia and the attempt to reform socialism*. In: Teich, M. – Kováč, D. – Brown, M. D.: *Slovakia in History*, pp. 299–314.
485 Skalnik Leff, C.: *National Conflict in Czechoslovakia, The Making and Remaking of a State, 1918–1987*, pp. 123–127.

Technically, the Constitutional Act on the Czechoslovak Federation 1968 was an amendment of the 1960 Constitution,[486] but in reality it was so far reaching, that it could be regarded as the third Constitution of the communist regime. The unitary Czechoslovak state was transformed into three units: the Czechoslovak Socialist Republic, the Czech Socialist Republic, and the Slovak Socialist Republic. Each of the units was represented by its own Parliament, Government and Supreme Court.

The Constitutional Act on the Czechoslovak Federation No. 143/1968 Sb. had a Preamble, which stated the main reasons for the federative arrangements and saw it as an important step towards truly friendly relations between the two equal and fraternal nations, Czech and Slovak, and as an expression of the right of self-determination of these nations.[487] This was accompanied by an ideological concept of the maintenance of the socialist order and proletarian internationalization. The concept of "social democracy" in resemblance of the ideas of the Prague Spring was mentioned, but it had no real importance in practice.

The Preamble was further implemented by Fundamental Provisions, dealing with the issue of the sovereignty of the two member states and the federation, their respective frontiers, state citizenship and equality of the Czech and Slovak languages. It stated that the unity of the federation was an issue of a common economy based on socialist principles, socialist ownership, single currency and uniform economic planning, including uniform management of the labour force.

The parliament of the Czechoslovak Republic was called the Federal Assembly and consisted of two chambers: the Chamber of the People and the Chamber of Nations. Both chambers were equal. In most cases it was necessary that both chambers should pass a bill. The Chamber of the People consisted of 200 deputies elected on the territory of the whole federation. The Chamber of Nations consisted of 150 deputies, of which half was elected in the Czech Socialist Republic and the second half in the Slovak Socialist Republic. Such a system was devised to represent the equal constitutional position of both Republics and was a safeguard that the smaller Slovak Republic could not be outvoted by the Czech Republic.

The Federation was represented by the President, as Head of State, and the Federal Government. The Constitution provided for the establishment of a Federal Constitutional Court (as well as for Constitutional Courts of Republics). However, this provision of the Constitution was not implemented in practice.

---

486 Simmonds, W. (ed.): *The Constitutions of the Communist World*, Brill, 1980, Czechoslovakia, Introduction by Th. J. Vondracek, Constitution of 1960, pp. 140–158.

487 For its text in English see *The Constitutional Foundations of the Czechoslovak Federation.* Prague: Orbis, 1978.

The Republics had their own parliaments, called National Councils, and their own Governments. The division of competences between the Federation and Republics was at first, in 1968, in the favour of the Republics; nevertheless such a trend was contrary to the intended process of normalization.[488] Therefore in December 1970 the competences of the Republics were limited, and political decision-making once again returned fully to the top apparatus of the Communist Party.[489]

The exclusive competences of the Federation consisted of foreign policy, defence, currency, federal reserves, federal legislation and administration within the scope of federal jurisdiction, control over the federal bodies and the protection of the federal constitutional rule. There were areas of joint jurisdiction shared by the Republics and the Federation, i.e. planning, finance, banking, price control, economic relations with other countries, industry, agriculture, transport, post and communications, development of science, labour, wages and social policy, socio-economic information, legal regulations governing national enterprises, standardization of measures, weights, internal order and state security, press, media and control.

The only matters which had not been specifically placed under the jurisdiction of the Czechoslovak Federation were under the exclusive jurisdiction of the Republics. This led, for example, to the implementation of almost identical laws and regulations in both Republics even in the sphere of their "exclusive" competences, i.e. in cultural, educational and scientific issues. The Republics had their own state budget and national development plans. This agenda of the Republics was under the strong influence and patronage of the centre.

Nevertheless, there were certain advantages of the federative model. Especially in Slovakia it was welcomed as a step towards the real emancipation of the Slovak nation; more liberal policies were pursued in Slovakia in comparison with the Czech lands in the 1970s and 1980s.[490] National Councils concentrated on the building of central bodies and agencies of the Republics and created the basis for a future possibility to renew both Czech and Slovak independent statehood.

The period of the Prague Spring also brought in considerable changes to policies regarding minorities. The assumption that minority problems in Czechoslovakia had been solved after WWII, and by introduction of the socialist system, proved unfounded, and minorities themselves, especially the Hungarian and Polish ones, intensified their activities. Constitutional Act

488 Žatkuliak, J.: *Slovakia's position within the Czechoslovak federation, 1968–1970.* In: Teich, M. – Kováč, D. – Brown, M. D.: Slovakia in history, pp. 315 – 329.

489 See also the pro-regime propaganda in Grospič, J.: *The Constitutional Foundations of the Czechoslovak Federation: The Constitution of the Czechoslovak Socialist Republic, the Constitutional Act Concerning the Czechoslovak Federation, the Constitutional Act Concerning the Status of Ethnic Groups in the Czechoslovak Socialist Republic.* Prague: Orbis, 1973.

490 See especially Pithart, P.: *Towards a Shared Freedom 1968–1989.* In: Musil, J. (ed.): *The End of Czechoslovakia,* pp. 204–222.

No. 144/1968 Sb., on minority rights, declared the equality of all Czechoslovak citizens irrespective of their language and nationality. Traditional minorities, i.e. Polish, Hungarian, Ukrainian and German, were promised special rights in the usage of language, establishment of minority schools, and promotion of their culture.[491] The Act confirmed existing rights in minority matters. Minorities were officially proclaimed a part of the Czechoslovak state, together with the Czech and Slovak nations, and all forms of forcible denationalization were forbidden.

After the Soviet invasion the minority problem was again frozen, and the special Acts envisaged by Constitutional Act No. 144/1968 Sb. for its implementation were not adopted.[492] Most of the promised rights were guaranteed to the minorities on the local and regional levels only. The Roma (Gypsy) population was not recognized as a minority and was still perceived mainly as a social (and also political) problem, which was for the Communist leadership difficult to address.[493]

---

491 Its text published in Grospič, J.: *The Constitutional Foundations of the Czechoslovak Federation: The Constitution of the Czechoslovak Socialist Republic, the Constitutional Act Concerning the Czechoslovak Federation, the Constitutional Act Concerning the Status of Ethnic Groups in the Czechoslovak Socialist Republic.* Prague: Orbis, 1973.
492 See Kalvoda, J.: *National minorities under communism: The case of Czechoslovakia.* In: Nationalities Papers: The Journal of Nationalism and Ethnicity, vol. 16/1, 1988, esp. pp. 9–28.
493 Broader context in Ulč, O: *Gypsies in Czechoslovakia: a Case of Unfinished Integration.* In: East European Politics and Societies, 2/ 1988, Sage Publications, pp. 306 and following.

/28/
The period of "normalization" 1969–1989

The period of "normalization" in the 1970s and 1980s was typical of a new wave of persecutions, mainly in the form of censorship, punishment and criminalization of all forms of real and latent opposition. New mechanisms of control over society were introduced combining policies of "stick and carrot".

Criminal law was again seen as a tool to ensure the fulfilment of the policies of the Communist Party. At first it was used to stop public protests against the end of democratic reforms and against the occupation of the country by "friendly troops". A special law was issued by the Chairman of the Federal Assembly in August 1969 to use extraordinary repressive measures against protesters and activists. The police were entrusted with the power to prolong the detention of organizers of protests for up to three weeks. Criminal proceedings were usually accompanied with the imposition of disciplinary measures upon those persons under labour law, and most of them lost their jobs. The first wave of persecution based upon these extraordinary measures directly touched 1,526 people, together with 609 others who were convicted in accordance with Chapter 1 of the Criminal Code, regulating crimes against the state.[494]

In May 1970 the Central Committee of the Communist Party confirmed use of a hard line in criminal law and proposed to not only abandon the liberal tendencies of the 1960s, but to also strictly apply the class approach once again.

In 1969 the issuance of passports was again strictly restricted and controlled. A special list of illegal emigrants was compiled; between 1970 and 1972 more than 9,000 emigrants were sentenced in absentia. Confiscation of their property followed, hitting primarily their apartments and family houses.

As of 1st January 1970 the Criminal Code was amended and a new concept of three categories of criminal acts – felonies, misdemeanours, and administrative transgressions – introduced by Act on Petty Offences No. 150/1969 Sb.

This enabled the regime to expand the types of punishment and types of political and economic offences. The reasons for the reform were again ideologically motivated. In 1973 Act No. 44/ 1973 Sb. governing special police supervision (so called "protective supervision") over convicts after their release from prison was passed; this law was misused mainly against the members of political opposition or selected groups of "notorious criminals" and the original intention of the act to intensify post-release care of the convicted was not fully met.

In the beginning of the 1970s the regime prepared a new wave of politically motivated trials, primarily against those who did not want to stop demanding reforms connected with the Prague Spring. Therefore reform communists, members of newly established non-communist organizations, and representatives of the student movement were among the first to be brought before courts. Punishments were severe, but the persecution was selective and did not take on the brutal form of the 1950s.[495]

The communist regime persecuted non-conforming young people and underground music. In 1976 a famous trial with the underground rock band called the Plastic People of the Universe took place.[496] The band was accused of public disorder, as its concerts had not been officially approved and permitted. The state prosecutor criticized their violation of socialist morality; the Court of Appeals not only confirmed the sentence but also stressed the difference between the official socialist culture and the declining values embodied in the song texts of the rock band.

However, the beginning of the period of normalization was not only a period of persecution. The regime tried to secure its position and applied a set of

---

494 See in more details Tůma, O. *The Half-life, the Communist's Regime Greatest Crises (1967-1971)*. In: Pánek, J. – Tůma, O. et, al.: *A History of Czech lands*, pp. 563–568.
495 Tůma, O.: *The Second Consolidation of the Regime and the Descent into Collapse*. In: Pánek, J. – Tůma, O. et, al.: *A History of Czech lands*, pp. 576–579.
496 See in more details Bolton, J.: *Worlds of Dissent: Charter 77. The Plastic People of the Universe, and Czech Culture Under Communism*. Harvard University Press, 2012, especially pp. 115–140.

policies known as "goulash socialism or goulash communism" implemented at first by János Kádár in Hungary.[497] Those who became loyal to the regime after 1969 were motivated by economic and social "bribes" to not take an active part in opposition activities.

In 1970 the new regime implemented a rise in pensions. Special provisions were intended to stimulate an increase in the birth rate. Higher family allowances, special loans for young families, and parental (in most cases maternal) leave were enacted. In 1975 the reform of pensions and a special law on the social security system followed. People were encouraged to buy consumer goods through special loans, and the number of Škoda cars sold, or weekend cottages newly built showed growth throughout the whole period of normalization.

Loyalty was manifested through official marches on International Labour Day, the International Day of Women, or in celebrations of the Bolshevik November Revolution. The farce elections showed 99 percent support for the Communist Party candidates. The Soviet system of "*nomenklatura*", i.e. special political lists of candidates for all leading political and economic positions within the states, was introduced.[498]

The period of normalization brought changes in civil law. Another important aspect of normalization was shown when the idealistic "socialist" approach of the 1960s was replaced by a more pragmatic approach. In the beginning of the 1980s the communist regime realized that the 1964 Civil Code and Code on Civil Procedure[499] was not functioning properly, and that it was impossible to apply it in practice because of its too radical and idealistic nature. A far reaching amendment was adopted (Act No. 131/1982 Sb.) to re-establish some of the traditional institutions of civil law, such as possession or easements, that had been removed in 1964.

After the 1975 Helsinki conference a new form of political opposition came into existence within communist Czechoslovakia. In 1977 the opponents of the regime, including former reform communists, writers and other influential intellectuals (including Václav Havel) signed a declaration known as Charter 77. They asked the communist government not to violate human rights and liberties and to fulfil its international obligations confirmed in Helsinki.[500] Czechoslovakia was a signatory party to the United Nations Pacts on Civil and

---

497 For the term see for example Kornai, J: *Evolution of the Hungarian Economy, 1848–1998: volume II. Paying the bill for goulash-communism*, Atlantic Studies on Society in Change (East European Monographs). Columbia University Press, 2000, especially pp. 121–123.

498 For its functions within Soviet society at that time see Hough, J. F.: *How the Soviet Union is Governed*. Harvard University Press, 1979, especially pp. 432–439 and 506–507.

499 On changes in civil procedure and notarial order see Bulletin of Czechoslovak Law, Volume 23, Union of Czechoslovak Lawyers, 1984, pp. 91 and following.

500 See for example Skilling, H. G.: *Charter 77 and Human Rights in Czechoslovakia*. London: Allen and Unwin, 1981 and Krejčí, J.: *Czechoslovakia at the Crossroads of European History*, pp. 192–193. Most recently Bolton, J.: *Worlds of Dissent: Charter 77. The Plastic People of the Universe, and Czech Culture Under Communism*, especially pp. 24–28.

Political, as well as Economic, Social and Culture Rights; Charter 77 urged the Government to guarantee these rights to its citizens not only in the Constitution but also in everyday practice. The persecution of the Plastic People of the Universe band was used as an example of how the right to free expression of opinion was in reality suppressed.

The Communist Party leadership reacted with a new wave of persecutions and propaganda aimed against the Charter 77 signatories, called "dissidents"; together with their families they were spied on and abused by the secret police, unlawfully detained, and in some cases convicted and imprisoned for alleged anti-socialist and anti-state "subversive" activities and "treasonous behaviour". Some dissidents were even forced to leave the country; most of them lost their jobs and were pushed into the outskirts of the society.

An opposition association, called the Committee for the Defence of the Unjustly Prosecuted, was established in 1978 to support oppressed dissidents and to monitor cases of injustice caused by the communist regime.[501] Its information, broadcast by the radio stations the Voice of America and Radio Free Europe, helped people in Czechoslovakia and in the free world to be informed about the true nature of the communist regime. The representatives of the Committee for the Defence of the Unjustly Prosecuted were themselves put before communist justice and sentenced in a trial, in which Václav Havel also was convicted. However, until the second half of the 1980s the dissident movement did not find support among the majority of society (the "grey zone").

When Gorbachev proclaimed new policies of the Soviet Communist Party, namely "*perestrojka*" and "*glasnost*",[502] Czechoslovak communists proposed only cosmetic changes in its leadership. In 1987 changes were proposed to be implemented in the economic system; the document was called "Complex Guidelines to Reconstruct the Economic Mechanism". A year later a special law on state enterprises was enacted. It, together with changes in the role of cooperatives and foreign trade, was planned to bring about greater effectiveness and innovative approaches into the rigid central planning. However, the economic changes would not work without adequate political changes.

It was quite clear that the socialist countries could not keep up with developments in the Western democratic countries. For the first time, opposition groups and initiatives found greater response, particularly among students. In Northern Bohemia the growing discontent led to a series of demonstrations

---

501 Krejčí, J.: *Czechoslovakia at the Crossroads of European History*, pp.192–193 and Bolton, J.: *Worlds of Dissent: Charter 77. The Plastic People of the Universe, and Czech Culture Under Communism*, pp. 215–217.

502 For the importance of these policies (together with abandonment of Brežněv doctrine) as preconditions to democratic transformation see Elster: J.: *Constitutionalism in Eastern Europe: An Introduction*. In: The University of Chicago Law Review, 58/1991 pp. 453–454.

against terrible air pollution. Opposition circles were supported by the Churches, which became more active.[503]

The draft of a new Constitution of the Czechoslovak Federation was discussed by the Communist Party leadership until November 1989. The draft was interesting from a constitutional perspective, because it was designed as a single constitutional charter for three entities – the Federation and both Republics.[504] The draft proposed some adjustments by the communist regime in accordance with the Soviet style of "*perestrojka*" but was insufficient to meet the growing appeal for fundamental changes. Partly because of the failure of Prague Spring and partly because of the changed internal and international situation the majority of the society simply did not want to reform the communist regime. People desired to replace it with a pluralistic democracy and a market economy with a social dimension.

---

[503] Tůma O.: *The Second Consolidation of the Regime and the Descent into Collapse*. In: Pánek, J. – Tůma, O. et, al.: *A History of Czech lands*, pp. 576–580.

[504] The draft constitutional law was under preparation in the Federal Assembly, www.psp.cz /eknih/1986fs/tisky/t0185_00.htm

/29/
Velvet revolution and period of "transformation"

In consequence of the profound changes in the international position of the whole Soviet Bloc, the year 1989 brought a domino effect of revolutions and changes within the socialist countries.[505] The Iron Curtain finally disappeared especially after Polish Roundtable Talks, the Czechoslovak "Velvet Revolution" and after the fall of the Berlin Wall. The Velvet Revolution started on 17th November 1989, when students called a demonstration to commemorate the fiftieth anniversary of the Nazi persecution aimed against Czech universities following the death of a medical student, Jan Opletal, in 1939.[506] On this anniversary students in Prague were again protesting against an oppressive regime – this time against Communism, demanding real democracy, human rights and liberties, as well as real social changes.[507]

---

505 See excellent account in Ash, T. G.: *The Magic Lantern: The Revolution of 89. Witnessed in Warsaw, Budapest, Berlin and Prague.* New York: Random House, 1990.
506 The best book on the 1989 Velvet Revolution was written in Czech by J. Suk (Labyrintem Revoluce). In English see his study *Czechoslovakia's Return to Democracy* in: Pánek, J. – Tůma, O. et al.: *A History of Czech lands*, especially pp. 589–591.
507 In English see for example Bradley, J. F. N.: *Czechoslovakia's Velvet Revolution. A Political Analysis.* New York: Columbia University Press, 1992.

The peaceful demonstration was stopped by police troops in the centre of Prague, and students were brutally beaten. Hundreds of young people were injured, and one student was reportedly beaten to death. Although the death was later proved hoax, the rumours themselves served as spark for active support of the students' demands by the general public. The events led to the student strike being supported by theatre actors and by popular protests which turned into mass demonstrations against the regime. The events of November 1989 soon led to the establishment of organizations of civic opposition against the communist regime. In Prague the "Civic Forum" was established, headed by Václav Havel; whereas in the Slovak capital of Bratislava the opposition formed the organization "Public Against Violence".[508] The united opposition demanded the abolishing of the article of the Constitution establishing the leading role of the Communist Party. The opposition called for a dialog with the modified Communist Party leadership, the release of political prisoners, and investigations into the police actions of 17th November. The communist regime collapsed within a few days without violence, thanks to a massive information and propaganda campaign which proved that the Communists had lost popular support. The Head of the Czechoslovak Government, Ladislav Adamec, agreed to form a new coalition government of national understanding and to abolish the leading role of the Communist Party in the Constitution. The fate of the communist regime was sealed by mass demonstrations in Prague and Bratislava and by a general strike. On 28th November the Communist Party of Czechoslovakia finally agreed in a Czechoslovak version of "Roundtable talks" to give up its monopoly on political power.[509] On 29th November 1989 Constitutional Act No. 135/1989 Sb. not only abolished the leading role of the Communist Party but also repealed provisions on the role of Marxism-Leninism in education, science and culture, and reformed the political system which was based on the National Front. The Civic Forum put forward the proposal for a new constitution, prepared by current Constitutional Court Chief Justice Pavel Rychetský in December 1989.[510] Václav Havel asked Western experts including professors from Europe and the United States to prepare papers and participate in conferences with the Czechs and Slovaks responsible for the drafting of the new constitution.[511]

On 10th December Communist President Gustav Husák appointed the first Government since 1948 not dominated by communist members and resigned.

508 Suk, J.: *Czechoslovakia's Return to Democracy*, pp. 589–583.

509 *Ibidem*, In more details see ten rounds of talks described by Calda, M.: *The Roundtable Talks in Czechoslovakia*. In: Elster, J. (ed.): *The RoundtableTalks and the Breakdown of Communism*. University of Chicago Press, 1996, pp. 135–177.

510 Stanger, A: Constitutional Transforamtion in Post-Communist Central Europe: A liberal revolution?. In: Suda, Z. – Musil, J. (eds.): *The Meaning of Liberalism*: *East and West, New York*: Central European University Press, 2000, pp. 237–240.

511 Cutlert, L. – Schwartz, H.: *Constitutional Reform in Czechoslovakia: E Duobus Unum?*. In: The University of Chicago Law Review, 58/1991, p. 511.

A symbolic figure of the Prague Spring 1968, Alexander Dubcek, was elected Chairman of the Federal Assembly on 28th December; Václav Havel became the first non-Communist President of Czechoslovakia since 1948 a day later. The Velvet Revolution had its historical paradoxes. Václav Havel was elected Czechoslovak President unanimously (including communist deputies) in the Federal Assembly.[512]

In 1989 there were no real political and social forces capable of preventing profound political and economic changes.[513] A period of transition from the authoritarian communist regime into a democratic system followed, although not without problems, controversies and discussions on effective policies. After the failure of the Prague Spring many Czechoslovaks had been doubtful regarding any possibility of reforming communism. However, there were not many patterns available in the transition period to follow so that political, economic and social changes could be carried out.[514]

New Czechoslovak leaders declared their commitment to maintain the democratic legacy of the Czechoslovak Republic for the period between WWI and WWII. Therefore some of the changes in the legal system were based on a return to the Central European (and therefore "civil law") legal tradition.[515] The communist ideology was rejected and replaced by ideas of liberal democracy, although there were for a long period of time visible remnants of the previous ideology.[516] New democratic foundations were used for a thorough modification of the existing Constitution, symbolized by returning to the democratic principles of the rule of law, human rights, real separation of powers, and free competition among political parties.[517] During the first half of 1990 the National Front was abolished, and the whole system of state administration ceased to be built upon the national committees with the prospect to re-introduce self-government.

In March 1990 a series of new laws on freedom of association, freedom of assembly, right of petition, and freedom of press were enacted and were

512 Paradox was noted also by foreign authors. See Ludwikowski, R. R.: *Constitution-making in the Region of Former Soviet Dominance*. Duke University Press, 1996, p. 164.

513 Most recently with regard to all strata of Czechoslovak society Krapfl, J.: *Revolution with a Human Face: Politics, Culture, and Community in Czechoslovakia, 1989–1992*. Cornell University Press, 2013, especially chapter I.

514 For analyses of the public opinion on transition schemes see Wolchik, S.: *Czechoslovakia in Transition: Politics, Economics and Society*. London: Pinter, 1991, especially pp. 116–119.

515 It was of course not the case of Czechoslovakia only, although the strategies of individual states varied. See interesting comparisons in Frentzel-Zagórska, J.: *From a One-party State to Democracy: Transition in Eastern Europe*. Amsterdam: Rodopi, 1993, especially pp. 93–97. This was reflected also in the third revised edition of John Merryman's famous book *The Civil Law Tradition*: Stanford: Stanford University Press, 2007, pp. 1–2, where he announces the end of "socialist law" after 1989 changes in Europe.

516 From a critical point of view Stanger, A.: *Leninist Legacies and Legacies of State Socialism in Postcommunist Central European Constitutional Development*. In: Grzegorz Ekiert – Stephen E. Hanson (eds.): *Capitalism and Democracy in Central and Eastern Europe: Assessing the Legacy of Communist Rule*. Cambridge University Press, 2003, pp. 182–207.

517 Ludwikowski, R. R.: *Constitution-making in the Region of Former Soviet Dominance*, pp. 164–165.

followed on by changes made to the judicial system and state prosecution. A new concept of ownership, in which all types of ownership and all owners were proclaimed equal, was confirmed in April 1990 when Constitutional Act No. 100/1990 Sb. was enacted and Article 7 of the Czechoslovak Constitution, which dealt with the socialist forms of ownership, was finally abolished. It also opened way for acquisition of property and property rights for foreigners and foreign legal persons under the conditions prescribed by law.[518]

As will be described in further detail below, the question of the new concept of ownership was embodied also in the Charter of fundamental rights (Article 11) and the Civil Code was fundamentally amended in this respect.

Further democratic changes in the Constitution were reflected in December 1990 in Constitutional Act No. 496/1990 Sb. regarding the return of property of the Communist Party and of the Communist Youth Organization to the Czechoslovak people and in February 1991 in Constitutional Act No. 91/1991 Sb. on the establishment of the Constitutional Court of the Czech and Slovak Federative Republic.[519] The Act was modelled according to the Federal Constitutional Court envisaged by the 1968 Constitution, and consisted of 12 judges, 6 Czech and 6 Slovaks. For its seat neither Prague nor Bratislava was chosen, but rather the Moravian capital Brno. Slovak Ernest Valko was elected its president. Its establishment was completed by Act on the Organization of the Constitutional Court of the Czech and Slovak Federative Republic and the Procedure of 7th November 1991, No. 491/1991 Sb., and by its Organizational and Procedural Statute from March 1992.

The main task of the Court was to perform constitutional review concerning the federal constitution and human rights as well as resolve disputes concerning competences and give authoritative interpretation of federal constitutional laws.[520] Even though the Court worked for a very short period of time, some of its judgments helped form foundations for the next independent Czech Constitutional Court.

It was necessary to find a new position for Czechoslovakia in the international field. Czechoslovakia ceased to be a party to the Warsaw Pact (although only from July 1991), as well as to the Council for Mutual Economic Assistance. After some discussion a majority of the society supported the idea of becoming a candidate for accession to the European Communities (later the

518 In more details Hoškova, M.: *The Evolving Regime of the New Property Law in the Czech and Slovak Federal Republic.* In: American University Journal of International Law. & Policy, vol. 7/1992, pp. 607–608.

519 For its English translation see Bulletin of Czechoslovak law, vol. 30, Prague, 1991, pp. 29–34.

520 For the position of the court in comparative perspective see Schwartz, H.: *The New East European Constitutional Courts.* In: Michigan Journal of International Law, vol 13/1991–1992, especially pp. 750–761. See also Brunner, G.: *Development of Constitutional Judiciary in Eastern Europe.* In: Review of Central and East European Law, No. 6/1992, pp. 542–551.

European Union) and NATO. However this process was delayed by the break-up of Czechoslovakia.[521]

First the composition of the Federal Assembly and National Councils in the Czech and Slovak Republics were changed after the resignation of the most discredited communist deputies and the nomination of new members from the candidates proposed by the Civic Forum and Public Against Violence organizations.[522] After adoption of new electoral laws in spring 1990, the first free elections by universal direct suffrage after 42 years of Communist system were held in June 1990.[523] The elections were won by Civic Forum and the new Federal Assembly re-elected Václav Havel as a President. Instead of the traditional four-year term the Assembly and Havel were elected for two years only, during which it was expected to prepare the new constitution and finish the first round of transformation legislation.[524]

The policies during the transitional period gained strong popular support and legitimacy. However, the Communist Party was not banned, and it became a part of the new political system together with civic and social democratic parties. The first changes concentrated mainly on the political system and the economy.

Changes in the political system and economy were closely connected with debates over new constitutional foundations for human rights.[525] The importance of human rights was officially confirmed on 9th January 1991, when Constitutional Act No. 23/1991 Sb., entitled the Charter of Fundamental Rights and Freedoms, was enacted. In its Preamble Czechoslovakia expressly recognized the inviolability of the natural rights of people and the universally shared values of humanity and democracy.[526] Bitter Czechoslovak experience from the periods of Nazism and Communism suppressing human rights and fundamental freedoms raised the importance of human rights as an important safeguard to not return to a totalitarian regime. Democratic values constituted the foundations of the Czechoslovak state, so that it would not be bound by any exclusive ideology or by any particular religious faith in the future. It also represents the combination of the above-mentioned return to the democratic

---

521 It was therefore only after 1993, when the Czech Republic became the first East European country to join the Organization for Economic Co-operation and Development (OECD), in 1995 and in 1997 The Czech Republic was, together with 10 other countries, invited to start negotiations on accession to the EU. In 1999 it became a member of NATO.
522 Kopecký, P: *Parliaments in the Czech and Slovak Republics: Party Competition and Parliamentary Institutionalization.* Ashgate, 2001, pp. 22 and following.
523 Suk, J.: *Czechoslovakia's Return to Democracy,* pp. 591–597.
524 Cutlert, L. – Schwartz, H.: *Constitutional Reform in Czechoslovakia: E Duobus Unum?,* p. 521.
525 Detailed analyses *Ibidem,* pp. 531–537.
526 Original text in English in: *Constitutional acts of Czech and Slovak Federal Republic and acts concerning the civil rights and freedoms adopted by the Federal Assembly of the Czech and Slovak Federal Republic.* Prague: Federal Assembly and Czechoslovak Academy of Sciences, 1992.

traditions of the interwar period[527] with the "reception" of the results of Western legal and political thinking achieved after WWII. Therefore this document could be regarded as the most important source of the Czech search for European identity.[528]

The sources for the Charter were found in Czechoslovakia's own traditions of democracy and self-government, as well as in the fundamental documents of the United Nations Organization and the European Convention on Human Rights.

All people were proclaimed free, equal in dignity, and enjoying equal rights. Their fundamental rights and basic freedoms were proclaimed as inherent, inalienable, and not subject to any repeal. Of particular importance was the principle that everyone was guaranteed the enjoyment of fundamental rights and basic freedoms irrespective of his or her gender, race, colour of skin, language, faith and religion, political or other conviction, national or social origin, affiliation to a national or ethnic minority, property, birth, or other status.

There were four main categories of rights: (a) fundamental human rights, (b) political rights, (c) social, economic and cultural rights and (d) rights of national minorities. Fundamental rights included the right to life, personal freedom, inviolability of the person and of his or her private life, inviolability of home, the freedom of speech, the protection of property, and religious freedom.

The Charter acquired a special position within the Czechoslovak legal system as all Czechoslovak laws, their implementation and interpretation, including constitutional laws, had to be in compliance with the Charter of Fundamental Rights and Freedoms.

In the period between 1990 and 1992 Czechoslovakia ratified several important international treaties in the field of human rights, including the Optional Protocol to the UN International Covenant in Civil and Political Rights of 1966, the UN Convention on the Rights of the Child of 1989, and especially the European Convention on the Protection of Human Rights and Fundamental Freedoms of 1950, with all its protocols. Czechoslovakia was also admitted as a member state to the Council of Europe.

After short discussions, the political and economic leaders of the new democratic Government decided to start an economic reform with a large scale and rapid privatization in order to create a free market economy built upon private ownership of the previously state-owned enterprises.[529] This was naturally linked with a liberalization of prices.

527 See also comments in Cutlert, L. – Schwartz, H.: *Constitutional Reform in Czechoslovakia: E Duobus Unum?*, pp. 531–532.
528 For wider philosophical context of this approach see especially Přibáň, J.: *Legal Symbolism: On Law, Time and European Identity*. Ashgate Publishing, 2007, especially pp. 159 and following.
529 In comparative perspective Aage, H.: *The Marketization of Planned Economies*. In: Clarke, T. (ed.): *International Privatization: Strategies and Practices*. Berlin, New York, De Gruyter 1994, especially pp. 165 and following.

The privatization process started with "small" privatization of small and medium sized enterprises based on Federal Acts No. 427/ 1990 Sb. and No. 541/1990 Sb.;[530] as early as 1990 this was combined with the restitution of property, i.e. returning property to its former private owners.[531] Restitution was regarded as both a just solution and another manner of privatization.[532] Initially, it was decided to return only property nationalized or confiscated after the communist coup, i.e. after 25th February 1948. The first of the restitutions laws, Act No. 403/1990 Sb., dealt with remedies for "certain property injustices", especially when property had been nationalized without compensation or when privately owned apartment houses and other properties were expropriated by National Committees. According to this Act aliens could also claim restitution or compensation provided that their claims had not been previously settled by bilateral international treaties (lump sum agreements) concluded by Czechoslovakia before 1989.[533]

There was also limited restitution of Church property, with a major portion to be decided later. In 1991 the most important of the restitutions laws, Act No. 87/1991 Sb. on out-of-court rehabilitation, was enacted. It brought some important changes to the original concept of restitution. Only Czechoslovak citizens with permanent residency in the country, who lost their personal property between February 1948 and 1990 (or their heirs) were eligible to get their property back. A special Act No. 229/1991 Sb., with similar conditions, was enacted for the restitution of land. This in fact meant that the restitution of some portions of the property of Jews and the restitution of the property of Sudeten Germans were excluded.

When it was not possible to return the property itself to the original owners or their heirs, compensation was paid. The rest of state property was privatized in a way called "the big privatization" (Act No. 92/1991 Sb.), organized mainly as a so-called "coupon" privatization.[534] This was combined with the direct sale of the property to foreign investors.

---

530 For the legal framework for small-scale privatization see Hoškova, M.: *The Evolving Regime of the New Property Law in the Czech and Slovak Federal Republic, p. 610.*
531 Fogelklou, A. – Sterzel, F.: *Consolidating Legal Reform in Central and Eastern Europe: An Anthology*, Uppsala: Iustus Förlag, 2003, pp. 56 and following.
532 Cepl, V.: *Restitution of Property in Post-Communist Czechoslovakia.* In: University of Liverpool, Centre for Central and East European Studies, Working Paper No. 3. b.d.
533 See Kuklík, J.: *Interference with proprietary rights between 1945 and 1948 and their reflection in so-called "indemnity agreements" and in privatization and "restitution" legislation After 1989.* In: Tomášek, M. (ed.): *Czech law between Europeanization and Globalization: New phenomena in law at the beginning of 21st century.* Prague: Karolinum Press, 2010, pp. and Kuti, C.: *Post-communist Restitution and the Rule of Law.* Central European University Press, 2009.
534 For the legal aspects see Gelpern, A.: *The Laws and Politics of Reprivatization in East-Central Europe: A Comparison.* In: University of Pennsylvania Journal of Business Law, 14/1993–94, pp. 317–322 and Hoškova, M.: *The Evolving Regime of the New Property Law in the Czech and Slovak Federal Republic*, pp. 611–612.

At first the principle of continuity prevailed for the legal system,[535] but it was clear that the law as a whole needed a thorough depuration of totalitarian residues and ideological deformations. On 13th November 1991 the special Act No. 480 of the Federal Assembly was enacted to declare the period between February 1948 and November 1989 as a period of loss of national liberty. It confirmed that the communist regime violated the human rights of its citizens and its own laws; however, legislation passed during the communist period remained in force unless specific changes were stipulated by new legislation.[536] A different approach was taken in respect of individual decisions of Czechoslovak courts from the communist period in criminal cases. A special law on judicial rehabilitation, No. 119/1990 Sb., was enacted already in April 1990 to deal with the most flagrant cases of communist injustice. Implementation of this law was met with some practical and also legal problems, especially how to decide whether a sentence was for a general crime or was a result of politically motivated persecution.[537] Only in July 1993 did the Czech Parliament pass Act No. 198/1993 Sb. which declared the communist ideology as totalitarian and illegitimate and the communist regime as illegal.

The most controversies from legal, political and also human rights points of view were caused by the so called Act on Lustrations (screening) No. 451/1991.[538] The Act laid down certain prerequisites for the holding of positions within the state administration, public organs and armed forces. The Act prevented the nominations of members of the Communist leadership and officers of the State security police as well as secret collaborators with the State security police. However the Act was amended several times and reviewed by the Constitutional Court and for example the categories of collaborators with the State security police had to be changed.

Most of the socialist codes remained in force, but important amendments were introduced.[539] On 13th December 1989 the Federal Assembly abolished most relics of communist ideology in the Criminal Code (Act No. 159/1989 Sb.), particularly those regarding crimes against the socialist order, against the interests of the Soviet Union; punishments were reduced in some other cases, and criminal procedure was changed. On the other hand, new crimes

---

535 For the critique of this decision with proposal of more radical reform see Scruton R.: *The Reform of Law in Eastern Europe*. In: Tilburg Foreign Law Review 7/1991–1992, especially pp. 13–14. With view from inside Cepl, V.: *Bottlenecks in the Transformation of Eastern Europe*. Washington University Journal of Law and Policy, vol. 4/ 2000, especially pp. 26–31.
536 See in more details Teitel, R. G.: *Transitional Justice*. Oxford University Press, 2000, especially pp. 11–22.
537 *Ibidem*, pp. 136–137.
538 *Ibidem*, pp. 163–171. See also excellent account in Přibáň, J.: *Legal Symbolism: On Law, Time and European Identity*, especially pp. 175–187.
539 On this problem see Knapp, V.: *Legislative Challenge for Former Socialist States in Europe*. In: Statute L. Review, 13/ 1992, especially pp. 97–104. Knapp was commissioned mainly with the preparation of amendments to the Civil Code.

regarding the protection of the environment were introduced. A wide-ranging amnesty by President Havel followed.

Six months later Act No. 175/1990 Sb. amended both the general and special parts of the Criminal Code; it stipulated a new aim of criminal law, namely to protect "the society and the constitutional order of the Czechoslovak Federative Republic as well as rights and lawful interests of citizens". The Act repealed ideological relics and terminology based on the socialist legal theory. The 1969 Act on petty offences was abolished.[540]

The most apparent deformations were removed from the Civil Code by the adoption of Act No. 509/1991 Sb.[541] The Act removed ideological aspects and some terminology of socialist law and restored the private law method of regulation in all spheres of personal and property relationships. New provisions were enacted and some new terms introduced; the Act could be regarded as a first step towards the return to the Central European civil law tradition. The concept of ownership was transformed to correspond with the provisions of the Charter of Fundamental Rights and Freedoms. Parts dealing with personal use and services were completely repealed. Another important amendment of the Civil Code was re-introducing the traditional concept of the law of obligations, especially of the law of contracts, and the law of succession was amended in a similar way.

A new Commercial Code (Act No. 513/1991 Sb.) was enacted. It returned the concepts of entrepreneurs and business companies to Czechoslovak law as well as the dichotomy of two major Codes for private law,[542] which we saw in operation in the interwar period.[543] It dealt with specific forms of obligations and some other relations applicable to business activities and commerce. The former International Trade Code and the Economic Code were abolished. The Code was divided into four parts.[544]

Part I dealt with general provisions defining the scope of the Code's applicability and with terminology. If the Commercial Code did not address a specific legal problem the general provisions of the Civil Code applied. Part II dealt with the status of business companies and cooperatives. Part III regulated

---

540 For the reform of Criminal law after 1989 see in English Fenyk, J.: *Czech criminal law and procedure*. Prague: Czech legal system in European context textbook, 2007, especially pp. 9–14. See also Kratochvíl, V. (ed.): *Criminal Law Reform in the Czech Republic in the Interdisciplinary Perspective: Contributions of the Intensive Lehrgang Within the Framework of TEMPUS-Programme in Brno, 14–21 March 1993*. Brno: Masaryk University, 1997.

541 Falada, D.: *Codification of private law in the Czech Republic*, pp. 64–66. The revised text was published in English by Trade links in 1995.

542 See Harmathy, A.: *Codification in a Period of Transition*. In: University of Califormia Davis Law Review, 31/1997/98, pp. 791–792.

543 For its text in English and commentaries see *The Czechoslovak Commercial Code*. Bulletin of Czechoslovak Law, volume 29, 1992, p. 3 and following. See also English translation of The Commercial Code by Trade Links in 1995. For short analyses together with historical excurse Bejček, J.: The New *Commercial Code of the* Czech Republic. In: The John Marshall Law Review, pp. 700–723.

544 *The Czechoslovak Commercial Code*, Bulletin of Czechoslovak Law, pp. 3–4.

contracts within the scope of commercial law whereas Part IV addressed final and transitional provisions.

For citizens who decided to start their private business the Act on Trade and Individual Proprietorship No. 455/1991 Sb. represented a real turning point. It meant a partial return to the liberal tradition of Austrian and Czechoslovak law of the interwar period, when it set legal preconditions for obtaining a license needed to perform a series of permanent, independently performed activities aimed at a profit. In certain cases, the Act required specific professional expertise for the licenses.

Important changes were introduced also to family law, although more sweeping reform was halted by the break-up of Czechoslovakia.[545] Act No. 234/1992 Sb., amending the Family Act, stipulated that spouses were free to decide whether to enter into marriage before a state authority or before the Church. The legislation was hurried through the Federal Assembly before elections and caused several problems in practice.[546] Changes to the community property of spouses, including possibility to reduce its scope, were introduced through amendments to the Civil Code.[547]

There was one important issue considered as a certain failure in the first two years of transformation. Czech and Slovak political representatives did not succeed in finding a suitable bilateral model for the coexistence of the Czech and Slovak nations within one common state.[548] Initial discussions spiralled around a name for the federation acceptable for both sides, around a new division of competences and around the concept of "authentic federation" advocated by Václav Havel as a contrast to "socialist" formal one.[549] By the end of 1990 a compromise was reached on the power sharing of the competences of federal bodies.[550]

In fact discussions on the name of the state resembled historical controversies between Czechs and Slovaks and showed the depth of the crisis of the common Czechoslovak state. The first proposal of a new name for the state, in March 1990, is a very good example of the inability to agree: two different versions were submitted, namely "Czechoslovak" in the Czech language, and "Czecho-Slovak" in the Slovak language. Under the new Constitutional Act

---

545 See Haderka, J. F.: *Czechoslovakia: Decline and Fall of the Federation and its Family Law.* In: University of Louisville Journal of Family Law 32/1993–1994, p. 283.

546 *Ibidem*, p. 288–289.

547 There were six such amendments until 1992, *Ibidem*, pp. 285–287.

548 In more details see Stein, E.: *Czecho-Slovakia, Ethnic Conflict, Constitutional Fissure, Negotiated Breakup.* Ann Arbor: The University of Michigan Press, 1997. See also Wolchik, S. L.: *The Politics of Transition and the Break-Up of Czechoslovakia.* In: Musil, J. (ed.): *The End of Czechoslovakia*, pp. 225–241.

549 In more details Rychlík, J.: *The possibilities for Czech-Slovak Compromise, 1989–1992.* In: Kraus, M. – Stanger, A. (eds.): *Irreconcilable Differences?: Explaining Czechoslovakia's Dissolution*, Rowman and Littlefield, 2000, especially pp. 50–54.

550 *Ibidem*, p. 54.

of April 1990 No. 101/1990 Sb. Czechoslovakia was quickly renamed as the "Czech and Slovak Federal Republic".

However, what was even more serious was the fact that the disputes on the division of competences and mutual relations between the Czech and Slovak Republics were followed with different views on the speed of political and economic reforms; for example, a possibility to prepare a new constitutional basis of the Federation in the form of a "state agreement" was discussed.[551] The issue of referendum became a new focus of the discussions and a special Referendum law was adopted as constitutional Act No. 327/1991 Sb. However this tool was not used in practice due to political obstacles both from the Czech and Slovak side;[552] the initiatives of Václav Havel from autumn 1991 and spring 1992 were ultimately to no effect.[553]

After parliamentary elections in June 1992 it became evident that the victorious political representations in both parts of the Federation lost any determination to maintain the common state. The inevitable outcome was "Velvet Divorce".[554] Moreover, the Slovak National Council adopted a Declaration on Slovak Sovereignty on 17th July 1992, and the Slovak Constitution on 1st September 1992.[555] This resulted in the organized and orderly split of the common state with the federal level of organs being eliminated.[556] Václav Havel resigned as Czechoslovak President with no prospect to be re-elected because of the Slovak political circles. The Federal Assembly adopted a series of laws on the dissolution of the Federation and on the split of federal property. The Czech and Slovak Republics concluded a series of international treaties. On 16th December 1992 the Czech National Council adopted the Constitution of the Czech Republic (Constitutional Act No. 1/1993 Sb.), together with the Constitutional Act governing measures to be taken in relation to the dissolution of the Czechoslovak Federation.[557] An independent Czech Republic and the Slovak Republic came into existence on 1st January 1993.

---

551 The proposal for a state treaty from February 1991 was depicted as "a bombshell" by E. Stein. Stein, E.: *Czecho-Slovakia, Ethnic Conflict, Constitutional Fissure, Negotiated Breakup*, pp. 105–108. See also See Žák, V.: *The Velvet Divorce – Institutional Foundations*. In: Musil, J. (ed.): *The End of Czechoslovakia*, pp. 245–267.

552 Stein, E.: *Czecho-Slovakia, Ethnic Conflict, Constitutional Fissure, Negotiated Breakup*, pp. 126–137.

553 *Ibidem*, pp. 139–145.

554 See Žák, V.: *The Velvet Divorce – Institutional Foundations*, pp. 262–264.

555 For its text in English see Ludwikowski, R. R.: *Constitution-making in the Region of Former Soviet Dominance*, pp. 578–604. For its analysis Stein, E.: *Czecho-Slovakia, Ethnic Conflict, Constitutional Fissure, Negotiated Breakup*, pp. 273–281, and Holländer, P: *New Slovak Constitution: A Critique*. In: East European Constitutional Review, 3/1992, pp. 16–17.

556 *New Czech, Slovak Leaders – Accelerate Separation*, Special Reports, *Ibidem* 2/1992, p. 9, and Franklin, D.: *Divorce Proceedings Continue between Czechs and Slovaks; Federal Bodies Lose Relevance, Ibidem* 2/1992, pp. 14–15.

557 For its text in English see Ludwikowski, R. R.: *Constitution-making in the Region of Former Soviet Dominance*, pp. 374–386, see also www.psp.cz/cgi-bin/eng/docs/laws/1993/1.html and www.usoud.cz/en/constitution-of-the-czech-republic

According to the Constitution, the Czech Republic is a sovereign, unified, democratic state based on the rule of law, founded upon the principle of respect for the rights and freedoms of an individual and of all citizens. The Charter of Fundamental Rights and Freedoms became an integral part of the constitutional order of the Czech Republic. The Constitution forms the basis and the cornerstone for the whole volume of Czech legislation. The principle of legal continuity was again applied, and most Czechoslovak laws applicable to the territory of the Czech Republic and not connected with the federal structure were accepted as laws of the Czech Republic. The era of Czechoslovak law came to its end, but new impetuses for discussions on continuity and discontinuity of law emerged together with Europeanization of Czech law as well as with the new role of the Czech Constitutional Court. However, this goes beyond the scope of this book which is devoted mainly to "closed cycles" of legal history.

References

The book is based on my research during which I was able to use various libraries and archives, although I tried to use mainly published sources for references.

I am especially grateful to the following libraries:

Library of the Law Faculty, Charles University in Prague
Library of UCL London.
The National Library in Wien
Library of Congress, Washington, D.C.
Staatsbibliothek zu Berlin

As well as the following archives:

Hoover Institution Archives, Stanford
The National Archives, Kew London
The National Archives, Prague

Law Library of Congress, Washington D.C. (materials related to the Mid European Law
  Project)
The School of Slavonic and East European Studies, University College London

The bibliography is intended mainly as a guide for those, who may wish to read more
and the references are focused primarily on the sources and literature in English.

PUBLISHED EDITIONS OF DOCUMENTS

Allgemeine kriminal-Gerichtsordnung. Edlen von Trattnern. Wien, 1788.

Andreas, G. – Guttenfeld, E. (edd.): Österreichisches Recht: *Textausg.* Österreichischer
  Gesetze, Verordnungen und Erlässe in einem Band; mit Hinweisen, Literaturangaben
  und einem ausführlichen Sachregister, 4th edition. Wien, 1950.

Bernatzik, E.: *Die österreichischen Verfassungsgesetze mit Erläuterungen.* 2 nd edition.
  Wien: Manzsche k.u k. Hof-Verlags, 1911.

Bílek, J. (ed.): Ius regale montanorum, právo královské horníkuov. In: *České horní právo.*
  Volume II., 1978.

Brandl, V. (ed.): *Kniha Rožmberská.* Prague, 1872.

Brandl, V. (ed.): *Kniha Tovačovská.* Brno, 1868.

Brauneder, W.: *Quellenbuch zur österreichischen Verfassungsgeschichte.* Wien: Manzsche Verlags, 2012.

Czechoslovak Yearbook of International Law. London, 1942.

Commentary on the Czechoslovak Civil Code by Th. J. Vondracek. Dordrecht: Martinus
  Nijhoff Publishers, 1988.

Constitution of the Czechoslovak Republic. Constitutional Act of May 9th, 1948. Prague:
  Czechoslovak Ministry of Education, 1948.

Constitution of the Czechoslovak Republic with Introduction by Jiří Hoetzel and V. Joachim.
  Prague: Politika, 1920.

Čáda, F. (ed.): *Nejvyššího sudího království českého Ondřeje z Dubé Práva zemská česká.*
  Prague, 1930.

Čáda, F. (ed.): *Zemská zřízení moravské z roku 1535 spolu s tiskem z roku 1562 nově vydaným.* Prague, 1937.

*Das österreichische Strafgesetz vom 27. Mai 1852 als Strafgerichts-Competenz-Tabelle für
  die neu organisirten Gerichtsbehörden im ganzen Umfange des Reiches* (e-book Google).
  Wien: C. Gerold und Sohn, 1855.

*Das strafgesetz über verbrechen, vergehen und uebertretungen: die strafgerichts-com-
  petenz-verordnungen und die press-ordnung vom 27. mai 1852 für das kaiserthum Oesterreich, Aus der kaiserlich-königlichen hof- und staatsdruckerei.* Wien, 1852, (e-book
  Google).

*Declaration of independence of the Czechoslovak nation by its Provisional Government,
  18 October 1918.* Printed for the Czechoslovak Arts Club by the Marchbanks press,
  New York, 1918.

Degras, J. (ed.): *Soviet Documents on Foreign Policy. Volume III., 1933–1941.* New York: Octagon Books, 1978.

Documents on British Foreign Policy, III. Series, volume 2. London, 1949.

Dodd, W. F. (ed.): *Modern Constitutions: A Collection of the Fundamental Laws of Twenty--two of the Most Important Countries of the World, With Historical and Bibliographical Notes.* Chicago: The University of Chicago Press, 1909.

Flodr, M. (ed.) : *Právní kniha města Brna z poloviny 14. století. volumes I.–III.* Brno: Brno City Archives, 1990–1993.

Flodr, M. (ed.): Gelhausen, J.: *Příručka práva městského (Manipulus vel directorium iuris civilis).* Brno: Matice Moravská, 2008.

Gebauer, J. (ed.): Kniha Rožmberská. *Listy filologické a paedagogické* 7, 1880.

Haider, B. (ed.): *Die Protokolle des Verfassungsausschusses des Reichsrates vom Jahre 1867.* Fontes rerum Austriacarum. Österreichische Geschichtsquellen. Abt. 2. Diplomataria et Acta. Bd. 88, Wien: Verlag der Österreichischen Akademie der Wissenschaften, 1997.

Hergemöller, B. U. (ed.): Maiestas Carolina Der Kodifikationsentwurf Karls IV. für das Königreich Böhmen von 1355. In: *Veröffentlichungen des Collegium Carolinum Bd. 74.* München, 1995.

Janiš, D. (ed.): *Práva a zřízení markrabství moravského z roku 1545. (Pokus moravských stavů o revizi zemského zřízení).* Historický úvod a edice. Brno, 2005.

Jireček, H. (ed.): *M. Viktorina ze Všehrd O právích země české Knihy devatery.* Prague, 1894.

Jireček, J. – Jireček, H. (eds.): *Zřízení zemská království českého XVI. věku.* Prague: Všehrd, 1882

Kreuz, P. – Martinovský, I. (eds.): *Vladislavské zřízení zemské a navazující prameny (Smlouva svatováclavská a Zřízení o ručnicích).* Edice. Příbram: Skriptorium, 2008.

Malý, K. et al. (edd.): *Práva městská Království českého: edice s komentářem.* Prague: Nakladatelství Karolinum, 2013.

Navrátil, J. (ed.): *The Prague Spring 1968: A National Security Archive Documents Reader.* Central European University Press, 1998.

Phillips, J. T. (ed.): *The Fundamental Laws and Constitutions of Seven Potent States and Kingdoms in Europe.* London, 1752.

Reich, E. (ed.): *Select Documents Illustrating Mediaeval and Modern History.* London, 1905.

Sammlung von civilrechtlichen Entscheidungen des k. k. obersten Gerichtshofes. Wienna, 1863, 1864, 1865 (2nd and 3rd volume accessible as google e-book).

Simmonds, W. (ed.): *The Constitutions of the Communist World.* Brill, 1980.

The Constitutional Foundations of the Czechoslovak Federation, Prague: Orbis, 1978.

The Chronicle of the Czechs. Cosmas of Prague, translated with an introduction and notes by Lisa Wolverton, Washington D.C.: The Catholic University of America Press, 2009.

SELECTED BOOKS AND ARTICLES

Agnew, H. L.: *The Czechs and the Lands of the Bohemian Crown*. Hoover Institution Press, 2004.

Ash, T. G.: *The Magic Lantern: The Revolution of 89. Witnessed in Warsaw, Budapest, Berlin and Prague*. New York: Random House, 1990.

Balazs, N. – Schaer, F.: *Autobiography of Emperor Charles IV. And his Legend of St. Wenceslas*. New York: Central European University Press, 2001.

Baltl, H.: Österreichische Rechtsgeschichte. Graz: Leykam Verlag, 1986.

Beneš, E.: *Memoirs of Dr. Eduard Beneš. From Munich to New War and New Victory*. London: Houghton Mifflin, 1954.

Beneš E. – Hauner M. (ed.): *The Fall and Rise of a Nation: Czechoslovakia 1938–1941*. New York: East European Monographs, 2004.

Beneš, Z. – Kural, V. et al.: *Facing history: the evolution of Czech-German relations in the Czech provinces, 1848–1948*. Prague: Gallery for the Ministry of Culture of the Czech Republic, 2002.

Bradley, J. F. N.: *Czechoslovakia's Velvet Revolution. A Political Analysis*. New York: Columbia University Press, 1992.

Brandes, D.: *Der Weg zur Vertreibung 1938–1945: Pläne und Entscheidungen zum "Transfer" der Deutschen aus der Tschechoslowakei und aus Polen*. Munich: Oldenbourg, 2005.

Brock, P.: *The Political and Social Doctrines of the Unity of Czech Brethen*. Leiden, 1957.

Brügel, J. W.: *Czechoslovakia before Munich. The German minority problem and British appeasement policy*. Cambridge University Press, 1973.

Brügel, J. W.: The Recognition of the Czechoslovak Government in London. In: *Kosmas – Journal of Czechoslovak and Central European Studies*, volume II., No. 1, 1984.

Bryant, Ch. C.: *Prague in Black: Nazi Rule and Czech Nationalism*. Harvard University Press, 2007.

Bolton, J.: *Worlds of Dissent: Charter 77. The Plastic People of the Universe and Czech Culture Under Communism*. Harvard University Press, 2012.

Burian, M.: *Assassination: Operation Anthropoid 1941–1942*. Prague: Ministry of Defence of the Czech Republic, 2011.

Butler, W. E.: *A Sourcebook on Socialist International Organizations*. Sijthoff & Noordhoff Alphen an den Rijn, 1978.

Carver, B. M.: *The Young Czech Party 1874–1901 and the emergence of a multi-party system*. New Haven: Yale University Press, 1978.

Cepl, V.: Bottlenecks in the Transformation of Eastern Europe. In: *Washington University Journal of Law and Policy*, vol. 4, 2000.

Cotic, M: *The Prague Trial. The First Anti-Zionist Show Trial in the Communist Bloc*. New York: Herzel Press, 1987.

Crampton, R.: *Eastern Europe in the Twenties Century – and after*. Routledge, 1997.

Cutlert, L. – Schwartz, H.: Constitutional Reform in Czechoslovakia: E Duobus Unum?. In: *The University of Chicago Law Review*, 58, 1991.

De Denken, J.-J.: *Social Policy in Postwar Czechoslovakia. The Development of Old-Age Pensions and Housing Policies During the Period 1945–1989.* Florence: European University Institute working papers in political and social sciences, 1994.

Dick Howard, A. E.: *Constitution Making in Eastern Europe.* Woodrow Wilson Center Press, 1993.

Dillon, K.: *King and Estates in the Bohemian Lands 1526–1564.* Brussels, 1976.

Douglas, R. M.: *Orderly and Humane. The Expulsion of the Germans after the Second World War.* Yale University Press, 2012.

Dvorník, F.: *The Life of Saint Wenceslas. Prince of Bohemia.* Prague, 1928.

Elster, J. (ed.): *The RoundtableTalks and the Breakdown of Communism.* Chicago: University of Chicago Press, 1996.

Elster: J.: Constitutionalism in Eastern Europe: An Introduction. In: *The University of Chicago Law Review*, 58, 1991.

Evans, R. J. W.: *The Making of the Habsburg Monarchy, 1550–1700. An Interpretation.* Oxford: Clarendon Press, 1979.

Evans, R. – Cornwall, M. (ed.): *Czechoslovakia in a Nationalist and Fascist Europe 1918–1948.* Oxford, 2007.

Falada, D.: Codification of private law in the Czech Republic. In: *Fundamina: A Journal of Legal History (South Africa).* Volume 15, Issue, 1, 2009.

Fenyk, J.: *Czech criminal law and procedure.* Prague: Czech legal system in European context textbook, 2007.

Filip, J.: *Celtic civilization and its heritage.* Prague: Academia, 1977.

Flossmann, U.: Österreichische Privatrechtsgeschichte. Wien: Springer, 2001.

Frommer, B.: *National Cleansing. Retribution against Nazi Collaborators in Postwar Czechoslovakia.* Cambridge University Press, 2005.

Gelpern, A.: The Laws and Politics of Reprivatization in East-Central Europe: A Comparison. In: *University of Pennsylvania Journal of Business Law*, 14, 1993–94.

Gori, F. – Pons, S. (ed.): *The Soviet Union and the Cold War.* London: Macmillan, 1996.

Grant Duff, S.: *A German Protectorate. The Czechs under Nazi Rule.* London: Macmillan, 1942.

Gsovski, V. – Grzybowski, K. (ed.): *Government Law and Courts in the Soviet Union and Eastern Europe. Volume, I. and II.* London – New York: Atlantic Books, 1959.

Gsovski, V. (ed.): *Church and State behind the Iron Curtain.* New York: F. A. Praeger, 1955.

Gooch, G. P.: *Maria Theresa: And Other Studies.* Archon Books, 1965.

Grant Duff, S.: *A German Protectorate. The Czechs under Nazi Rule.* London: Macmillan, 1942.

Haderka, J. F.: Czechoslovakia: Decline and Fall of the Federation and its Family Law. In: *University of Louisville Journal of Family Law* 32, 1993–1994.

Harmathy, A.: Codification in a Period of Transition. In: *University of California Davis Law Review* 31, 1997/98.

Hausmaninger, H.: *The Austrian legal system.* Hague: Kluwer Law International, 1998.

Heyman, F. G.: *George of Bohemia. King of Heretics.* Princeton University Press, 1965.

Hikl, M.: *The Civil Codes in Communist Czechoslovakia*. Toronto: The Czechoslovak Foreign Institute in Exile, 1959.

Hikl, M.: *The Penal Codes in Communist Czechoslovakia*. Toronto: The Czechoslovak Foreign Institute in Exile, 1957.

Hrachová, S.: Social Security and National Insurance Act in Postwar Czechoslovakia (1945–1948). In: *Prague Economic and Social History Papers*. Prague: Faculty of Arts, Charles University, vol. 13, 2011.

Höbelt, L.: 1867: The Empire Loyalists' Last (But One) Stand. In: *Parliaments, Estates and Representation* 23, 2003.

Höbelt, L.: Devolution Aborted: Franz Joseph I and the Bohemian "Fundamental Articles" of 1871. In: *Parliaments, Estates and Representation* 32, Issue 1, 2012.

Charvát, P.: *The Emergence of the Bohemian State*. Leiden and Boston: Brill, 2010.

Jančík, D. – Kubů, E. – Šouša, J.: *Arisierungsgewinnler. Die Rolle der deutschen Banken bei der „Arisierung" und Konfiskation jüdischer Vermögen im Protektorat Böhmen und Mähren 1939–1945*. Wiesbaden, 2011.

Jaszi, O.: *The Dissolution of the Habsburg Monarchy*. The University of Chicago Press, 1929.

Jech, K. (ed.): *The Czechoslovak Economy 1945–1948*. Prague: State Pedagogical Publishing House, 1963.

Kalvoda, J.: National minorities under communism: The case of Czechoslovakia. In: *Nationalities Papers: The Journal of Nationalism and Ethnicity*, vol. 16/1, 1988.

Kann, R. A.: *The Multinational Empire, Nationalism and National reform in the Habsburg Monarchy 1848–1918. Volume II. Empire reform*. New York: Columbia University Press, 1950.

Kann, R. A.: *A History of the Habsburg Empire 1526–1918*. Berkeley: University of California Press, 1974.

Kaplan, K.: *Report on the Murder of the General Secretary*. London: I. B. Tauris, 1990.

Kavka, F. – Petráň, J. (ed.): *A History of Charles University I, II*. Prague: Karolinum Press, 2001.

Kejř, J.: *The Hussite Revolution*. Prague: Orbis Press Agency, 1988.

Kelsen, H.: *The Communist Theory of Law*. New York: F. A. Praeger, 1955.

Klápště, J.: Czech lands in Mediaval Transformation. In: *East Central Europe in the Middle Ages 450–1450. Volume 17*. Leiden, Boston: Brill, 2012.

Kočvara, Š.: Criminal Code. In: *Law of June 12, 1950. No. 86 Coll., as amended. Crimes Against the Republic*, Washington, 1960.

Kočvara, Š.: *The Sovietization of Czechoslovak farming, Standard Charter of the Unified Agricultural Cooperative in Czechoslovakia of February 17, 1953*. Mid European Law Project, Library of Congress. Washington, 1954.

Kočvara, Š.: *Czechoslovakia: Local Councils (People's Committees) at the Village Level (outline of Principal Laws)*. Library of Congress, Washington, 1956.

Koenigsberger, H. G.: *Estates and Revolutions: Essays in Early Modern European History*. Cornell University Press, 1971.

Kolmer, G.: *Parlament und Verfassung in Oesterreich. 8. Vol*. Wien, Leipzig: Carl Fromme, 1902–1914.

Kopecký, P: *Parliaments in the Czech and Slovak Republics: Party Competition and Parliamentary Institutionalization.* Ashgate, 2001.

Korbel, J.: *The Communist Subversion of Czechoslovakia 1938–1948. The failure of Coexistence.* Princeton New Jersey, 1959.

Korbel, J.: *Twentieth-Century Czechoslovakia: the Meanings of Its History.* New York: Columbia University Press, 1977.

Kosík, K.: *The crisis of modernity: essays and observations from the 1968 era.* Rowman & Littlefield, 1995.

Kovtun, G. J.: *The Czechoslovak Declaration of Independence: A History of the Document.* Washington D.C., 1985.

Kraus, M. – Stanger, A. (ed.): *Irreconcilable Differences?: Explaining Czechoslovakia's Dissolution.* Rowman and Littlefield, 2000.

Krejčí, O.: *History of Elections in Bohemia and Moravia.* New York: Columbia University Press, 1995.

Krejčí, J.: *Czechoslovakia at the Crossroads of European History.* London: I. B. Tauris, 1990.

Kuklík, J. – Němeček, J.: *Od národnostního státu ke státu národností? Národnostní statut a snahy o řešení menšinové otázky v Československu v roce 1938.* Prague: Nakladatelství Karolinum, 2013.

Kuklík, J. et al.: *Faculty of Law of Charles University in Prague.* Prague: Havlíček Brain Team, 2008.

Kuklík, J.: *Znárodněné Československo: od znárodnění k privatizaci – státní zásahy do vlastnických a dalších majetkových práv v Československu a jinde v Evropě.* Prague: Auditorium, 2010.

Kuklík, J.: *Do poslední pence.* Prague: Nakladatelství Karolinum, 2007.

Kuklík, J.: The Recognition of Czechoslovak Government in Exile and its International Status 1939–1941. In: *Prague Papers on History of International Relations. Volume 1.* Prague: Faculty of Arts, Charles University, 1997.

Kuklík, J. – Němeček, J. – Šebek, J.: *Dlouhé stíny Mnichova: Mnichovská dohoda očima signatářů a její dopady na Československo.* Prague: Auditorium, 2011.

Kuklík, J. – Němeček, J.: Czechoslovak government in Exile 1942. In: Němeček, J. et. al. (edd.): *Zápisy ze schůzí československé vlády v Londýně II. (1942).* Prague: Institute of T. G. Masaryk, 2012.

Kuklík, J. – Němeček, J.: Czechoslovak government in Exile 1943. In: Němeček, J. et. al. (ed.): *Zápisy ze schůzí československé vlády v Londýně III.1 (1943).* Prague: Institute of T. G. Masaryk, 2013.

Kühn, Z.: *The Judiciary in Central and Eastern Europe. Mechanical Jurisprudence in Transformation?* Leiden, Boston: Martinus Nijhoff Publishers, 2011.

Láníček, J.: *Czechs, Slovaks and the Jews 1938–48: Beyond Idealisation and Condemnation.* Palgrave Macmillan, 2013.

Langášek, T.: *Ústavní soud Československé republiky a jeho osudy v letech 1920–1948 (Constitutional Court of the Czechoslovak Republic and its fortunes in years 1920–1948).* Plzeň: Aleš Čeněk, 2011.

Lehner, O.: *Österreichische Verfassungs- und Verwaltungsgeschichte*. Trauner Verlag, 2007.

Lettrich, J.: *History of Modern Slovakia*. New York: F. Prager, 1955.

Loebl, E.: *Sentenced and Tried. The Stalinist Purges in Czechoslovakia*. London: Elek Books, 1969.

Long, M.: *Making History. Czech Voices of Dissent and Revolution of 1989*. Oxford, 2005.

Ludwikowski, R. R.: *Constitution-making in the Region of Former Soviet Dominance*. Duke University Press, 1996.

Lukacs, J.: *The Great Powers and Eastern Europe*. New York: American Book Company, 1953.

Lukeš, I.: *On the Edge of the Cold War: American Diplomats and Spies in Postwar Prague*. Oxford University Press, 2012.

Luža, R.: *The Transfer of the Sudeten Germans. A Study of Czech-German Relations 1933–1962*. London: Routledge, 1964.

Macartney, C. A.: *The House of Austria. The Later Phase 1790–1918*. Edinbourgh, 1978.

Macartney, C. A.: *The Habsburg Empire 1790–1918*. London, 1968.

MacDonald, C. A.: *The Killing of SS Obergruppenführer Reinhard Heydrich*. New York: The Free Press, 1989.

Mamatey, V. S. – Luža, R. (eds): *A History of the Czechoslovak Republic 1918–1948*. New Jersey: Princeton University Press, 1973.

Marečková, M.: *Czech Legal and Constitutional History. Brief Summary*. Prague: Linde, 2006.

Mařík, V. – Urbanec, A.: *The Czechoslovak trade unions and labour legislation*. Prague: Práce, 1967.

Mastný, V.: *The Czechs Under Nazi Rule: The Failure of National Resistance 1939–1942*, Columbia University Press, 1971.

May, A. J.: *The Hapsburg Monarchy, 1867–1914*. Cambridge, MA: Harvard University Press, 1951

Milotová, J. – Kubů, E. – Jančík, J. – Kuklík, J. – Šouša, J.: *The Jewish Gold and Other Precious Metals, Precious Stones, and Objects Made of Such Materials – Situation in the Czech Lands in the Years 1939 to 1945*. Prague: Sefer, 2011.

Musil, J.: (ed.) *The End of Czechoslovakia*. Central European University Press, 1997.

Okey, R.: *The Habsburg Monarchy c. 1765–1918. From Enlightenment to the Eclipse. European Studies Series*. Basingstoke, 2001.

Olechowski, T.: *Rechtsgeschichte, Einführung in die historischen Grundlagen des Rechts*. Wien: Facultas verlags und buchhandels, 2006.

Opočenský, J.: *The Collapse of the Austro-Hungarian Monarchy and the Rise of the Czechoslovak State*. Prague, 1928.

Ott, E.: *Beitrage zur Receptionsgeschichte der römisch-canonischen Processes in den Böhmischen Landern*. Leipzig, 1897.

Paar, M.: *Die Gesetzgebung der österreichischen Monarchie im Spiegelbild der Normen und der staatsrechtlichen Literatur. Series II. Law*. Frankfurt – Wien: Peter Lang, 2008.

Padower, S. K.: *The Revolutionary Emperor. Joseph the Second, 1741–1790*. London, 1934.

Pánek, J. – Tůma, O. et al.: *A History of the Czech lands.* Prague: Karolinum Press, 2009.

Parker, R. A. C.: *Chamberlain and Appeasement: British Policy and the Coming of the Second World War.* London: Macmillan, 1993.

Pauknerová, M. – Tomášek, M.: *Nové jevy v právu na počátku 21. století (New Phenomena in Law at the Beginning of the 21st Century). IV. Proměny soukromého práva.* Prague: Karolinum Press, 2009.

Pauknerová, M. *Codification of Czech Private Law in the Middle and on the Outskirts of Europe.* Liber Amicorum Valentinas Mikelenas, Vilnius: Justitia, 2008 (2009).

Pech, S. Z.: *The Czech Revolution of 1848.* The University of North Carolina Press, 1969.

Pelikán, J.: *The Czechoslovak Political Trials 1950–1954. The Suppressed Report of the Dubček Government's Commission of Inquiry 1968.* Stanford University Press, 1971.

Perman, D.: *The Shaping of the Czechoslovak State.* Diplomatic History of the Boundaries of *Czechoslovakia* 1914–1920. Leiden, 1962.

Polišenský, J. V.: *The Thirty Years War.* University of California Press, 1971.

Přibáň, J.: *Legal Symbolism: On Law. Time and European Identity.* Ashgate Publishing, 2007.

Redlich, J.: *Das Oesterreichische Staats- und Reichsproblem.* Volume II. Leipzig, 1926.

Rechcígl, M. (ed.): *Czechoslovakia Past and Present: Political, international, social, and economic aspects. Volume I.* Published under the auspices of the Czechoslovak Society of Arts and Sciences in America, by Mouton, 1968.

Ripka, H.: *Czechoslovakia Enslaved. The Story of the Communist Coup d'Etat.* London: Victor Gollanz, 1950.

Robinson, O. F. – Fergus, T. D. – Gordon, W. D.: *European Legal Histroy. Sources and Institutions.* London: Butterwords, 1994.

Rothkirchen, L: *The Jews of Bohemia and Moravia: Facing the Holocaust.* University of Nebraska Press, 2006.

Scruton, R.: The Reform of Law in Eastern Europe. In: *Tilburg Foreign Law Review* 7/1991–1992.

Seton-Watson, R. W.: *25 Years of Czechoslovakia.* London, 1945.

Seton-Watson, R. W.: *A History of the Czechs and Slovaks.* London, 1943.

Seton-Watson, R. W.: *The New Slovakia.* Prague, 1924.

Schambeck, Herbert (Hg.): *Österreichs Parlamentarismus. Werden und System.* Berlin: Duncker & Humblot, 1986.

Shaffern, R. W.: *Law and Justices from Antiquity to Enlightenment.* New York: Rowman and Littlefield, 2000.

Schwartz, H.: The New East European Constitutional Courts. In: *Michigan Journal of International Law* 13/1991–1992.

Skalnik Leff, C.: *National Conflict in Czechoslovakia. The Making and Remaking of a State 1918–1987.* Princeton University Press, 1988.

Skalnik Leff, C.: *National Conflict in Czechoslovakia. Nation versus State.* Westview Press, 1997.

Skilling, H. G.: *Czechoslovakia's Interrupted Revolution.* Princeton University Press, 1976.

Skilling, H. G.: *Czechoslovakia 1918–88. Seventy Years from Independence.* Oxford: St. Antony's College, 1991.

Skilling, H. G.: *The Governments of Communist East Europe.* New York: Crowell Comparative Government Series, 1966.

Skilling, H. G.: The Czechoslovak Constitutional System: The Soviet impact. In: *Political Science Quarterly,* June 1952.

Smetana, V.: *In the Shadow of Munich. British Policy towards Czechoslovakia from the Endorsement to the Renunciation of the Munich Agreement (1938–1942).* Prague: Karolinum Press, 2008.

Staar, R. F. : *Communist regimes in Eastern Europe.* Hoover Press Publications, 1982.

Stein, E.: *Czecho-Slovakia, Ethnic Conflict. Constitutional Fissure. Negotiated Breakup.* Ann Arbor: The University of Michigan Press, 1997.

Stone, N. – Strouhal, E. (ed): *Czechoslovakia: Crossroads and Crises 1918–1988.* New York, 1989.

Strakosch, H. E.: *State Absolutism and the Rule of Law: The Struggle for the Codification of Civil Law in Austria, 1753–1811.* University of Sydney Press, 1967.

Suda, Z. – Musil, J. (ed.): *The Meaning of Liberalism: East and West.* New York: Central European University Press, 2000.

Táborský, E.: *Czechoslovak Democracy at Work.* London: Allen and Unwin, 1944

Táborský, E.: *The Czechoslovak Cause. An Account of the Problems of International Law in Relation to Czechoslovakia.* London: Witherby, 1944.

Táborský, E.: *Communism in Czechoslovakia: 1948–1960.* Princeton University Press, 1961.

Táborský, E.: *President Edvard Benes. Between East and West 1938–1948.* Stanford: Hoover Institution Press, 1981.

Tapie, V. L.: *The Rise and Fall of the Habsburg Monarchy.* London: Praeger Publisher, 1971.

Taylor, A. J. P.: *The Habsburg Monarchy 1809–1918. A History of Austrian Empire and Austria – Hungary.* London: Hamish Hamilton, 1948.

Teich, M. (ed.): *Bohemia in History.* Cambridge University Press, 1998.

Teich, M. – Kováč, D. – Brown, M. D. (ed.): *Slovakia in History.* Cambridge University Press, 2011.

Teichová, A.: *The Czechoslovak Economy 1918–1980.* London: Routledge, 1988.

Teitel, R. G.: *Transitional Justice.* Oxford University Press, 2000.

Terry, S. M. (ed.): *Soviet Policy in Eastern Europe.* New Haven: Yale University Press, 1984.

Textor, L. E.: *Land Reform in Czechoslovakia.* London: Allen and Unwin, 1923.

The 17th November: the Resistance of Czechoslovak Students: Almanac about the Resistance of Czechoslovak Students in the Years 1939–1945. Prague: Orbis, National Union of Czechoslovak Students, 1945.

Tschuppik, K.: *The Reign of the Emperor Francis Joseph 1848–1916.* London: G. Bell and sons, 1930.

Ulč, O.: The *Judge* in a *Communist State*; *A View from Within.* Ohio University Press, 1972.

Ulč, O.: Gypsies in Czechoslovakia: a Case of Unfinished Integration. In: *East European Politics and Societies* 2/1988.

Unger, J.: *System des österreichichen allgemeinen Privatrechts.* Leipzig: Breitkopf u. Härtel, first edition, six volumes 1856–1864.

Valiani, L.: *The End of Austria-Hungary. The Definitive Account of the Collapse of a Great Empire.* London, 1973

van den Berg, P. A. J: *The Politics of European Codification. A History of the Unification of Law in France, Prussia, the Austrian Monarchy and the Netherlands.* Groningen: Europa Law Publishing, 2007.

Vaněček, V.: *The Universal Peace Organization of King George of Bohemia: A fifteenth Century Plan for World Peace 1462/1464.* Prague: Czechoslovak Academy of Sciences, 1964.

Von Glaise-Horstenau, E.: *The Collapse of the Austro-Hungarian Empire.* London, 1930.

Voráček, E. (ed.): *The disintegration of Czechoslovakia in the end of 1930s: policy in the Central Europe.* Prague: Institute of History, 2009.

Vyšny, P.: *The Runciman Mission to Czechoslovakia. Prelude to Munich.* Basingstoke Palgrave Macmillan, 2003.

Wandruszka, A.: *The House of Habsburg: Six hundred years of a European dynasty.* Greenwood Press, 1975.

Wandruszka, A. – Urbanitsch, P. (ed.): *Die Habsburgermonarchie 1848–1918. Volume II, Verwaltung und Rechtswesen.* Wien: Verlag der Österreichischen Akademie der Wissenschaften, 2003.

Wandycz, P. S.: *Czechoslovak-Polish Confederation and the Great Powers 1940–1943.* Bloomington, Indiana, 1958.

Wheeler-Bennett, J. W.: *Munich: Prologue to tragedy.* New York, 1948

Winters, S. – Pynsent, R. B. – Hanak, H.: (edds.) T. G. *Masaryk*, 1850–1937. 3 volumes, London: St. Martin's Press, 1989–1990.

Wiskemann, E.: *Czechs and Germans. A Study of the Struggle in the Historic Provinces of Bohemia and Moravia.* Royal Institute of International Affairs, Oxford University Press, 1938

Wolchik, S. L.: *Czechoslovakia in Transition: Politics. Economics and Society.* London: Pinter, 1991.

Wolverton, L.: *Hastening toward Prague, Power and Society in the Medieval Czech lands.* Philadelfia: University of Pennsylvania Press, 2001.

Zeman, Z. A. B.: *The Break-Up of the Habsburg Empire 1914–1918. A Study in National and Social Revolution.* New York: Octagon Books, 1977.

Zeman, Z. A. B.: *The Making and Breaking of Communist Europe.* Oxford: Blackwell, 1991

Zeman, Z. A. B.: *Prague Spring: A Report on Czechoslovakia 1968.* London: Penguin Books, 1969.

Zinner, P. E.: *Communist Strategy and Tactics in Czechoslovakia, 1918–1948.* New York, 1963.

Žemlička, J.: *Přemysl Otakar II. - Král na rozhraní věků - Přemysl Otakar II. A King on the Turn of Ages.* Prague: Nakladatelství Lidové noviny, 2011.

FOR THE LITERATURE ON CZECH AND CZECHOSLOVAK LEGAL HISTORY IN CZECH SEE ESPECIALLY

Baxa, B.: *Dějiny práva na území Republiky Československé.* Prague, 1935.

Bobek, M. - Molek, P. - Šimíček, V. (ed.): *Komunistické právo v Československu. Kapitoly z dějin bezpráví.* Brno: Masarykova univerzita, Mezinárodní politologický ústav, 2009.

Kapras, J.: *Právní dějiny zemí koruny České. Díl 1-3.* Prague, 1913-1920.

Kapras, J.: *Přehled právních dějin zemí České koruny.* Nákladem vlastním: Prague 1935.

Kuklík, J. et al.: *Dějiny československého práva 1945-1989.* Prague: Auditorium, 2011.

Malý, K.: *České právo v minulosti.* Prague: Orac, 1995.

Malý, K. et al.: *Dějiny českého a československého práva do r. 1945.* Prague: Leges, 2010.

Malý, K. - Soukup, L. (ed.): *Vývoj práva v Československu v letech 1945-1989.* Prague: Nakladatelství Karolinum, 2004.

Malý, K. - Soukup, L. (ed.): *Vývoj české ústavnosti v letech 1618-1918.* Prague: Nakladatelství Karolinum, 2009.

Malý, K. - Soukup, L. (ed.): *Československé právo a právní věda v meziválečném období 1918-1938 a jejich místo ve střední Evropě.* Prague: Nakladatelství Karolinum, 2010.

Malý, K. et al.: *Městské právo ve střední Evropě.* Prague: Nakladatelství Karolinum, 2013.

Vaněček. V.: *Dějiny státu a práva v Československu do roku 1945.* Prague: Orbis, 1975.

Malý, K. - Kučera K.: *Právněhistorická bibliografie: výběr českých a slovenských prací z let 1966-1973 k dějinám státu a práva.* Prague: Nakladatelství Karolinum, 1974.

Petráš, R. - Starý, M.: *Právněhistorická bibliografie: výběr českých a slovenských prací z let 1990-2000 k dějinám státu a práva.* Prague: Nakladatelství Karolinum, 2005.

Sivák, F.: *Slovenské a ceské dejiny štátu a práva v rokoch 1918-1945.* Bratislava: Universita Komenského, 1999.

Vojáček, L. - Schelle, K.: *Právní dějiny na území Slovenska.* Key Publishing, 2007.

INTERNET SOURCES

Bundeskanzelramt RIS - Rechtsinformationssystem
www.ris.bka.gv.at
cms.flu.cas/cz/badatele/ sources on line - Czech medieval sources online (especially Archiv český čili staré písemné památky české i moravské, vol. I-XXXVII. edited by F. Palacký, J. Kalousek, G. Friedrich, Codex Diplomaticus et Epistolaris Regni Bohemiae, vol. I-III. edited by G. Friedrich, Codex juris Bohemici, vol. I.-V. edited by Hermenegild and Josef Jireček and Codex juris municipalis regni Bohemiae, vol. I.-IV. edited by J. Čelakovský, G. Friedrich, A. Haas)

www. psp.cz (digital repository, Joint Czech and Slovak Digital Parliamentary Library,
   Czech – Bohemian Assemblies Digital Library)
www.usoud.cz

JAN KUKLÍK

CZECH LAW
IN HISTORICAL
CONTEXTS

Published by Charles University in Prague, Karolinum Press
Ovocný trh 3–5, 116 36 Prague 1, Czech Republic
http://cupress.cuni.cz
Prague 2015
Editor Vice-rector Jan Royt
English text editing Marta Chromá a Jim Critz
Layout by Jan Šerých
Typeset by DTP Karolinum Press
Printed by Karolinum Press
First edition

This book is written under the auspices
of institutional support PRVOUK P04.

ISBN 978-80-246-2860-8
ISBN 978-80-246-2916-2 (pdf)